INDIAN FALL

*The Last Great Days
of the Plains Cree and
the Blackfoot Confederacy*

D'ARCY JENISH

VIKING

VIKING

Published by the Penguin Group

Penguin Books Canada Ltd, 10 Alcorn Avenue, Toronto, Ontario, Canada M4V 3B2

Penguin Books Ltd, 27 Wrights Lane, London W8 5TZ, England

Penguin Putnam Inc., 375 Hudson Street, New York, New York 10014, U.S.A.

Penguin Books Australia Ltd, Ringwood, Victoria, Australia

Penguin Books (NZ) Ltd, cnr Rosedale and Airborne Roads, Albany Aukland 1310, New Zealand

Penguin Books Ltd Registered Offices: Harmondsworth, Middlesex, England

First published 1999

10 9 8 7 6 5 4 3 2 1

Printed and bound in Canada on acid free paper ∞

CANADIAN CATALOGUING IN PUBLICATION DATA

Jenish, D'Arcy
    Indian fall: the last great days of the Plains Cree and the Blackfoot confederacy

ISBN 0-670-88090-6

1. Piapot, 1816–1908. 2. Big Bear, 1825?–1888. 3. Crowfoot, 1830?–1890.
4. Poundmaker, 1842–1886. 5. Cree Indians – Prairie Provinces – History – 19th century. 6. Siksika Indians – Prairie Provinces – History – 19th century. 7. Northwest, Canadian – History. I. Title.

E99.C88J46 1999   971.2'004973   C99-931236-7

Visit Penguin Canada's website at www.penguin.ca

CONTENTS

ACKNOWLEDGEMENTS

MANY PEOPLE ASSISTED in the creation of *Indian Fall* and I would like to take this opportunity to say thanks. Hugh Dempsey was always generous with his time and advice. Robert Hendriks and Keith Davidson graciously shared their knowledge and insights. Brock Silversides and Tim Novack of the Saskatchewan Archives Board kindly directed me to photos and other material. Clifford Crane Bear and Clarence Wolf Lake of the Siksika First Nation, Vera Kasakeo and Tyrone Tootoosis of the Poundmaker First Nation, and Ray Lavallee and Daryl Obey of the Piapot First Nation provided invaluable assistance. I am indebted to my old friends Ric Dolphin and Steve Hopkins and to my colleague Mike MacLean for their timely contributions. I would like to thank everyone at Penguin who worked on the book, especially Jackie Kaiser, a remarkable editor. Finally, I must pay tribute to my wife, Hélène, and my children, Jesse, Isabel and Patrick, whose patience and perseverance made the whole project possible.

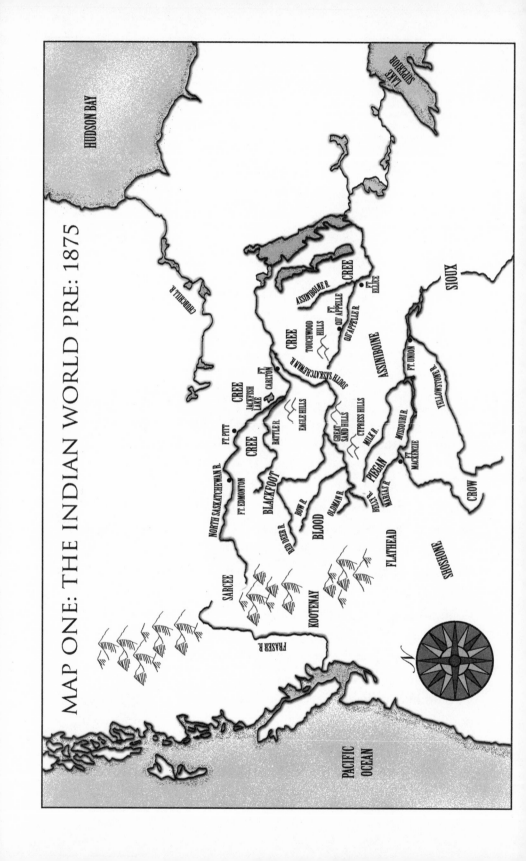

MAP ONE: THE INDIAN WORLD PRE: 1875

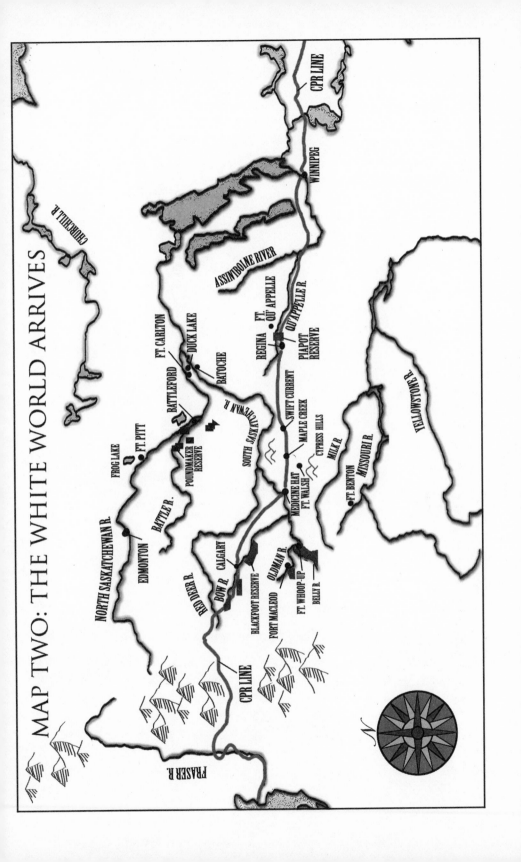

MAP TWO: THE WHITE WORLD ARRIVES

D ominion Over All

"One of the distinguishing natural traits of the (North) American Indian ... is his uncompromising tenacity for unbounded freedom."

George Catlin, *Life Among the Indians*, 1875.

IF YOU GREW UP, AS I did, in a raw, windy, tumbleweed town in southern Saskatchewan in the late 1950s or early 1960s, you inevitably learned that the land you inhabited had once, not so long ago, been the domain of the plains Indians of North America and the great thundering herds of buffalo that sustained them. You learned that the opening and settling of these broad, bountiful prairies had been a big, extravagant enterprise that ended in defeat for the native peoples and victory for the whites. You learned this at an early age, first through Hollywood westerns, which usually got the basics right (time and place, winners and losers) but not much else. Whatever their shortcomings, westerns were a staple in our town. We watched them at the theatre on Main Street and at the drive-in on the highway or on the two TV stations— one from Regina and the other from Minot, North Dakota —which you could pull in if your father erected a rickety, gawky-looking antenna on the roof of the family home.

If you were really lucky, as I was, and happened to be able to play child's games on virgin prairie—a rare piece of land unbroken by the plough—you might discover physical evidence of these plains Indians. You might climb and cavort on cone- or cross-shaped clay mounds that were barren of any vegetation and nearly immune to the erosive effects of wind and rain because they had been baked to the consistency of brick by the prairie sun. Or you might find yourself standing amid tepee rings, stones placed in circular patterns where the members of some native band had once erected their lodges. And if you kept your eyes glued to the ground, you might even find a mallet-shaped tomahawk stone. You could pick it up, feel its heft and its smooth surface and imagine: here was an object once used to drive in tepee stakes, to break open buffalo bones, or to fracture the skull of an enemy warrior.

Even if you never watched a western or happened upon native artefacts, you were bound to hear about the plains Indians and the buffalo and the coming of the white man in history class. Our straight-up, stripped-back lessons were nowhere near as exciting as the westerns, due largely to the relative lack of wars and battles, bloodshed and death on the Canadian side of the border. Our teachers explained, with a certain pride, that the opening of the Canadian West had been a more peaceful process than the opening of the American West because our government had imposed law and order on the region before hordes of settlers arrived, whereas, south of the border, settlers poured in first and the result was anarchy. But even though there was less murder and mayhem, there was an undeniable grandeur to the settling of our portion of the Great Plains of North America.

We learned that the opening of the Canadian West was a saga spanning two continents, several centuries and thousands of miles of wilderness. We learned that it was based on the pursuit of furs, the construction of railways and the transformation of oceans of grass into fields of wheat. The story began in the late seventeenth century as a commercial battle between two great European powers, France and England, and the prize that they competed for was an industrious rodent known as *Castor canadensis*—the Canadian beaver—whose lustrous fur coat could be turned into warm, waterproof felt hats for the prosperous and fashionable citizens of those two nations and the populace of other northern European countries.

We learned that the English pursued the beaver from the shores of Hudson Bay; the French, from the banks of the St. Lawrence River. For 104 years or so, English traders employed by the Governor and Company of Adventurers of England Tradeing Into Hudson's Bay, commonly known as the Hudson's Bay Company, were content to sit in their bayshore posts and let the Indians of the western interior paddle down to them every spring in canoes packed to the gunwales with furs. The two parties then bartered and haggled until the furs had been exchanged for muskets, powder, shot, blankets, kettles, knives, axes and other manufactured goods.

The more aggressive and entrepreneurial French dispatched crews of muscular but scruffy men in canoes, who departed from Montreal and paddled up rivers and across lakes into the heart of the continent, eventually capturing so much of the trade that they awakened their slumbering English rivals. There then began a race to construct trading posts from the mouths almost to the headwaters of the great river systems of the West—the Red, the Saskatchewan, the Athabasca and the Peace—and four decades of cut-throat competition that nearly ruined both sides until common sense prevailed and a typically Canadian compromise was reached. In 1821, the Montreal-based Northwest Company threw in the towel and merged with its older, better-financed rival, the Hudson's Bay Company. Then, with an utter disregard for the limits of the resource, the unchallenged, unfettered Bay men trapped out one region after another until there were no longer enough beaver to sustain their trans-Atlantic enterprise.

As the fur trade was in decline, the railway age was beginning its long ascent. Trappers and traders soon gave way to bearded, barrel-chested, cigar-smoking tycoons in top hats, the railwaymen who played the country's politicians like puppets on strings and employed crews of lean, sinewy labourers to place the ties, lay the tracks, drive in the spikes, and actually build the iron road that linked our gangly, disparate Dominion from coast to coast. Once the job was done—once the last spike was driven into the ground on November 7, 1885, in Craigellachie, British Columbia, and the trains began to run— the railwaymen were swept off the stage by the homesteaders. One and a quarter million of them poured onto the plains in the four decades following Confederation—restless settlers from central Canada and land-hungry European peasants in sheepskin coats who came in search of freedom, opportunity and a brighter future.

The struggle of the homesteaders, their titanic effort to turn thousands of square miles of virgin prairie into millions of acres of productive farmland, was the final phase of this long saga of furs, railways and wheat and it lasted well into the twentieth century. The life of a homesteader was distinguished by brief advances, an economic boom here or a bumper crop there, and repeated setbacks, caused by late spring or early autumn frosts, swarms of rapacious grasshoppers, vicious hailstorms that could flatten a crop in minutes and wild fluctuations in wheat prices. And all of these were just a warmup for the droughts, dust bowls, bankruptcies and assorted calamities of the Dirty Thirties.

We learned all this and more in our history classes, but we learned precious little about the native peoples we had displaced. We learned little of their cultures, their religious beliefs or their means of governing themselves. We learned next to nothing of the various nations among the plains Indians, the territories they inhabited and their relationships with each other. And we never learned the names of their great leaders.

In retrospect, this is not so surprising. The opening of the Canadian West to white settlement is a story that has been told many times. Popular and professional historians have portrayed the transformation of the Prairies as a triumphant accomplishment, and the fur traders, railway builders, mounties and homesteaders who threw their energy and initiative into this vast enterprise have been treated as heroes. But where the opening of the West was a triumph for Canadians of European descent, it was a catastrophe for the original inhabitants—the Plains Cree, the Sarcee, the Assiniboines, the Saulteaux and the tribes of the Blackfoot Confederacy (the Bloods, Piegans and Blackfoot). Their fate was settled in the second half of the nineteenth century, and they would surely remember those years as an era of disappearing resources, loss of territory, the end of their way of life and the near total destruction of their cosmos. Whole bands were ravaged by European diseases, booze, hunger, starvation and warfare. Yet, in our tales of nation

building, the experiences and perspectives of the native inhabitants often become little more than a colourful background
against which the main story is played out.

Perhaps it is only natural for writers of history to focus on
those who have won rather than those who have lost, on that
which was built rather than that which was destroyed. And yet,
we cannot escape the fact that, before the transformation of the
West could occur, two conditions had to be met: the great
herds of buffalo that fed, clothed and sustained the native
peoples had to be exterminated; and the people themselves had
to be subdued, made to surrender their ancestral lands, and
forced to settle on reserves.

We frequently find comfort in the notion that our forefathers were neither as ruthless nor as unscrupulous as their
American counterparts. But to do so is really to focus on the
means rather than the objectives. For the objectives in both
countries were the same: to create new societies in territories
that were immense but sparsely populated. In both countries,
these new societies were built on the ruins of older aboriginal
communities. Some might argue that this was inevitable, that
there was a cultural chasm that could never be bridged, that
natives and whites lived in worlds as different as summer and
winter. Yet for all our genius for compromise, there was no
compromising with the natives of the Great Plains. Their
world had to go.

The men who fathered the Dominion of Canada dreamed of
turning a runt of a country—four thinly settled colonies, clustered on the eastern half of a continent—into a dynamic and
prosperous nation stretching from Atlantic to Pacific. *A mari
usque ad mare.* He shall have dominion also from sea to sea.

Those words, which come from the eighth verse of the
72nd Psalm, became our national motto thanks to Samuel

Leonard Tilley, a teetotalling New Brunswicker and devout Anglican who trained as an apothecary but chose politics as a career. Tilley supported prohibition, promoted railways and won a bare-knuckle, backwoods, wildly partisan fight to lead his province into Confederation. Tilley read his Bible every morning, and when he and his fellow fathers of Confederation were gathered in London in early 1867 to finish drafting the document that would become the British North America Act, he remembered the line from Psalm 72. And so it was that our fledgling nation acquired a title, a motto and a purpose.

The first order of business of the new government was to achieve dominion over those lands of immense horizons and unbounded potential that lay north of the forty-ninth parallel and stretched from the western end of Lake Superior to the Rocky Mountains. Before there could be railways and home-steads, before there could be cities and towns, before this new nation could hope to fulfil its purpose—to stand from sea to shining sea—Canada had to acquire the North-West from the Company of Adventurers, who had been "the true and absolute Lordes and Proprietors" since May 2, 1670, according to the charter issued to them on that date by the distant monarch, King Charles II.

Negotiations involving Canada, the Company and Great Britain began in December of 1867 and ended in the spring of 1869 with an agreement to transfer the North-West for the grand sum of £300,000. The dry legalese of the document conceals the true purpose of the agreement—the pursuit of a national dream—and fails to mention that the pursuit of this dream would create a dispossessed class of people and lead to the destruction of their nations. It makes no mention of the Plains Cree, the tribes of the Blackfoot Confederacy, the Assini-boines and others; they were not signatories to the agreement because, to use a contemporary phrase, they were not consulted. And the swirl of events unleashed by this accord, an armed uprising and open challenge to the legitimacy of the new confederation and the resolve of its leaders, ensured that the thoughts, feelings and positions of those we had dispossessed would never be considered.

There has been plenty written about the impact of the railways, settlers and agriculture on the existing communities of the prairies and about resident opposition to these intrusive developments, but the vast majority of this writing and thinking has been devoted to the Metis and their leader, Louis Riel, the West's most famous rebel. The literature on Riel and the rebellions has had a powerful influence on public perceptions. We can easily believe that the West was wrested from the Metis rather than the native peoples. We tend to associate western discontent during this period with the Metis, who saw their lives as semi-nomadic buffalo hunters coming to an end and at the same time feared that they would lose their land holdings first in the Red River valley and later the Saskatchewan River valley. These grievances, rooted in land and lifestyle, were exacerbated by language and religion, the two central sources of tension and conflict in central Canada. The antagonists in the rebellions were French-speaking Catholics and English-speaking Protestants, and the conflicts between them led to violence, bloodshed and death; not nearly as much, however, as the murderous war between the Plains Cree and the Blackfoot, the two most powerful indigenous nations on the Canadian prairie. This war raged almost continuously throughout the middle decades of the nineteenth century.

The names and dates of Riel's rebellions are lodged securely in our memories. They adorn the covers of books. They are drilled into our heads as schoolkids. Every high school student who studies Canadian history learns the story of Thomas Scott, the belligerent Ontario Orangeman who was executed by Riel's provisional government in March 1870, the only man to lose his life in the Red River Rebellion. But how many of us have heard of the bloodbath that took place one day in October 1870, at the Battle of Belly River?

By mid-century the eradication of the buffalo had begun in earnest, largely due to the introduction of the American repeating rifle and American demand for buffalo hides. The Crees were the first to suffer. They were the most northern of the prairies tribes and lived at the edge of the great beast's range. It was here that the herds dwindled fastest and disappeared first. Armed and mounted Cree warriors began making deeper, more daring forays into Blackfoot country to hunt, to make war and to smash through their old enemy to reach the remaining herds.

The Battle of Belly River, which occurred near what is now the city of Lethbridge, Alberta, was supposed to be the Crees' decisive assault upon an adversary weakened by smallpox. This was going to be the day the Cree crushed the Blackfoot. This, they were certain, would end their hunger and desperation, and they rode confidently into battle armed with wooden bows and English muskets.

They ambushed a Blood camp under cover of darkness and a furious battle ensued that lasted all night. As the sun rose, Blackfoot and Piegan reinforcements arrived from nearby camps up and down the river. They drove the Cree aggressors into a coulee and eventually flushed them out. "You could fire with your eyes shut and would be sure to kill a Cree," a guide and interpreter named Jerry Potts, who fought alongside the Blackfoot, said later. By the end of the day, about forty Blackfoot and anywhere from two hundred to four hundred Cree were dead. Cree blood reddened the shores of the river, Cree bodies floated downstream on its swift, mountainous waters, Cree resolve was shattered. The last armed conflict between Canada's Indian peoples was effectively over.

Most of us are unfamiliar with this battle and the decades of warfare that preceded it. The telling and re-telling of one of our most cherished national sagas—the opening, settling and building of the West—has swept these events into the shadows. And yet the story of the Plains Cree and Blackfoot Confederacy—the two nations whose warriors fought their last major battle near the banks of the Belly River—is as big as the prairie itself. It is a tale of tragedy and heroism, sorrow and grandeur. *Indian Fall* tells that story through the lives of four great nineteenth-century chiefs—Piapot, Big Bear, Crowfoot and Poundmaker. They were born in a native world, but died reluctant, unhappy citizens of the newly minted Dominion of Canada. These four men lived through the transformation of the West. Each experienced or played a role in the most significant events of their time—the native wars, the extermination of the buffalo, the signing of treaties and the 1885 rebellion—and each helped shape the outcomes of these events. Each was a different type of leader. Each stood for something quite different among his people.

Piapot earned his reputation as leader of a band known as the Young Dogs, a motley mix of Cree and Assiniboine warriors who were skilled buffalo hunters and cunning horse thieves, and who considered themselves pure men of the plains, but he achieved lasting renown as a healer and holy man. Big Bear was a political activist who foresaw the disastrous consequences of surrendering title to native lands. He was the last Plains Cree leader to sign a treaty and the last to take a reserve, but he was first in the fight for native rights.

Crowfoot was a warrior who fought in nineteen battles and was wounded six times before he was twenty years old. But he achieved lasting fame as a peacemaker by convincing his Blackfoot brethren to lay down their arms and sign a treaty, rather than fight the white man and risk annihilation. And Poundmaker, the adopted son of Crowfoot, a man of striking physical appearance—he was over six feet tall, with a handsome, slender face and waist-length hair—was an orator whose captivating eloquence impressed native and white listeners alike.

Piapot, Big Bear, Crowfoot and Poundmaker grew up at the best of times, the first half of the nineteenth century, when their peoples were the real lords and proprietors of the most northerly regions of the Great Plains of North America. But they served as leaders in the second half of that century—in what proved to be the darkest of times for their people.

PART

ONE

B*uffalo*
Days

National Archives of Canada c3863

CHAPTER

ONE

Kisikawasan

Flash in the Sky
Born about 1816

THE WOMAN AND HER grandson, a child about two years of age, are alone on a broad, windy plain. They have been on their own so long, here on the southern frontier of Cree country, near the territory of the neighbouring Assiniboines, that she has stopped counting the days. She has struggled to feed herself and the boy during the long, hot summer. But now the days are getting cooler and winter is not far off. She still hopes to be rescued, but she is frightened. She has no idea how or when their ordeal will end, but she knows exactly how and when it began.

The trouble started early in the summer when a party of hunters from her band encountered a desperate and barely coherent white man wandering alone on the prairie. He had been abandoned by his companions, a group of explorers, and he was ill, so the hunters took pity on him and brought him in to their camp. But despite their attempts to minister to him, his condition deteriorated and soon his sickness spread. Members of the band began suffering from fevers and cramps, headaches and nausea. Then red, pus-filled blisters erupted on their arms and faces. Elders knew immediately that it was *omikiwin*, the disease of the scabs, the most frightening marauder that their people, the Plains Cree, had ever known. This scourge—small-pox—was introduced to their world many years earlier by other white men, and previous outbreaks had taught them that it spared no one, neither men nor women, neither young nor old. Cree medicines and healing rituals were powerless against this invisible menace.

Panic had swept their camp like a wind-driven grass fire, and the people had scattered. Husbands and wives had parted. Brothers and sisters went separate ways. Parents abandoned their children. They had no choice because no one knew who was infected and who wasn't. Some fled on foot and some on horseback, some with possessions, some with nothing but the clothes they were wearing. They left behind the sick and the dying, and one small child too young to fend for himself.

The boy wandered around the nearly deserted camp, bewildered and terrified, and bawling at the top of his lungs. He cried until he could cry no more, until exhaustion overtook him. Then he lay down and slept. Out on the prairie, his grandmother had heard his cries. She remembered the dream she had had shortly after his birth, the dream that he would one day be a great man, a leader of his people. So she returned, gathered her grandson in her arms and retrieved a few tattered lodge coverings.

With these, she erected a makeshift shelter among some bushes and gnarled, knotty trees, a thicket that resembled a forlorn little island in a vast shortgrass sea. She erected the shelter upwind of the camp to avoid the stench of bloated and rotting corpses. From there, she watched the remains of the camp, so recently full of life and vitality, become a ghastly and desolate place. She watched wolves prey on the dying. She watched scavengers pick clean the remains of the dead. And as the days passed, she watched the sun, the wind and the rain do their work—baking, drying and bleaching—until all that remained were skeletons scattered on the prairie.

The woman and her grandson are among the lucky ones. They have been spared a grisly end, only to face new perils. They spend most of their time in the thicket, where the air resonates with the sound of insects, where there is shelter from the searing midday sun and the chilly night-time air, and where, if necessary, there are places to hide. She sits to conserve her strength and passes the time telling her grandson stories about his family, their people and this land they live in. She tells these stories in soft, whispery tones, so the sound of her voice rarely rises above the hum of the insects. And she is always alert.

She stands periodically to scan the horizons, looking for signs of her people. A plume of smoke might signify the camp of a Cree band, or an encampment of friendly Assiniboines. But horsemen could be either friends or enemies. She listens intensely for any tell-tale sounds. The snap of a twig, the swish of grasses or the sudden flight of startled birds might mean someone is lurking nearby. She knows that if there happens to be an enemy war party in the vicinity, scouts will be prowling the land. And scouts are men who specialize in stealth, who can appear out of nowhere, brandishing knives or clubs and ready to use them.

Almost daily, while her grandson sleeps, she wanders on the vast expanse around her to forage for food and look for fuel. She collects buffalo bones, which she boils to make a broth, and picks prairie turnips, which can be baked, roasted or eaten raw. And occasionally she takes a break from her labours. She pauses to enjoy a gully smothered in wild roses or a knoll clothed in lilies. She pauses to gaze at the wind-sculpted clouds and the fleeting shadows they cast on the shortgrass sea.

It is during such a moment of reflection and rapture that the boy's grandmother spots them. At first, they are no more than tiny, barely discernible specks in the distance, and she tells herself that she has seen them before, that they are bushes or trees. But she knows intuitively that they are horsemen. She also knows that if she has seen them, they may have seen her, so she drops to her knees and crawls back to the thicket. It takes her a long time, long enough for the sun to climb higher in the sky and for a warm breeze to become a hot wind.

Once she is back, she sits and watches. She sees them disappear and re-appear in the subtle ripples and folds of the prairie. She sees them become larger, their forms more distinct. These men could be triumphant Cree braves on their way home from plundering and pillaging an enemy village. Or they might be warriors from an enemy tribe looking to inflict havoc and mayhem on a Cree band. Whoever they are, they are coming straight toward her and the boy.

They ride at a steady, deliberate pace, as though anxious to cross this exposed stretch of land. Soon, she can hear the sound of hooves, carried by the wind. As the riders get closer, the clatter becomes louder and sharper until it erupts like thunder in her ears. The men have arrived but they haven't seen her and the boy. They are inspecting the site of the camp and the bones strewn here and there. Then as their leader turns his horse to gallop away, one of his followers implores him to stop. He points at the thicket, as though he had seen something. The woman knows they have been discovered, and she goes cold from head to foot. These men are Sioux hunters. This, she is certain, means death.

Two of the men come into the thicket and lead her out, with the baby boy in her arms. Then they all stand silently, this Cree woman and those Sioux hunters, eyeing each other warily while the sun shines, the wind blows, and the moments pass. One man holds a knife to her throat, but the head man tells him to put it away. He scrutinizes the woman, who appears strong and healthy despite the lean, haunted look on her face, and then he gestures to one of his subordinates: Bring her a horse.

Perhaps he is impressed with her composure. Perhaps it is her courage. Or perhaps he sees something in the boy he likes. For whatever reason, the head man will not put them to death. But neither will he leave them behind. He will take the child and his grandmother south as prisoners. At first, she is too surprised to feel relieved. But by dusk, after a long ride with the boy nestled in front of her, her fear begins to subside, and suddenly she shakes so hard that she almost falls off the horse.

By the end of the journey, she is bone tired and sore all over. It is about a three-day ride to Sioux country and the better part of another day to their captors' village. There, like it or not, they are to begin new lives, the boy adopted by a family who will raise him as their own, and his grandmother assigned to the household of a prosperous male, where she will be one of several wives. And the Sioux welcome the newcomers because it is not uncommon for parties of warriors or hunters to bring back people they have found lost or abandoned on the prairie.

THESE EVENTS OCCURRED in about 1818. The woman, whose courage and ingenuity saved both their lives, was in her late thirties or early forties. Her name was never recorded. But the boy, who was born to an Assiniboine father and a Cree mother, was called Kisikawasan, or Flash in the Sky. He may have been named for an illustrious warrior, a powerful shaman or a famous chief. Or perhaps there was something special about the birth of this boy. Perhaps he was born on a night when the sky was ablaze with falling stars or the shimmer of aurora borealis. Or maybe his mother had delivered him in a rush of wind and rain, as thunder ricocheted around the heavens, and lightning lit up the land.

Kisikawasan was not far removed from infancy when smallpox destroyed his family's band, making him an exile and changing his life. He lived among the Sioux until he was about fourteen. His grandmother frequently reminded him that he was a member of the Cree nation. But he learned the language of his captors and adopted their ways. He probably had his first taste of war with them. And he undoubtedly expected to spend the rest of his life among them. The distance between their country and his was great, and travel on the plains dangerous, too dangerous for small parties unable to defend themselves. So, as a bright, ambitious youngster, Kisikawasan would have acquired the values and outlook of the Sioux.

He would have learned that they had four core values— bravery, fortitude, generosity and wisdom—and that every Sioux man was expected to possess these qualities to some degree. Bravery was taught first because warfare was an integral part of Sioux culture. Boys were groomed to be warriors. They learned to handle bows and arrows, lances and clubs at a young age, and mock warfare was a favourite pastime. War games were rough and arduous to prepare a boy for the day when he would ride with the warriors of his band.

Fortitude was closely related to bravery. It meant that an individual could handle the pain of a wound or a fracture, that he could endure hunger and prolonged exposure to the elements, and that he was willing to disfigure or maim himself as a sign of respect when a comrade or a beloved family member died. Generosity was a constant in the life of the Sioux. Hunters shared the spoils of the kill with the weak and infirm. The young gave what they could to the old. The wives of prosperous men made clothing for widows and orphans. Gift-giving was part of every feast and ritual. A person who hoarded material possessions was considered a misfit and was usually ostracized.

Finally, boys in Sioux society were taught that they should strive to attain wisdom—the most intangible of the four virtues. The wise were believed to have acquired their powers through contact with the spiritual world. Only the wise could command the respect necessary to provide advice, settle disputes, inspire their peers, act as a mentor or lead a war party. And only a select few possessed the wisdom required to become expert in the complex shamanism and spirituality of the Sioux.

Kisikawasan and his grandmother might have spent the rest of their lives with that Indian nation, which controlled thousands of square miles of land drained by the Missouri River and its tributaries in present-day North and South Dakota. But as chance would have it, a party of enemy warriors one day attacked their village. The attack was sudden and unexpected. Yet, amid the chaos and cacophony of battle—the cries of attackers and defenders, the frantic screams of women and children running for shelter, the shrieks of the wounded and

the gasps of the dying—amid all this the boy and his grandmother recognized that the raiders were no enemies of theirs.
They were Crees.

This was an opportunity to return to their people, and they
seized it, despite the inherent dangers. They would be put to
death—with no questions asked—if caught deserting by the
Sioux. And what if the Cree did not recognize them? There
lay another danger. How they managed to elude one side and
convince the other cannot be said. But, when the Cree warriors withdrew from the battlefield that day and galloped away
from the Sioux village, Kisikawasan and his grandmother rode
with them. They, no doubt, were elated, and their rescuers
flabbergasted.

In the Cree scheme of things, to return home with a war
party intact—that is, no men wounded and none dead—earned
all the participants, but particularly the leader, recognition and
respect from the band. To attack an enemy camp and ride
home victorious was even better. When a pack of pilfered
horses was led into the village, the work of the day would stop,
and women, children and elderly men would come out to greet
them. It would be an occasion for gift-giving and feasting and
dramatic recountings of the expedition.

But to return with two members of your tribe—an adolescent boy and an older woman liberated from the Sioux—this
was unheard of. It was astonishing. Imagine the reaction when
the war party rode into their camp chanting battle songs or
singing the story of their attack on the Sioux. Imagine youthful
warriors in war bonnets and battle paints pulling up and dis-
mounting, greeting family and friends, and presenting
Kisikawasan and his grandmother. News of their return would
have spread quickly. There would have been visits to and from
other bands, perhaps the renewal of old friendships or reunions

with family. There would have been feasts and celebrations, wonder and rejoicing, and, for Kisikawasan, a new name. He would be known as Nehiyawapwat, or the Cree Sioux.

However, his youthful friends soon came up with a nickname, one that hinted at the story of his life, his long exile, and how he, through guile and courage, had escaped from the Sioux. He became known as Payipwat—Hole in the Sioux. There was no need to say more, no need to search for a lofty or poetic name. In those days, the Sioux were a powerful nation, feared by many. They had become masters of their country by conquering other nations and driving them away from the upper Missouri. The Sioux and the Cree were bitter enemies, a state of affairs that had lasted many years, longer than anyone could remember. Few outsiders encountered that nation and walked away unharmed. But Payipwat was one who did.

His life as a Sioux had ended. Yet he had many stories to tell about them. He had much to say about their ways, their warriors, their battles and what might be called the mystique of the Sioux. He had witnessed their generosity. He had seen their bravery and their unusual ability to endure hardship. He had been exposed to their shamans and spiritual leaders. All of this had made an indelible impression on his youthful mind. He could never forget the attention and respect they commanded from all who met them, the receptions they received at the trading posts on the Missouri, and the wild pride in their eyes when they rode across the plains on handsome, painted ponies. He would always remember the size and the swirl of their sun dances.

These were some of the things he brought with him when he rejoined his people and began rediscovering their world. He started this phase of his life among the Cree bands that wintered in the Qu'Appelle River valley near present-day Regina.

These people came to be known as the Calling River People. They, and the valley where they loved to camp, took their names from a legend about a pair of youthful and tragic lovers, a legend Payipwat surely heard, for it was a famous tale.

According to this legend, a famous chief who had lived in the valley several generations earlier, before white men arrived in the country, had a daughter whom he loved dearly. She was beautiful, clever and talented. This girl was a skilful cook. She was adept at turning hides into leather. And many admired her decorative work with beads and porcupine quills. She was the chief's only daughter and naturally attracted the interest of many young men. But the one she really cared for was an idle youth who had not distinguished himself in any way. He returned her affection and was determined to marry her. The chief insisted, however, that before the young man wed his daughter he should demonstrate skill and courage in confrontations with the enemies of their people. He issued a challenge to the suitor: Go to the land of our enemies on your own, and with your own hand take several scalps. Bring them back and you may marry my daughter.

So great was the young man's love that he left immediately and gave no thought to the dangers ahead. He journeyed far and was gone a long time, so long that many assumed he was dead. But the youth was more courageous and resourceful than anyone had imagined. He approached enemy camps with great stealth and waited patiently until a warrior wandered off alone. Then he approached silently, knocking him out with a stone tomahawk. He knelt over his fallen foe, used a crude stone knife to make a circular incision in the man's scalp, and yanked free a tuft of hair. At that, he had to flee, using all the craft and guile he had at his disposal, because the victim was quickly discovered and an alarm raised.

Word of these daring acts spread quickly. Enemy warriors became more vigilant. And each attack became more dangerous for the young man. Nevertheless, he eventually obtained the scalps and set off on the long journey home. Upon returning, he found that the chief and his band had moved their camp several miles upriver. The young man was so eager to see the girl he loved that he immediately borrowed a canoe to complete his journey. It was late in the day, and darkness fell while he was on the water.

But he kept paddling until he reached a portion of the river where the banks were shrouded in trees. By then, it was midnight and intensely dark. He was just about to dip his paddle into the water when the melancholy voice of a young woman broke the stillness by calling out his name.The young man stopped and shouted: *O-wan-na ka tap-wat?* Who calls? But there was no response. Just as he was about to start paddling, the voice cried out again. This time, he went ashore and shouted loudly: *O-wan-na ka tap-wat?* Who calls? Again, there was no response. The youth set off once more, only to be interrupted a third and final time.

Just before daybreak, he reached the camp and strode proudly into the circle of tepees. Then he noticed a crowd of mourners near the chief's lodge. Inside, he found the old man and his wife with their hair hanging loose, a sign of grief, and family and friends seated around the lodge weeping. The youth showed his respect by sitting down. He shook hands with the chief, presented the scalps, and asked for his daughter. But the head man merely pointed to a buffalo robe that hung from one side of the tepee, shielding a body laid out behind it. "Last night, just as the moon rose, her spirit left her," the grieving father said. "Before she died, she mentioned your name three times, and called for you to come quickly."

The young man rose without speaking and lifted the robe. He knelt beside the body of the young woman, leaned over and kissed her on the forehead. With that, he shook the chief's hand and left. He paddled back to the place where he had heard her voice, and there he drowned himself so that he could be united with the spirit of the woman he loved.

The chief decided that these tragic deaths should not be forgotten. He declared that the river would, in the future, be known as *o-wa-na ka tap-wat oo-se-pe*, the river of one who calls. And this was the Cree name for the waterway in the mid-1770s when French-speaking white men began paddling upstream in canoes laden with tea, sugar and trinkets, blankets, clothing and axes, muskets, ammunition and liquor.

These men were Nor'westers, employees of that vast and daring enterprise known as the Northwest Company, which every spring shipped trade goods more than a thousand miles inland by canoe from its headquarters in Montreal and used these same boats and waterways to carry out cargoes of valuable furs trapped the previous winter. These Nor'westers were lively souls. They were quick and agile with a paddle or a song but they could not get their minds or their tongues around *o-wa-na ka tap-wat oo-se-pe*. Instead, the river of one who calls became simply the Qu'Appelle—the Who Calls river.

The Nor'westers built several posts along the Qu'Appelle, and some of these were still occupied and open for business when Payipwat was born. But by the time he was rescued from the Sioux and returned to his homeland, the French-speaking traders were gone, their posts abandoned, and the wooden structures falling apart. This was the result of decisions made years earlier and thousands of miles away. In 1821, the Hudson's Bay Co. of London absorbed the Northwest Co. of Montreal, bringing to an end the cut-throat competition that threatened to ruin both firms. Hundreds of fur trading posts immediately became obsolete, including those in the Qu'Appelle Valley, and they were closed.

For the next forty years or so, various Cree bands and their allies among the Assiniboines were the sole inhabitants and unquestioned masters of the rich and splendid Qu'Appelle Valley, as well as the surrounding plains that seemed to stretch to eternity in every direction. The valley was like an oasis carved from west to east across a nearly treeless, relentlessly flat land.

Cree bands particularly liked a section of the valley where the river widened at intervals to form a chain of lakes, now known as the Fishing Lakes. These waters were often thick with whitefish, which were easy to catch and delicious to eat. At times, immense flocks of migrating waterfowl took over the lakes and the surrounding shorelines to rest and feed. Throughout the summer there were saskatoons, chokecherries, pin cherries and gooseberries to harvest. And during the long, hard winters, buffalo sought refuge in the wooded valley bottom. There, two hundred to three hundred feet below the adjacent prairie, the big beasts found protection from the bite of wind-driven snow and cold.

Payipwat lived for several years—precisely how many is not known—among the Crees of the Qu'Appelle Valley. For generations, these bands had wintered in the valley, and broken camp at *ayikipicim*, the frog moon, as the cold began to loosen its grip on the land and life returned to the prairie. They wandered the plains through spring, summer and fall, their course set not by the winds or the stars but by the movement of the herds. After the moon of the falling leaves—*pinackopicim*—as winter was preparing to hammer the land and all its inhabitants, they returned to the Qu'Appelle.

The Qu'Appelle Cree had thoroughly embraced life on the

prairie, unlike their brethren who lived along the North Saskatchewan and retained some of the habits and characteristics
of their forest-dwelling predecessors. They had largely given
up trapping beaver and other fur-bearing animals, a pursuit
closely associated with the northern forests. Nevertheless, they
continued to play an important role in the fur trade, supplying
pemmican and dried meat to feed the men of the canoe
brigades who transported furs to Hudson Bay and Montreal.
Horses and guns had made the Qu'Apelle Cree proficient
hunters who could slaughter more buffalo than they needed for
their survival. The women converted the surplus kills into pemmican—a combination of dried meat, berries and fat—which
could be stored in rawhide containers and consumed the following winter or exchanged for the new and tantalizing goods
available at the trading posts.

Invariably, the annual travels of the Calling River Cree
included a trip to a fur trade establishment. For three decades
after the closure of the Qu'Appelle posts, the nearest place to
conduct business was Fort Ellice, which stood about five miles
below the confluence of the Qu'Appelle and Assiniboine
Rivers, near the present-day Saskatchewan–Manitoba border.
This post was opened in 1831, about the time Payipwat
returned to the Cree and, according to the Hudson Bay trader
Isaac Cowie, it was "beautifully situated at a point on the level
of the prairie where the deep and picturesque valley of the
Beaver Creek joined the broad valley of the Assiniboine, which
could be seen wending its way for miles to and fro in the park-
like bottom lands."

A man named John Richards McKay, who was born at
Moose Factory on James Bay, took over the post in 1833 and
ran it for twenty-five years. In his book *The Company of Adventurers*, which recounted his years as a Hudson's Bay employee,

Cowie described McKay as fair, friendly and courageous, not to mention colourful. He even had an Indian name—Little Bear Skin. "The admiration of the many tribes who resorted to Fort Ellice was aroused by feats in which he displayed his skill and dexterity as a horseman, a swordsman and a sure shot, and by other sprightly and spectacular accomplishments." Above all, he was a successful trader who managed to attract such a diverse clientele that he required interpreters who spoke Cree, Assiniboine, Saulteaux, Sioux, Mandan and a couple of other native tongues.

Fort Ellice drew its clientele from a huge swath of prairie covering much of present-day southwestern Manitoba, southern Saskatchewan and North Dakota. With the closure of the Qu'Appelle posts, many of the Indians who lived on these lands had begun trading at newly established American forts on the upper Missouri River, but McKay lured them back to the Hudson's Bay Co.

The Indians made annual or semi-annual treks to Fort Ellice from their homelands on the unbounded, uncharted plains. They arrived with their cargoes of pemmican, robes and a few furs, and they sometimes stayed a couple of weeks. They sang and danced and drank—late into the night and occasionally till dawn—keeping the traders awake and disrupting their routines. They socialized with friends and acquaintances from other tribes who happened to be there at the same time. Once the trading was complete, they left with their highly prized European goods. Where they went and where they had come from, how they lived and how they died, were largely unknown to traders like McKay and his colleagues. They were men of commerce. They were preoccupied with balance sheets and bottom lines and advancing their careers within the Company of Adventurers.

Payipwat was undoubtedly part of the traffic to and from
Fort Ellice each summer. He was part of the multi-tribal bazaar
that sprang to life briefly on the prairie outside the post. Afterward, he returned to his world, where there were no traders,
no balance sheets and no bottom lines. There wasn't a single
road or fixed dwelling, or any other sign of white civilization in
all the prairie between Fort Ellice and the Rocky Mountains,
lands that these British traders claimed as their own.

Payipwat came of age, went to war, took his wives and
became a leader in a world that was almost totally Indian. But
there are no accounts of these developments, neither written
nor oral. Instead, there is a great hiatus, a thirty-year stretch,
from the early 1830s till the early 1860s, one-third of his long
and colourful life, about which almost nothing is known. Two
things can be said with a fair degree of certainty, however: he
emerged from these years of obscurity as leader of the Young
Dogs, a band of rogues, renegades and wild men of Cree and
Assiniboine extraction; and it was in this capacity that he
became one of the most durable and celebrated native leaders
of his day.

Payipwat was then in his early fifties. He had six wives and
spoke five languages—Cree, Assiniboine, Sioux, Saulteaux and
Blackfoot. He was a well-known and highly respected spiritual
leader. He had acquired the rudiments of his faith as a boy
growing up among the Sioux and he had practised devoutly all
his life. He worshipped the *kice manito*, the Creator who had
willed the universe into existence and controlled everything in
it. He was capable of contacting the *atayohkanak*, the spirit
powers who inhabited all living things, all inanimate objects,
and natural phenomena like wind and rain, thunder and lightning. And because of this, people said he possessed strong
medicine. They sought him out when they needed help from

the spirit powers—before going off to war, or embarking on the hunt, in times of sickness or hunger.

Payipwat was a man of character and presence. He caught the attention of the traders and explorers who were beginning to push farther and farther into the broad, unbroken plains that had for so long been the sole domain of wandering bands of buffalo-hunting Indians. These white men took note of him, and they gave him the name by which he became famous. They turned Payipwat, an eight-letter, three-syllable mouthful, into Piapot, just two letters shorter but oh so smooth to an English tongue. And to his native followers and admirers, he had become someone else as well. Piapot was no longer Hole in the Sioux. He had become One Who Knows the Secrets of the Sioux.

Cowie was one of the white men who encountered Piapot in the late 1860s, and he was the first to write about him. Cowie was part of the wave of traders who travelled deep into the Indian country of the prairie, drawn there by the diminishing size and range of the buffalo herds. In the memoir he wrote of his years with the Hudson's Bay Co., Cowie observed that in the 1830s buffalo "were frequently so numerous right at Fort Ellice as to require a watchman round the hay yard to keep and drive them out of it in the winter when the snow was deep."

By 1852, the Bay had opened a provisioning post in the Touchwood Hills, 150 miles northwest of Fort Ellice, for quicker and easier access to the herds, and in 1863 the company built a fort in the Qu'Appelle Valley for the same reasons. Cowie was posted there as a clerk for several years. In June and July of 1868, he was part of an expedition that travelled southwest from Fort Qu'Appelle to trade with a group of Crees, Assiniboines and Saulteaux—perhaps as many as three thousand people—who had formed one large camp of 350 lodges.

They were hunting buffalo a few miles north of the Cypress Hills on the edge of Blackfoot country and had come together for protection against their old enemies.

It was there that Cowie first met Piapot and his Young Dogs. He described Piapot as "an honorable man and a good hunter," even if the native leader was "ambitious and thereby made troublesome." However, he had no kind words whatsoever for the Young Dogs. To a man like Cowie, there were two kinds of Indians: the good ones—those who were proficient hunters and regular customers at the trading posts; and the bad ones—those who spent their time stealing horses, making war and giving company employees a hard time. Then there were Piapot's followers. They were in a class by themselves, according to Cowie. The Dogs, as he called them, were outcasts even among the Indians, and they had a reputation that "might be most fittingly expressed by calling them sons of the female canine."

The Hudson's Bay man did not explain the origins of the Young Dogs, how they acquired their name, or how Piapot came to be associated with them. Perhaps they arose out of the multi-tribal bazaar that occurred at Fort Ellice each summer. Perhaps he left his people to ride off with them. Or perhaps they rode away from their bands to join him. Either way, the Young Dogs appear to have been distinguished more by the wildness of the Assiniboines than the enterprising character of the Crees, who had long been enthusiastic participants in the fur trade and had always been peaceful in their dealings with whites.

The Assiniboines, according to both British and American traders who wrote of this era, were courageous and daring fighters, and incorrigible horse thieves. But for all their thieving, they always owned fewer horses and guns than their larger, more powerful neighbours and perpetual enemies—the Blackfoot to the west and the Sioux to the south. And they were reluctant participants in the fur trade, according to Edwin Denig, a trader from Pennsylvania who was married to an Assiniboine woman. Even by the mid-nineteenth century, when British posts had long been established on the North Saskatchewan, and American posts were firmly entrenched on the Missouri, the Assiniboines were much less enamoured of the products of white civilization than other tribes of the plains. "It is but a few years since any of them could be persuaded to wear a coat or pantaloons, or even a hat or shirt," Denig wrote in 1854. "Their saddles, dresses, utensils are all made in the same way as they were in the days of stone axes and bone awls. They see and know well enough that something better can be done, particularly when iron tools are furnished them and every sort of material can be had, but they will not exert themselves and even ridicule other nations for imitating the manners, dress and manufactures of whites."

That determination to resist the material goods of white civilization, that resolve to maintain their own ways and a pure Indian identity, may have been the force that drove the Assiniboine members of the Young Dogs. Perhaps Piapot saw this and admired it. Perhaps he saw it as the source of their strength and power. And he may have brought his own unique elements to the mix, qualities he had acquired from the Sioux—a Sioux pride in being Indian that was strong enough to resist the white pressure to abandon the life of the roving, free-spirited warrior in order to become a placid hunter and reliable customer at the nearest trading post, and a Sioux haughtiness that could make a man formidable in the face of enemies who were more numerous and better armed. Perhaps he had given a band of wild, reckless young men the mindset that made them strong and courageous. Maybe this was why they regarded Piapot as One Who Knows the Secrets of the Sioux.

In any case, it is clear from Cowie's version of his encounter with the Young Dogs in the summer of 1868 that they were the most threatening of all the Indians camped near the Cypress Hills, and that they had no use for white interlopers. Indeed, they would have murdered Cowie and stolen his wares were it not for the intervention of the Crees and Saulteaux.

The trouble occurred the day after he arrived. Cowie was there to trade, and he opened the session by distributing gifts to customers he trusted and valued, which was the established practice. He then spent most of the morning and a good part of the afternoon in a large tepee doing business with Indians who were desperately short of tea, tobacco and ammunition.

The session ended unexpectedly when two members of the Young Dogs, Yellow Head and Big Beak, both apparently under the influence of alcohol, strode into the lodge and sat down squarely in front of Cowie. They had come from their warriors' lodge and demanded gifts equivalent to those that the Hudson's Bay clerk had given out earlier in the day. Cowie prudently decided to appease them and placed two pints of tea and a yard of rolled tobacco on a buffalo robe between them. But Yellow Head, a noted warrior who was said to have as many as ten wives, merely scowled and threw the offerings back at him. Then he stood up, approached Cowie and slapped him on the cheek.

Cowie sprang to his feet in a rage and, with one well-placed blow, broke his adversary's nose and knocked out two teeth. At that instant Yellow Head's fellow warriors, who had remained outside, slashed the lodge coverings to shreds. Cowie found himself surrounded by forty Young Dogs who had guns and bows aimed at him. "I quickly caught the butt of my revolver and was drawing it, determined to die fighting," he wrote in his book, "when up sprang all the Crees, who had remained so long passive spectators, and three of them seized me, and bore me, struggling desperately to the earth. There they struggled with and held me down till I was utterly exhausted."

When the disturbance had ended, the Crees took Cowie to their warriors' lodge where the head men of several bands were meeting in council. A Cree leader named The Broken Sword spoke for his people and the Saulteaux, and Cowie later reproduced the chief's speech in his book. "White man," The Broken Sword began, "the Young Dogs are very bad people. They have tried to rob and murder you to-day. The Whites are our friends and the Young Dogs are people whom we detest. We have seen to-day that your arm is strong and your heart is strong and—if you will say the word—we, the Crees and Saulteaux of Qu'Appelle and Touchwood Hills, will fall upon them and kill the whole odious and villainous tribe of them. We have held and surrounded you to prevent your being killed by these rascals. Now you are free to do as you like, and we will do as you say."

An interpreter named La Pierre convinced Cowie not to take up The Broken Sword's offer, so a tense peace prevailed in the camp. But the Young Dogs had made a lasting impression on the white trader, and the stories he heard later about them only reinforced his antipathy. He often heard the tale about the natural disaster that befell the Young Dogs in the mid-1860s, a few years before he encountered them. This incident was said to have occurred during a buffalo hunting expedition to the Great Sand Hills, which lay between the Cypress Hills and the South Saskatchewan. Several Cree bands were camped together. But they would not permit the Young Dogs to erect their lodges—about forty to fifty in all—among them.

"So it happened that the Young Dogs camp was pitched about a mile from that of the Crees... that summer day. In the afternoon, a cloud no bigger than a man's hand arose in the north-west, came on swiftly and enlarging till it burst in roaring thunder and forked lightning, with a torrential downpour over the site of the doomed camp of the Young Dogs. That downpour was not of water, but of a liquid acid, which quickly reduced to ashes everything on which it fell. A few, near the shores of a small lake on which the camp stood, sought refuge from the burning rain in its waters, but while their bodies were protected by the water their heads above it were reduced to ash.

"When the storm ceased, the Crees, who then ventured to the scene, found the forms of men lying under covers of robes and skins, and the moment these were touched they crumbled into dust and ashes. Carts, lodges and poles left standing also crumbled away at a touch or a breath of wind. The miraculous nature of the occurrence is heightened by the statement that every living creature in that camp miserably perished, except a young and beautiful Cree maiden, who had a day or two before been kidnapped and taken into his harem by one of the Dogs. She is said to have escaped by diving till she crossed the lake."

Cowie first heard this story from a fellow trader and long-time friend, William Traill, and he heard it often from Crees he met during his travels. Like most white men of his era, Cowie dismissed most Indian tales of strange adventures and supernatural occurrences. Yet he related this one without a trace of scepticism. In fact, he visited the site of the disaster in the fall of 1873 and found what he took to be physical evidence of it. "The grass, turf and soil, down to the clay subsoil beneath, were also consumed and ... the circle in which the camp had stood could still be distinguished by the barren clay supporting scattered growth of weeds in a depression which was surrounded by grass-grown prairie."

So something unusual had happened there. Whether it was acid falling like rain from the sky, men turned to ash, and earth scorched and barren is not the point. The real question is this: why did Piapot and his followers inspire such a strange story?

Unfortunately, that question cannot be satisfactorily answered. The historical record of these times is too thin. The Young Dogs, who roamed the Canadian prairie during the last great days of the Plains Cree and the Blackfoot Confederacy, must forever remain men of the imagination rather than figures on the printed pages. They remain one of the mysteries of this period, and their leader Piapot an enduring enigma. But a revealing anecdote about him has survived, and it suggests that he was a proud and enterprising man with a sly sense of humour.

Piapot had been snubbed, the story goes, by the white traders of the Hudson's Bay Co., who refused to recognize his leadership and to award the benefits, however small, that came with such recognition. The Bay men had a habit of bestowing their blessings on certain native leaders by issuing what the Cree called *mis-ny-gan*, or "little writings." The chief trader at a post would give a chief a handwritten note saying, for example, that "the bearer, Piapot, is an influential warrior among the Cree and Assiniboines of the Qu'Appelle, who has always been friendly to the whites, and deserves a piece of tobacco from any of the Company's people when they meet."

But no officer in the company, not even a junior trader at a minor post, would ever have considered writing such a testimonial for Piapot. This had nothing to do with his character or abilities, because, as Cowie says, the Young Dog leader was "an honorable man and a good hunter." In fact, he and his wives and their offspring were capable of producing hundreds of pounds of pemmican every summer, which they could trade at the posts. But this made no difference to the employees of the company.

It so happened, however, that a man of English and native extraction was travelling alone on the prairie and wandered into the Young Dogs' summer camp one day. He not only knew how to write. He had a pencil and paper with him. So Piapot prevailed upon him to write a *mis-ny-gan*. Seated in the chief's lodge, the stranger put pencil to paper and went to work, as the Young Dog leader dictated, and his family watched intently. "I am PIAPOT. . . ." the visitor wrote slowly, almost as though he were etching on wood, his big, calloused hands being more adept a firing a rifle than wielding a pencil. And when the man had finished, Piapot allowed everyone to admire the document briefly before folding it carefully and stowing it away in a pouch for safekeeping.

That is where Piapot's *mis-ny-gan* remained until he led his band into a Hudson's Bay post for the fall trading session. They made a colourful caravan as they came in from the plains. Hunters rode their best buffalo runners and wore their fanciest clothes. Women and children followed on the pack horses, which dragged travois loaded with pemmican and personal possessions. Dogs barked, babies cried and, when the trading post appeared on the horizon, the men fired guns to announce their arrival.

The session opened, as these affairs always did, with plenty of pomp and an undercurrent of politics. The leading men of the band met the chief trader within the post, they being seated on the floor and he being ensconced in a chair. Greetings and gifts were exchanged. The Hudson's Bay man may have distributed tea and tobacco to those in attendance. And the men who hunted diligently, who never made trouble, who were known as good Indians, they hoped for something special: wool pants, a colourful coat or a feathered hat. It was during such a gathering that Piapot presented the note he had dictated to the mixed-blood stranger. He was determined to set the record straight about who he was, and this is what he told them: I am PIAPOT, LORD of the HEAVEN and EARTH.

Piapot undoubtedly acted partly in jest when he dictated the note. He would never have confused himself with a higher power because he believed too deeply in the Creator. But he was astute enough to see that the Bay men were using petty praise and small gifts to keep the chiefs docile and loyal to the company. Piapot likely resented this practice and so made a mockery of it.

In the not-too-distant future, after white men had come into the country in large numbers, taken over the land and begun to wield power, he would see many other things he resented. These newcomers would try to impose their ways and their values on his people. They would try to destroy his faith. By then, he was an old man, but he would stand up for his people. And he would fight the last battle against the white man—the battle for cultural survival.

Mistahimusqua
Big Bear
Born about 1825

OLD PEOPLE KEPT HIS story alive. Old people who were born in the days of freedom, who had roamed the plains, hunted buffalo, made war on the Blackfoot. Old people who were there when the treaties were signed, when the Indians settled on reserves, when the troubles of 1885 occurred, and when trains full of white homesteaders arrived to occupy their homelands.

The old people had fantastic memories. They were gifted storytellers. They might sit on a hillside on a summer evening, surrounded by members of their band, and tell stories as the sun set slowly in the big prairie sky. Or on cold, silent winter nights, they might sit at the kitchen table in a tiny tar-paper shack on the reserve and reminisce about the old days as the light from a kerosene lamp flickered against the walls and danced across the rapt faces of their little audience. They would tell stories about their adventures, about the dangers they had faced and the wondrous things they had seen. They would talk about the warriors they had known and the head men they had served. Men like Little Pine and Lucky Man, or Sweetgrass and Red Pheasant. Men who had signed treaties on behalf of their people and loaned their names to the reserves where their bands had settled.

On those summer evenings and winter nights, the old people talked often and with reverence about the man called Mistahimusqua. Mistahi meant big, and musqua was the word for bear. He was a great chief, someone would say. Nobody fought for our people like he did. He was the last to sign a treaty, another would add, the last to settle down. Those who had stood by Big Bear would remind the others how they had all been gaunt and ragged, starving and desperate during the final days of freedom.

Inevitably, there were debates about that dreadful morning in April 1885, when Big Bear's men had massacred most of the inhabitants of the white settlement of Frog Lake. It was all Wandering Spirit's doing, one would say, referring to the war chief. No, my friend, the old person across the table would reply, it was Big Bear's son, Imasees. He put the men up to it. When that point had been thoroughly talked through, someone would say: Remember how it all ended? Remember the flight north through the bush, from Frenchman's Butte to Loon Lake, with our people and the Woods Cree and the white prisoners, all being chased by the mounted police and the Canadian soldiers. And who could forget, because Big Bear's band had been destroyed, and the old chief had wound up behind bars.

When they talked of these things, one of the old people would always say Big Bear had foreseen the trouble with the white man. He had seen it in a vision, when he was not much more than a boy. Then that person would tell the story of this premonition, or one of Big Bear's other visions and conclude by saying, unequivocally, that he was a man of unusual spiritual power. They talked about the personal qualities that made him a great leader—his warmth and humour, his bravery and generosity. They would entertain youthful listeners with tales of his battles with the Blackfoot and his miraculous escapes from that fearsome tribe.

The talk spanned generations. The old people shared the stories with their children, who passed them on to their offpring. The talk began in the late nineteenth century and continued well into the twentieth. By the time the old people had gone to their graves, few of the stories about Mistahimusqua had been recorded. Most were preserved only in the memories of the children and grandchildren of the old-timers. And they remained there, locked up in memory, until the early 1970s when, by chance, the Calgary writer and historian Hugh Dempsey met an aging Cree man named Four Souls, who lived on the Rocky Boy Indian Reservation in northern Montana.

Four Souls, a retired ambulance driver, was in his early seventies. He met Dempsey at a social gathering and told him that he was the son of Imasees and the grandson of Big Bear. Four Souls knew many stories about his forefathers and he shared them with Dempsey, who had made a career of studying the history and culture of Canada's plains Indians, and immediately knew that none of these stories had ever been published. In the years that followed, Dempsey began looking for others who had heard stories. He visited Cree reserves along the North Saskatchewan River and met seven elderly Cree men whose stories formed the basis of Dempsey's biography of Big Bear, published in the early 1980s.

Big Bear was the son of a chief named Mukatai, a Cree word for Black Powder. Mukatai was Ojibwa by birth but his people had left their homelands in the forests north and west of Lake Superior, migrated to the Saskatchewan country, probably in the late 1700s or early 1800s. There, they settled among the Cree. Mukatai had married a woman of either Cree or Ojibwa descent, but her name was neither remembered nor recorded. He had become leader of a band consisting of about a dozen Cree and Ojibwa families, about a hundred people in all.

Mukatai and his followers divided their time between prairie and parkland, between grasslands and woodlands, between hunting buffalo and trapping beaver and other fur-bearing animals. They spent the summers out on the plains and the winters camped on the shores of Jackfish Lake, a small, irregular-shaped body of water surrounded by rolling, wooded hills that provided shelter from icy winter winds, fuel for the fires and abundant game. It was there, in the winter of 1825, during *api-htapipunpicim*, the mid-winter moon, or perhaps *mikiciwpicim*, the eagle moon, that Mistahimusqua was born.

Big Bear's birthplace is easy to locate on a map of Saskatch-ewan. Start at the city of Saskatoon and run a finger westward along Highway 16 through Radisson, Ruddell and Denholm and a handful of other one- and two-elevator prairie towns. At North Battleford, situated at the forks of the Battle and the North Saskatchewan Rivers, let the eye wander north on Highway 4, and there is Jackfish Lake. It is six to seven kilome-tres wide at most, and about ten kilometres long, and busy as a beehive every summer. Its shores provide a retreat for cottagers and campers, a playground for boaters and swimmers, but a year-round home for hardly anyone, except the native people who live on two reserves on the east side of the lake.

Jackfish Lake has become what hundreds of other Canadian lakes have become over the past century or so: cottage country. But in Big Bear's youth, the lake and the surrounding country-side were in the heart of Cree country. For several hundred miles to the east, the south and the west, virtually the only inhabitants were bands of Crees. They moved at will on these lands. They controlled them. These lands belonged to the Cree people, who had been placed there by the Creator. And the Creator had provided the herds of buffalo so that the Cree, his children, would have food to eat, skins for their lodges, robes to sleep in and many other goods that made their lives comfortable.

As a boy, Big Bear would rarely have encountered a white man. At the time of his birth, there was only one Hudson's Bay Co. trading post—Fort Carlton—in the vicinity of Jackfish Lake. Carlton stood on a broad, flat tableland adjacent to the North Saskatchewan, about eighty miles east of Jackfish, a three- to four-day walk. A few years after Big Bear's birth, the company had built Fort Pitt, about the same distance upstream, or west of Jackfish.

The traders seldom ventured far from their fortified store-houses and counting houses to conduct business. They let the Indians come in from the surrounding countryside. Big Bear's father was well known at the posts, particularly Carlton. In the spring, Mukatai and other men of the band would paddle downriver, or walk there with their loads of furs harvested over the winter, and these they would trade for tea, tobacco, ammu-nition and other goods for the summer buffalo hunt out on the prairie. In the fall, he would lead his band back, with pemmican to trade for winter supplies.

While his father was away trapping, hunting or trading, Big Bear stayed home. His life, until he was seven or eight years old, revolved around the camp, a small, intimate community of extended families—grandparents, parents and children, aunts, uncles and cousins—and probably a few people who were tied to the band through friendship or marriage rather than blood. It was a community of many shared responsibilities and joint undertakings, of few secrets and very little privacy. In such a setting, there would be potential for squabbles, jealousies and resentments, and these Mukatai would have to resolve or arbitrate.

For a boy like Big Bear, life in this little world was unstructured and uncluttered. There were no clocks, calendars or schedules, not many rules, not many constraints of any kind on a boy's freedom. The day usually began with a wake-up call from an old man, who would rise just before daybreak, step outside his tepee and shout, "If the sun finds you working when he comes up, you will live long, and be healthy."

At that, the camp would begin to stir. The women would kindle the fires and start preparing the morning meal. And a boy like Big Bear could contemplate a day of games and adventures, perhaps some mock warfare against the hated Blackfoot, or perhaps a morning spent following the trail of some small animal, then stalking it with a child's bow and arrow. He and the other boys in the band could play till they were exhausted and eat when they were hungry, because when food was plentiful there was always a meal simmering in a pot over the fire.

In the winter, the hills and woods around Jackfish Lake served as their playground, and they could wander as far as the weather or their stamina would permit. In the summer, the prairie became the playground. This seemingly simple land-scape was a place of surprising beauty and abundance. Sage and songbirds sweetened the morning air. Berry bushes swayed and sagged with the weight of chokecherries and saskatoons. Hawks soared overhead. Vast colonies of gophers burrowed beneath the earth. And the hot summer days seemed as endless as the prairie itself.

It was a landscape to stir the wanderlust in a young boy's soul. But for all its grandeur and beguiling beauty, the prairie could be a dangerous place in the summer. Enemies of the Cree prowled the land at that time of year, and a crowd of boys who wandered too far or wide might look over their shoulders just as a party of Blackfoot warriors rode over the crest of a hill and swooped down on them.

So the women kept the children close to the camp during the day. Later, a head man or an elder announced the end of the day's activities by walking through the camp and shouting, "Get my grandchildren ready to watch the sun go out of sight." Watching the sunset was a nightly ritual for many Cree young-sters. The world was transformed before their eyes as shadows filled the gullies and ravines and darkness rose from the land. Creatures of the night emerged from their dens and, a long way off, wolves howled from the hilltops. If the earth seemed to be in motion, so was the sky. The blazing blue of the sum-mer afternoon gave way to crimsons, purples and golds. As the children gazed at the spectacle in the sky, the old man might ask in low, rich voice, "Grandchildren, have I ever told you the story about Wesakaychak and the great flood?"

Wesakaychak, the story went, was born when the earth was young and wild and unfit for people. He was the first human child, but was orphaned when he was only half-grown. Alone in a wilderness, he had many adventures. He was abducted by a malevolent old creature named Waymisosiw, who was similar to Wesakaychak, but hairier and too rough in appearance to be a real human being. Wesakaychak was attacked by a crimson eagle but killed the bird. He encountered a great serpent and slew it, too. Finally, he destroyed a giant moose that tried to crush him with its mighty antlers.

Wesakaychak prevailed over these creatures because he was clever and courageous and had a good heart. He wanted to make the world comfortable for human beings, so he created all the animals used by man. He invented the bow and arrow. He knew that people needed light and heat so he captured a heavenly body—the sun—to shine on the earth. But there were evil creatures in the world who wanted to undo Wesakaychak's good works, so they planned to cause a great flood. Wesakaychak learned of the scheme and instructed the animals to build a large raft, and they finished it just as the flood waters began to rise. Many animals reached the raft. Some fled to the tops of the hills, and these Wesakaychak rescued. But many others perished.

In time, even the hills were covered, and the world was drowned. After many days, calm returned to the earth, and Wesakaychak summoned the otter, the beaver and the muskrat. First, he sent the otter off to see if he could find any sign of land. But the otter returned empty-handed. Next, the beaver took his turn, and he, too, came back with nothing. Then, Wesakaychak sent the muskrat. He was gone longer than the other two. Finally, he returned, so exhausted he could barely swim, but clutching a shred of green. "I touched the top of a tree," he cried with jubilation in his voice, "but I was faint, and could not reach the bottom to get some earth. I will make another try."

After resting, the plucky muskrat set off again. Suddenly, one of the birds who had been flying about looked at the horizon and shouted, "Muskrat is coming back." It was true. The little animal soon arrived, nearly dead with exhaustion, but clutching a clump of mud. Wesakaychak took the mud, made it into a ball and blew on it, whereupon it grew rapidly. With his paddle-like tail, beaver began to beat the mud out flat while Wesakaychak blew on it. In time, they could not see where the land touched the water. Wesakaychak rested, but asked a grey wolf to run around the land to judge its size.

In two days, wolf came back and reported that it was not yet large enough. Again Wesakaychak began to blow. The wolf was sent to investigate once more but did not return for many days. When he came back, he reported that the land still was not large enough. So Wesakaychak went to work again. This time, when he was finished, he sent the crow, who did not return. Then, Wesakaychak concluded that the earth was large enough, and he stopped.

Thus, out of the flood, the earth was reclaimed and the animals multiplied again. Many of the forms of life that had been vicious and dangerous to man had disappeared. But the muskrat, the beaver and the otter were rewarded and were told that henceforth they would be equally at home on land or water. And they are to this day. The grey wolf left to roam this new world, but some of his offspring stayed with Wesakaychak, and today their descendants—those most faithful companions and protectors of man, the dogs—are to be seen wherever Indian lodges stand.

Stories such as this were an essential part of Big Bear's upbringing. But a youth couldn't learn everything through stories. He had to absorb some of life's most important lessons from the land and the creatures that lived on it. The playgrounds of Big Bear's boyhood, the prairie and the parkland, those endless grasslands and rolling, wooded hills, were his classroom. He would have had several mentors because his father, being a chief, had many other duties and responsibilities to fulfil. And besides, Black Powder never stayed put for long. Dempsey, in his authoritative biography of Big Bear, described Mukatai this way: "The man was a wanderer. One day, he might turn up at Edmonton House, and two months later he could be in his lodge in the Eagle Hills. Spring might find him in his bark canoe, bringing furs from his winter catch, but in autumn he could be astride his best buffalo runner, acting as though he had spent his whole life on the plains."

There were always camp elders who were willing to share their knowledge of the woods and the plains. Or a youth in his late teens or early twenties, who had established himself as a capable hunter and a daring warrior, may also have taught Big Bear. Cree boys and young men often formed such pupil-teacher relationships, and the two would become the closest of companions. They referred to one another as *niwitcewahakan*— he with whom I go about.

Every Cree boy was expected to become a proficient hunter and a courageous warrior, and Big Bear was no exception. As an adult, he would inevitably be called upon to defend his community. And if he wanted to enhance his position within the band, a Cree man had to participate in raiding parties to steal horses from enemy tribes, or join war parties in which the objective was to attack the village of an enemy and inflict as much damage as possible.

But hunting was his first and most important obligation because a man had to provide for his family year round. A boy like Big Bear would learn to snare rabbits, lynx and prairie chickens. He would learn to trap wolves, coyotes and badgers.

He would acquire the patience and stealth required to stalk deer and antelope, perhaps even moose and elk. And he would spend much time and energy learning to hunt buffalo.

In the winter, when food was scarce, hunters would look for opportunities to drive one or two buffalo away from a herd and then they would spend hours or even days on foot pursuing these animals, driving them across a snow-crusted plain until they were too exhausted to run any farther. Then they would move in for the kill. Or they would drive the animals into snowdrifts that immobilized them and made them easy targets.

But for sheer exhilaration, nothing surpassed the communal summer hunts. Many Cree bands spent the summers camped along the South Saskatchewan River, near the range of the magnificent herds. Scouts would search out the buffalo and return when they had found them. The hunt was a simple affair. The men would ride out together on their swiftest horses, stopping just out of sight of the herd. Warriors would line everyone up to ensure an equitable start and to prevent someone from stampeding the herd. They would give a signal and the hunters would be off, chasing thousands of wild-eyed, panic-stricken beasts across the prairie.

Many men preferred the bow, and the most skilled among them could draw arrrows from their quiver, load their weapon and discharge deadly projectiles all in one fluid motion, despite the thunder and dust of the herd and the ever-present risk of being tossed from a horse and trampled to death. Those who used guns would keep bullets or musket balls in their mouths, spit them into the barrel of their firearm, add a smattering of powder and pull the trigger when they could almost reach out and touch the heaving sides of one of these huge beasts.

Hunting was sometimes a hazardous business. In the winter, men could get caught in a sudden storm and freeze to death chasing a buffalo. And guns occasionally exploded, leaving a hunter with a maimed hand or missing fingers. Yet a boy was expected to accept such risks, without complaint, as well as the dangers that came with warfare and horse-stealing expeditions.

But for Big Bear, there was more. He was the son of a chief. Other members of the band expected that he would succeed his father. They would give him advice and encouragement. They would watch him closely, because to become a chief was no simple matter. He would have to earn his father's position. He would have to be industrious, generous and courageous. He would have to win the respect of the elders and inspire confidence in those who might accompany him on raiding missions or war parties. He would have to outshine other brave and ambitious young men in the band.

The surest way to meet these challenges was to perform well in battle, and when Big Bear was growing up there was no shortage of opportunity to excel at warfare. In those days, the Plains Cree and the tribes of the Blackfoot Confederacy were almost continually at war. Occasionally, these two nations would negotiate a truce, sometimes at the behest of the Hudson's Bay Co., whose employees reasoned that the Indians would be more productive trappers if they spent less time fighting. One such accord was reached in 1828 but fell apart four years later. Horses and a desire for vengeance were the twin sparks that re-ignited the hostilities. Hudson's Bay employees watched from the sidelines and scrupulously avoided getting caught between the combatants. Occasionally, they recorded in the journals of their respective posts some observation about the carnage caused by Indian warfare.

In March 1832, a trader at Fort Pitt observd that a Cree party had attacked a Blackfoot camp and "killed four young men . . . owing to these Blackfoot having stole their horses." In

March 1834, a trader at Edmonton House commented that "a war party of Stone [Assiniboine] and Beaver Hill Cree Indians amounting to about 100 attacked a Camp amounting to 30 Tents of Blood Indians on the Banks of the Red Deer River." Another trader, stationed at Fort Carlton, added that the Cree–Assiniboine party "had killed a good many and brought off 96 horses and 6 women." The following year, in the spring of 1835, a trader at Fort Carlton noted that a Cree–Assiniboine party numbering between three thousand and four thousand warriors had assembled for a campaign against the Blackfoot. A journal entry states that part of this force "about 300 in number had a battle with 22 Circies [Sarcees] Indians killed 10 of them of the Cree party 3 were killed and 10 wounded."

The traders mentioned only those battles that they deemed noteworthy or that happened to come to their attention, and many did not. Big Bear, who was growing up in this environment, would certainly have heard about more raids and skirmishes than the Bay men did. He would have heard his father and other men discussing them. He would have heard the youthful warriors around the camp recounting their military deeds. He would have seen them packing their weapons, war bonnets and facial paints in preparation for a raid. He would have watched as they danced and sang their war songs for several evenings prior to leaving. He might even, as a ten- or eleven-year-old boy, have pleaded with them to take him on the warpath, and he certainly would have dreamed of the day when he was old enough to meet the enemy on the battlefield.

And then, in July 1837, the warfare ended temporarily. Smallpox swept the northern plains and killed over ten thousand native people in the space of a few weeks. The disease first appeared in a mulatto man employed on a steamboat named the *St. Peter's*, which was slogging upstream to Fort Union at the confluence of the Missouri and Yellowstone Rivers in modern-day Montana. It spread from him to the Indians when a party of Assiniboines came to trade at a post along the river. Then it raced through one nation after another, with ghastly results.

The Mandan, a small agrarian tribe on the Missouri, were virtually obliterated. Only thirty-one of sixteen hundred survived. The Crows, who lived south of the Missouri on the Yellowstone River, lost one-third of their three thousand members while the Minnetarees were reduced from a thousand to five hundred and the Arikaras from three thousand to fifteen hundred. Entire villages of Assiniboines perished. Six to eight thousand Blackfoot, a third of the population of the Confederacy, had succumbed to this swift, silent, unseen killer by the time it reached the Cree villages of the North and South Saskatchewan Rivers, where it finally began to run out of destructive energy.

"The prairie has become a graveyard," an American eyewitness to the devastation wrote. "Its wildflowers bloom over the sepulchres of Indians. The atmosphere for miles around is poisoned by the stench of the hundreds of carcasses unburied. The women and children are wandering in groups, without food, howling over the dead. The men are flying [off] in every direction. Deserted lodges are seen on every hill. No sound but the raven's croak or the wolf's howl breaks the stillness. The desolation is appalling, beyond the powers of the imagination to conceive."

The epidemic hit Black Powder's camp and Big Bear, then just twelve years old, was among the victims. He survived, but bore the telltale scars—faint pockmarks on his face—for the rest of his life. A short time after he had recovered, Big Bear had the first of three visions that would mark him as a youth with strong connections to the spiritual forces that inhabited the earth and all its creatures. He saw a day when white men began coming into the country in large numbers. They were soon as numerous as the Indians. They coveted the Indian lands and began pushing them out. These images, fragmentary but disturbing, came to Big Bear in a dream.

He told his parents and the band elders what he had seen, and they perhaps turned to one of the shamans for an explanation. Others would have dismissed it as foolish, an understandable response. At the time, there was no reason for anyone to think that the Crees could lose their land to the white man. Either way, the boy's dream was puzzling and provocative, and it occurred at a significant juncture in his life. He had just survived smallpox. And he was nearing the age when he could begin to accompany the warriors on horse-stealing raids and attacks on enemy camps.

By age thirteen, many Cree boys had had a taste of armed conflict. On their first few expeditions, they usually served as apprentices. They carried supplies for the warriors, their dried meat, extra moccasins and tobacco, or they acted as personal assistants to the leader. When the raid itself occurred, these novices were often ordered to remain at the party's base camp, several miles from the enemy village, and they did not share in the spoils.

But the more capable and ambitious boys would not be held back for long. A youth who displayed valour in battle or daring in a raid for horses might be deemed to be a Worthy Young Man, a title usually bestowed by the elders of the band. The band's warrior society might then look favourably on such a youth and invite him to join. The warriors maintained a lodge that was erected in the centre of the circle of tepees and served as a gathering place for members. They had their own songs and dances, and a number of responsibilities: they guarded the camp, defended when enemies attacked, protected the band when moving from place to place, policed the buffalo hunts, and made war on their enemies.

Big Bear undoubtedly distinguished himself on the battlefield. Otherwise, he would never have become a chief. Yet very little of his war record survived in the memories of his contemporaries and the stories they passed on. Instead, people remembered his visions and his spiritual powers. Almost a century after Big Bear's death, an elderly Cree named Stanley Cuthand provided Dempsey with an account of one of those visions. It involved a cave full of horses and a test of character. In a dream, a spirit guided Big Bear to the entrance of the cave and promised him all the horses he would ever need. All he had to do was walk through the immense herd of jostling and skittish animals to the centre of the cave. There he would find the one horse that was to be his. But he had to resist the temptation to take others and he had to remain calm. "The horses will rear up and kick at you," the figure warned him. "But if you show any fear, you won't get to the horse in the middle." Big Bear was almost there when a stunning, black stallion reared above him, its front hooves flailing ferociously. Momentarily startled, Big Bear flinched. He recovered instantly to find himself alone with the spirit. "It's too bad you crouched," the strange figure said. "You had your chance but now you'll never be rich in horses as long as you live."

And the spirit's words came true. Big Bear captured many horses through raids on enemy camps. But he never kept more than he needed for himself. The rest he gave as gifts to other members of the band. In this way, the prophecy of the vision was fulfilled, and Big Bear came to be seen as a generous individual, another quality that he had to possess if he ever hoped to lead his people.

To his contemporaries, Big Bear's most significant vision occurred when he was in his early teens, and it gave him great power in battles and other confrontations with the enemies of the Cree. It may have occurred during a vision quest, a prevalent practice among the Ojibwa and people of Ojibwa descent. The vision quest was a solitary retreat to a hilltop or a secluded place. For several days, the individual fasted and prayed for a visit from one of the myriad spirit powers or *atayohkanak*, who served as intermediaries between man and the *kice manito*, the supreme being who controlled everything in the universe but never appeared directly to human beings. A spirit who visited a boy became his protector or guardian, but only in certain situations, which were spelled out in the vision.

Many boys went on vision quests, but not all were successful. Hence, those who had a vision were seen as having strong connections with the spirit world. In Big Bear's case, the spirit of the most powerful creature on earth—the bear—appeared to him. The spirit gave him a power song—"My teeth are my knives, my nails are my knives"—which Big Bear could chant to calm his fears and to summon his courage as he prepared for battle. It told him how to make a medicine bundle, which would protect him in skirmishes and fights with the enemy. The bundle contained the hide of a bear paw, with the claws intact, sewn to a square piece of red flannel, which could be worn around the neck.

The spirit provided elaborate rituals for wrapping the bundle, for unwrapping it and for putting it on. Many years later, a Cree man named Fine Day, who was born about 1850 and later settled on one of the reserves along the North Saskatchewan, explained the rituals to a visiting American anthropologist named David Mandelbaum. "Before Big Bear would put it on," Fine Day said, "he would dig a hole in the ground about a foot deep. Out of this hole he would take some mud and plaster it over his eyes and then scratch it so that there were streaks. Then he would sing the bear song: 'My teeth are my knives; my nails are my knives,' and then put it on and go out and fight."

Once the effectiveness of the bundle had been proven, it became a valuable object. Other young men would ask Big Bear to transfer it to them before they set out on a raid and would offer him gifts for the privilege of wearing it. Big Bear wore his bundle only in battle, according to Fine Day. So he would not have been wearing it on the summer day he had one of his most celebrated encounters with the Blackfoot.

The incident occurred when the band was camped near the forks of the South Saskatchewan and the Red Deer Rivers, as far south, as far west and as close to Blackfoot country as Mukatai ever took his people to hunt buffalo. On the day in question, the hunters rode into the early morning sun and away from the land of their enemy. But they left behind several young warriors, Big Bear included, to guard the women and children. By early afternoon, Mistahimusqua was bored and restless. He announced that he would ride west a way and look for buffalo, and that's when he met the Blackfoot.

Elders in Cree camps, and later on the reserves, told the story of Big Bear's miraculous escape many times before Dempsey heard it on a February day in 1983 and put it down on paper. His source was an old Cree man named Alphonse Little Poplar, who was living near North Battleford, Saskatchewan. Little Poplar, who has since died, got the story from a fellow Cree, Eli Pooyak, who heard it from his grandfather, Gopher Shooter, and an uncle named Mimiquas. They heard it from others, perhaps people who had known Big Bear at the height of his fame, or perhaps someone who was there when Big Bear told the story for the first time.

Big Bear returned from his encounter with the Blackfoot well past sunset, and long after the hunters had returned for the day. He likely sang his power song as he approached the camp, rousing the dogs and alerting the people that he was back. Relieved and jubilant band members would have greeted him and peppered him with questions—Where were you, Big Bear? What happened? How did you get back? They would have followed him to his parents' tepee where he would have stood before a small, spellbound audience to recount his adventure.

He told them how he had ridden west until he was alone with the wind, the grass and the rolls and swells of the country. The wind caressed his face and whispered in the grass and swept away all thoughts of buffalo and Blackfoot. He was charmed by the beauty and unfamiliarity of the place and before long had travelled much farther than he should have. He was climbing a ridge when the sound of hooves startled him. He looked over his shoulder and saw a party of warriors, maybe a dozen of them, charging after him. They were Blackfoot, and they were coming on fast.

Big Bear kicked his pony in the flanks and away he went, over the ridge, down the other side and into a gully. He had a short lead, time enough to slide off the pony and let it race away. He crawled through the grass, into the middle of a thicket of willows and there he lay, as still and silent as a stone, hardly daring to breathe. He heard Blackfoot gallop down the slope and pull up. He saw them dismount and he watched them scour the grass. Then, he saw them coming toward him. He watched them walk back and forth at the edge of the thicket, and he was certain they could hear the thump of his heart. He expected they would push their way into this tangle of grass and brush, but then their leader called them off. They mounted their horses and rode off.

Big Bear stayed where he was until he was certain they were gone. Then he set out on foot because the Blackfoot had taken his horse. Had they found him, they would have taken his life, and maybe a few slices of his scalp as a trophy. But his survival proved that he was powerful. He had a spirit helper who would protect him from enemies. The elders undoubtedly recognized that Big Bear had all the attributes necessary to become a chief. and they would have taken him aside for some friendly words of advice about the burdens of leadership. This was a common practice, according to Fine Day.

"When a young man showed [by his deeds] that he would be a chief some day, the old men would go to see him and say, 'Now young man, you are climbing higher and higher and are on the way to become a chief. It is for your own good [that we speak]. It is not an easy thing to be a chief. He has to have pity on the poor. When he sees a man in difficulty, he must try to help him in whatever way he can. If a person asks for something in his tepee, he must give it willingly, and without bad feeling. We are telling you this now because you will meet these things, and you must have a strong heart.'"

Big Bear was then in his late teens. He was a young man of less than average height, with slender shoulders and a lean physique. He wore shoulder-length hair and he had a broad, rugged face. He was, no doubt, proud and ambitious but not so consumed with himself that he ever tried to usurp his father, or break away to form his own band. Like many of his peers, he was in his early twenties when he gave up the life of a warrior, with all its freedom, danger and adventure, for that of husband and father, with the attendant duties and responsibilities.

Mistahimusqua married Sayos, an Ojibwa woman whose family had migrated west and settled among the Cree just as Black Powder's people had done, and the young couple were soon parents. She gave birth to a daughter, Nowakich, followed by a boy, Twin Wolverine, and a second son, Imasees, or Bad Child, also known as Apistakoos, or Little Bear, all within five to seven years. Mistahimusqua eventually went on to take four more wives, although Sayos is said to have remained his favourite. Nothing is known of the others, not even their names, nor whether they bore any children by him. As the head of a large household, Big Bear worked hard to provide for his family, and he immersed himself in spiritual activities for he was a deeply religious individual.

From the latter half of the 1840s and through the 1850s, he was able to devote himself to his family and his faith because the world in which he lived was relatively stable. The Cree remained at war with the Blackfoot, but the conflicts were smaller and less costly for both sides, as far as loss of life, than they had been in the 1830s and early 1840s. And then in 1857, a truce was negotiated. At the same time, there were no new epidemics, and no winters of hunger and famine.

By 1860, the peace and stability were in jeopardy. War erupted again between the Cree and the Blackfoot. The hostilities began in October 1860, when Cree warriors killed and scalped a Blackfoot chief. The Blackfoot retaliated by attacking and killing twenty Crees camped near Fort Pitt. Hudson's Bay Co. employees recorded the worst incidents in their journals, and they captured the turbulence of the times, as well as the futility of attempting to bring peace to the northern plains. An entry from Edmonton House, dated March 28, 1861, reads: "The Blackfeet have been unbearable for the last 3 Years or more, always getting worse & worse destroying our crops, stealing our Horses and doing everything they could to annoy us, in order to provoke a quarrel so as to Kill us. They now threaten openly to Kill whites, Half-breeds or Crees whereever they find them and to burn Edmonton Fort." Another entry, dated January 26, 1862, says a Cree band attacked a Blackfoot camp, killed eighteen people and made off with the horses. On March 8, 1862, Bay employees witnessed a similar skirmish that occurred just outside the post.

The warring tribes negotiated another truce in mid-December 1862 when Sweetgrass, one of the foremost leaders of the North Saskatchewan Cree, and fifty warriors escorted their principal peacemaker, Maskepatoon, or Broken Arm, to Edmonton House. Two days later a delegation from the tribes of the Confederacy—the Blackfoot, the Bloods and the Piegans —arrived, along with their Sarcee allies. The leaders made speeches, promised to keep the peace, exchanged gifts of tobacco, shook hands and left quickly when the talks were concluded. "Long may it last," a Bay man wrote of the pact.

It held until November 1863 when a Cree war party attacked a Sarcee camp and reignited the old tit-for-tat war-fare, a state of affairs that continued until the spring of 1865. Once again, disease knocked the combatants off their feet and temporarily ended the hostilities. Measles swept through Cree camps in the district around Edmonton while scarlet fever hit the Blackfoot. Toward the end of March 1865, a man named Jean L'Heureux, an assistant to the Oblate missionary Father Albert Lacombe, arrived at Fort Edmonton carrying a note from Lacombe "informing of great mortality among the Pagans, Bloods and Blackfeet, from scarlet fever more than 1,100 persons, men, women and children had died among the Blackfeet."

At some point amid all this turmoil, Big Bear's father died. The date and cause of Black Powder's death are not known. He had been chief for many years and had served his people well. That is clear from the fact that he enjoyed the loyalty and support of his followers through times of plenty and times of hardship. He was one of the leading chiefs among the bands that inhabited the North Saskatchewan, and he had produced a son who was an eminently capable successor.

Big Bear was about forty when he assumed the leadership. He did not inherit his father's status, however. He was a minor chief, the leader of a small band of about a dozen families, or one hundred people. He was content with that and wanted nothing more than to be allowed to provide for his family, raise his children and worship his god. But that would not be possible. The Plains Cree were about to be jolted by unimaginable change, a new order that would end their way of life and attack the entire Cree cosmos. Out of the cauldron of crisis and catastrophe, Big Bear would emerge with one of the largest followings on the Canadian prairie, and he would lead a heroic but doomed crusade to preserve the dignity and autonomy of his people.

A*stohkomi*
Shot Close
Born about 1830

COLUMNS OF SMOKE, AS
straight as lodgepoles, rose from the tepees. They rose slowly,
curled and curtsied, then vanished into a ravishing blue sky.
The air was perfectly still on this summer morning, a rarity in
the land of the Bloods. The various Blood bands, the Fish-
Eaters, the Black-Elks, the Lone-Fighters and others, lived on
and roamed across hundreds of miles of territory in what is
now southern Alberta. Most days, a wind came from the other
side of the mountains that shimmered on the horizon. It
slipped over peaks perpetually capped in snow. It tiptoed across
the foothills, teasing the tops of pine and aspen forests, and
ruffling the feathers of eagles perched on crags and outcrops.

Then it slammed into the prairie and raced across that flat, treeless expanse like a herd of runaway horses galloping toward the land of the Assiniboines.

Sometimes the wind howled. Sometimes it whistled. And sometimes it hummed. But on this occasion, it didn't even whisper or sigh. The air was dead calm. Dogs were scattered here and there within the circle of tepees. Sleeping. Sunning themselves. Chasing flies. A few elderly men loitered about the camp or played with the children. Young boys came and went freely, sometimes stopping to eat before racing off to resume their games or to roam the surrounding prairie. Barebottomed toddlers with pudgy faces and fat legs frolicked and played while mothers and grandmothers, sisters and aunts worked nearby.

The women were busy as always. They kept the camp. They tended the fires and cooked the meals. They gathered wood and buffalo chips for fuel, and returned to the camp, stooped and panting, with heavy loads slung over their backs. They fetched water and picked berries. They cut the flesh of animals into thin strips and hung it on racks to dry. They pounded dried meat and berries and animal fat into a mash called pemmican that would be stored and eaten in the winter or while travelling long distances. They scraped fat and flesh from the hides of buffalo, deer, elk and many other animals, then stretched and pegged them to the ground so the wind and sun would tan them. They rubbed in a concoction of buffalo brain, fat and liver to soften them. And when the hides were fully prepared, the women cut, snipped and sewed. They made shirts, leggings and moccasins for the whole family. They made rawhide ropes, saddle covers and saddlebags.

Women were engaged in most of these tasks that morning. They talked and laughed while they worked, and they kept a close watch on the children. Among the women was a young mother named Axkyahp-say-pi—Attacked Toward Home—who had given birth to her second son a few months earlier. The infant slept soundly at her side and she could glance at his soft, smooth face as she worked. But she had to look up often to keep track of her older son, Astohkomi, or Shot Close.

He was a little over two years old and had a toddler's unlimited curiosity about the world. He wanted to touch everything: hot objects around the fires; the racks for drying meat; the camp dogs, some of whom had nasty temperaments. He was quick on his feet, but still wobbly. Even a brief foray within the camp circle was an adventure. The sight of him stumbling, and struggling back to his feet brought a smile to her face. And the peaceful breathing of the little brother left her glowing with pride and happiness.

They were strong, healthy boys. Attacked Toward Home looked at them and saw their father, Istowun-eh'pata, or Packs A Knife. He was a proud, handsome man, a warrior who had fought in many battles. She thought of him often. She wondered where he was, and when she would see him again. These questions had drifted through her mind since his departure, and they always left her uneasy. Packs A Knife had ridden off with a party of warriors earlier in the summer to steal horses from the Crow Indians, old enemies of the Bloods, the Blackfoot and the Piegans.

Attacked Toward Home knew that the land of the Crows lay far to the southeast, a seven- to ten-day ride from her own country. Her husband and his companions had to travel through the territory of the Piegans, but likely avoided the camps of their allies. Raiding parties worked best when they were made up of fewer than a dozen men, led by a trusted and experienced warrrior, because speed and stealth were essential.

They could travel by day, with little or no fear of being attacked, until they reached the Missouri River, which was the southern limit of Piegan territory, and Blackfoot country.

Beyond that, they were in a no-man's land and had to proceed cautiously, sometimes travelling at night, until they crossed the Yellowstone River, a tributary of the Missouri in present-day southern Montana. Then they were in Crow country and had to move at night to avoid detection. During the day, their scouts prowled the countryside looking for enemy camps.

The Crows were a small nation, not nearly so numerous as the tribes of the Blackfoot Confederacy, but they were very rich in horses. Many men owned herds of eighty to a hundred, everything from weedy packhorses to sleek, handsome buffalo runners, and a man with only twenty was considered poor. Crow men were generally tall and handsome. They wore their hair long, sometimes waist length. They braided their locks and decorated them with strings of beads and shells. Axkyahp-say-pi knew all these things because the men of her band talked often about their raids on the Crows and their accomplishments on the battlefield. And the Crows frequently came north to recover their animals or avenge their losses. This state of affairs had lasted for many years, as long as Axkyahp-say-pi could remember. It had cost numerous lives on both sides, and no truce had ever interrupted the hostilities.

So she had good reason to be uneasy and may have been wrestling with such fears when a young man who had stayed behind to guard the camp and the band's herd of horses rode into the circle of tepees with exciting news. The raiding party had returned and would soon be here. They were still too far off to be seen, but the youth had observed a signal from the warriors while he and several younger boys were out on the prairie grazing the horses. The signal—sunlight reflected off a mirror—had come from a hilltop that was barely discernible on the horizon. The youth had held his own mirror to the sun to reveal the location of the camp.

The news caused a great commotion. The work of the day stopped. Everyone scanned the horizon. And they wrestled with their fears. The return of the men might mean rejoicing. There might be horses to give away, a victorious scalp dance that night, brave deeds to celebrate and to recount around the fires. Or there might be grieving because raids could also end in defeat.

And then someone spotted them, still miles away on the horizon. They could see that the men were not driving any horses ahead of them. And that raised a disturbing question: Had all the warriors survived? The question was quickly answered. Even at a distance, the band members could see that the raiding party was smaller by several members than the one that had left weeks earlier. They could hear the warriors chanting songs of mourning as they rode. The women responded by wailing and moaning, and Axkyahp-say-pi wept and shrieked as loud as anyone because she could see that Istowun-eh'pata was not among the warriors who galloped into the camp.

Something had gone drastically wrong. Axkyahp-say-pi soon learned that her husband's comrades had been forced to leave him where he fell. Had anyone tried to retrieve his body, they too would have paid with their life. And they all knew what happened to a dead man left behind on the battlefield. If the hatred between the combatants ran deep enough, or if the victors merely wanted to make a point, they might decapitate the corpse, or sever the hands and feet, and parade around their camp with body parts impaled on pikes.

But regardless of the indignities visited upon his body, Istowun-eh'pata's spirit would enjoy a serene afterlife in the

Sand Hills, that arid and desolate tract of land east of the confluence of the Red Deer and South Saskatchewan Rivers beyond the eastern frontier of Blackfoot country. There, he would be reunited with old friends. He would ride horses, hunt buffalo and enjoy the company of handsome women.

Axkyahp-say-pi grieved as the women of her nation had always mourned their men. She hacked off her hair. She put on ragged old clothes and for many days she left the camp at dawn, went to some secluded place and stayed there till dusk. She smeared herself in dirt and mud. She lamented her loss by scratching her calves with sharpened flint.

Eventually, she rejoined the band. Axkyahp-say-pi gathered her meagre household possessions and returned to the lodge of her father, whose name was Scabby Bull. He was likely in his early to mid-forties and still a capable hunter. He became a surrogate parent to Astohkomi and his younger brother, Iron Shield, making their first bows and arrows, teaching them the rudiments of stalking small game, and introducing them to horses and riding.

Axkyahp-say-pi and her boys lived in Scabby Bull's lodge for about three years. Then, one day, a party of warriors visited their camp. They were Blackfoot and belonged to a band known as the Biters. They lived beyond the territory occupied by the Bloods, and beyond the Red Deer River, near the northern frontier of Blackfoot country. The young men had horses with them, animals they had obtained in a successful raid on the Crows, and they were returning home.

The men of Axkyahp-say-pi's band welcomed these warriors. The chief, Crying Bear, who was the brother of her late husband, opened his lodge to as many as he could accommodate. He hosted feasts for them and the leading men of his band. The feasts were great social events. The chief and his guests ate heartily, smoked their pipes and shared stories about the recent raid, past battles and other deeds of courage and daring. Crying Bear entertained as lavishly as possible, which was one of the obligations of a chief. It was also an opportunity to enhance his reputation as a prosperous and generous man. So he performed his duty gladly, giving no thought to the cost.

For the members of the band, the arrival of the visitors was a cause of tremendous excitement, and a welcome relief from the routines of their small, insular world. Many of them went for long periods of time, perhaps the entire winter and spring, without encountering anyone from outside the band. The presence of guests gave them an opportunity to catch up on news about tribal affairs, to exchange gossip about mutual friends and acquaintances, or to strike up new friendships.

The Blackfoot warriors stayed several days, then departed, all but a young man called Akay-nehka-simi, or Many Names. He had struck up a friendship with Crying Bear's sister-in-law, the widow Axkyahp-say-pi, and stayed behind. After a brief courtship, she agreed to be his wife, and her father approved the union. There was no wedding ceremony, and no exchange of vows. Among the Blackfoot, a marriage was solemnified by an exchange of gifts. In this case, the young warrior presented Scabby Bull with two horses. And with that, Many Names and Attacked Toward Home became man and wife.

A short time after the marriage, the couple decided to move north to live among his people. Initially, they intended to take Iron Shield, the younger of the two boys, with them and leave Astohkomi, by then five years old, with his grandfather. But the child objected so strenuously that Many Names decided everyone, including his father-in-law, would make the journey. They strapped all their possessions to a travois and hitched it to a packhorse. They gathered the rest of their horses and their dogs, and they set out. The children rode most of the time, Iron Shield aboard the travois and Astohkomi on a horse, while the adults alternated between walking and riding.

They travelled through the heart of the wild and beautiful land that was Blackfoot country. Mountains gleamed on the western horizon. Prairie stretched as far to the east as the eye could see. Immense azure skies belittled mountain and plain and everything beneath them. The little caravan of humans, horses and dogs encountered herds and packs and flocks—fleet, fragile-looking antelope who were both skittish and curious; stately, handsome deer who collectively raised their heads as the caravan passed, then went back to grazing; massive and indifferent buffalo, who looked at a distance like clumps of dark, brooding boulders. They sensed—and occasionally glimpsed—the wolves that continually lurked behind them, or just beyond their field of vision. They heard the chatter of waterfowl that rose from every slough and pond. And they crossed plains and valleys where there were no creatures, nor any wind or motion or sound, just a mesmerizing stillness, an all-encompassing, spellbinding silence broken only by the distant and occasional cackle of crows and magpies.

This was their land, this place of splendour and plenty. Their people had lived here for as long as anyone could recall, perhaps since the time of creation. Napi, the Old Man, had created the earth and everything in it, according to the legends of their tribe. He created the mountains, the rivers and the lakes. He made grass grow on the plains and trees in the valleys. He made the birds that sometimes darkened the skies, the animals that walked on the land, and the fish that swam in the rivers. And he made himself a wife, Old Woman, from a lump of clay.

Napi and Old Woman created the people, gave them eyes

and mouths, made them walk upright. They decided that the people should die rather than live forever. They showed the people how to gather roots and berries, how to make bows and arrows, how to hunt buffalo and other animals, and how to produce comfortable clothing from animal skins. Once the work of creation was finished, Old Man ascended a mountain near the headwaters of a river and was seen no more. But the people named the river the Old Man, in his honour, and it still bears that name to this day.

The Blackfoot loved this land that Old Man had created for them. The land and its creatures provided them with food, clothing and shelter—and many other things they needed to live comfortably. It inspired stories and legends. They defended it tenaciously when necessary. And Blackfoot men like Scabby Bull and Many Names, both experienced hunters and warriors, travelled with ease and confidence in their country. They knew the trails, the landmarks and the sacred places. They knew where to cross the Bow and the Red Deer Rivers, and where to find drinking water out on the dry, windy prairie.

The journey to the camp of the Biters band took five or six days. They knew they were near the end when they detected the smell of smoke in the breeze. Soon the aroma of wood fires became more pronounced, and the melodious sound of drums and rattles and singing drifted across the plain. And when they reached the crest of a barely perceptible swell in the prairie, there was the camp spread out before them, with the prairie beyond it, the mountains lying low on the horizon and a fat, early evening sun bathing everything in a soothing, amber glow. The dogs detected them first and began howling. Then the children took note and ran to meet them, and finally the entire camp was coming out to welcome the newcomers.

Attacked Toward Home, her father and the children quickly

settled into their new community. But the move north was the start of a new phase in their lives, and Many Names marked the occasion by renaming his elder stepson. Soon after their arrival, Astohkomi became Kyiah-sta-ah, or Bear Ghost.

He remained Bear Ghost for the rest of his boyhood. He was Bear Ghost when he learned to ride and when he began to develop his skills as a hunter. He was Bear Ghost when he sat in the family lodge listening to the tales of plunder and warfare that his stepfather and grandfather and other men often told. He listened attentively to their stories, and to the advice they had for him.

"If you want to be somebody," they would tell the boy, "you must be brave and unflinching in war. You must not think it is a good thing to grow old. The old people have a hard time. They are given the worst side of the lodge. They are sometimes neglected. They suffer when the camp moves. Their sight is dim, so they cannot see far. Their teeth are gone, so they cannot chew their food. Only misery and discomfort await the old. It is much better, while you are young and strong, while your body is in its prime, while your sight is clear, your teeth are sound and your hair is long and black, to die in battle, fighting bravely."

Bear Ghost absorbed these values. They inspired him. This is evident from his performance on the battlefield. He is said to have gone to war early (at age thirteen) and often (nineteen times). Initially, he was likely an apprentice. But Kyiah-sta-ah soon had a taste of combat. Little is known of his early battles, but over time he acquired a reputation for being a young man of unlimited courage and no fear. He earned the trust and respect necessary to lead rather than merely participate in war parties. His feats on the battlefield were talked about by his peers, their offspring and several generations of Blackfoot. They became part of the oral history of the tribe.

There were men and women living on reserves in southern
Alberta in the middle of the twentieth century who heard these
tales. They passed them on to Hugh Dempsey, and he recounted
them in his 1972 biography of this celebrated Blackfoot warrior. The accounts of his war record were, by their nature,
anecdotal and were often missing the details—like dates, places
and outcomes—that structure and anchor written history. But
the stories revealed the spirit of the man.

Bear Ghost had been to war only a few times when he first
distinguished himself. What he actually did was not preserved
in the tales of the Blackfoot storytellers, only the fact that he
took a new name. Kyiah-sta-ah became Istowun-eh'pata. He
took the name of the father he barely knew and hardly remembered. He rode off to war as Bear Ghost. He rode home as
Packs A Knife. And soon he acquired another name.

On that occasion, Istowun-eh'pata rode south to the land of
the Crows with a large party of warriors drawn from the three
tribes of the Confederacy. They found a sizeable Crow encampment near the Yellowstone River, and the leader assembled his
warriors in a concealed position some distance away in preparation for the attack. As the young men waited silently, with
adrenalin surging through them, their hearts racing and their
minds focused, some prayed to their spirit helpers or whispered their power songs. The leader waited until his warriors
were ready to burst with tension, then he drew their attention
to a large and distinctive tepee with four red stripes painted
around the base. It was a Piegan dwelling that a Crow raiding
party had stolen.

"See that painted lodge," the leader said to his men. "Whoever gets to it and strikes it will be the future leader of his
people in hunting and war."

With that, he unleashed his warriors. They erupted with

speed and ferocity. They charged the camp, with faces painted and heads adorned in war bonnets, howling like ravenous wolves and enraged grizzlies. Crow women and children shrieked with panic. The sound of gunfire filled the air. Musket balls whizzed in every direction. Oblivious to the risks, Istowun-eh'pata and several other young men raced toward the painted lodge. Istowun-eh'pata outran the others. He was almost there when a lead ball hit him in the arm. The projectile missed the bone, but ripped into his flesh and knocked him down. Undeterred, he sprang to his feet, reached the tent and lashed it with his riding whip.

When the raid was over and the party had retreated from the Crow camp, Istowun-eh'pata told his story, and others confirmed it. Touching the tepee was an act of unusual bravery. It was also an act laden with cultural significance. The design on a tepee was painted according to the dreams of its owner. There were often geometric figures at the base and circles near the top, representing earth and sky respectively. In between, sometimes there were images of animals such as buffalo or otter, who had appeared to a man in dreams and provided him with supernatural powers. Designs were sometimes destroyed when the owner died. They could also be sold or traded to other members of the tribe. But to have a painted lodge stolen—this was offensive to the Blackfoot.

By striking the tepee, the youthful Istowun-eh'pata had recovered the design for his tribe, and it was now his. He had performed admirably, and he decided to celebrate the occasion by changing his name. "Because of this deed," he announced, "I will take the name of Isapo-Muxika."

And the warrior who had led the excursion conferred his blessing. "Yes," he said to the wounded youth, and those who looked on, "you have struck the tepee, and you will become a leader of your people."

Isapo-Muxika meant "Crow Indian's Big Foot." It was a whimsical name, which had belonged to only one man, a renowned warrior who had been murdered many years earlier by the Shoshones, implacable enemies of the Blackfoot who lived south of the Missouri and west of the Rockies. The first Isapo-Muxika was a leader of the Biters band. He acquired the name during a raid on the Crows. He and his men were travelling surreptitiously through the territory of their old foe and found a recently abandoned camp. On the banks of a creek, they saw a footprint in the soft, sandy soil. They were astonished by the size of it, so each man took a turn placing his own foot in the print. But they were all too small. Then their leader tried. He was a perfect fit, so he became known as Crow Indian's Big Foot.

Some time later, he led fourteen warriors to the land of the Shoshones to negotiate a peace treaty. But as they crossed the mountains in mid-winter, a Shoshone war party ambushed and slaughtered all fifteen members of the delegation. The Blackfoot retaliated by sending south a huge party, numbering several thousand warriors, according to some accounts, and they avenged this atrocity with a ferocious attack on a Shoshone camp of eight hundred lodges. These events occurred in about 1828, two years before the Blood baby Astohkomi was born. In the intervening years, nobody had taken the name Isapo-Muxika, which was a measure of the man's honoured place within the Blackfoot world.

Now there was a new Isapo-Muxika. He was still in his teens, but would prove himself a worthy heir to that name. He would fulfill the prophecy made on the day he dodged musket balls and ignored a painful wound to strike the red tepee. He would become a leader. White men would amend his name, and call him Crowfoot and he would make that name famous. All of that was far in the future. The youthful Isapo-Muxika was an exuberant warrior, with many more battles to fight, particularly with the Cree, who lived to the north and east of his people, and had been at war with them for as long as anyone could remember.

Blackfoot elders delighted in recounting his exploits against the Cree even after the days of freedom were over. In one case, he was a member of a party that set out on a raiding mission from the Biters camp. They travelled on foot and had gone only a short distance when they met a Cree party on a similar expedition. The two sides exchanged gunfire, then the Crees ran for shelter in a nearby wood. Crowfoot immediately gave chase. He discarded his gun and caught one Cree warrior in a thicket. Seizing his enemy by the hair, he yanked his head back, raised his free hand, and plunged his knife into the man's chest. The Cree dropped to his knees and fell face first to the ground. As the blood flowed from the dying man's body, Crowfoot knelt and scalped him.

It was through such deeds that Crowfoot acquired his reputation for valour, character and ability. But he paid a high price for it. He was shot in the back in a battle with the Shoshone and lived the rest of his days with a musket ball lodged within him. He was shot in the knee, after which riding became painful and unpleasant. He was wounded in the arm while fighting the Crows, and he suffered three other serious wounds, though the details are lost in time. He absorbed most, if not all these blows by age twenty, when his days as an active warrior ended.

It was roughly 1850, and he had risen to prominence at a

time when the Blackfoot nation was at the peak of its power, when the three tribes of the Confederacy were feared by all who lived and travelled on the northern reaches of the Great Plains of North America. The Blackfoot had begun to assert themselves a century earlier after acquiring guns and horses. The guns arrived via the rivers, the North Saskatchewan and the Missouri. They arrived as trade goods, supplied first by the British and Canadian traders, and much later by the Americans, or the Long Knives, as the Indians called them, a term that may have referred to the long, extremely sharp knives that American trappers carried. Horses arrived from the south. They were introduced by the Spanish and migrated north from tribe to tribe through trade or thievery.

The Blackfoot were among the last to obtain horses. Hence, for many years, they were at a disadvantage in conflicts with southern neighbours like the Kutenais, the Shoshones and the Flatheads, and suffered many defeats. Similarly, they acquired firearms later than the Crees and Assiniboines, who became involved earlier in the fur trade. However, by 1750, the Blackfoot had gained access to reliable supplies of both guns and horses. The hostile tribes around them were not so fortunate. The Crees, and to a lesser extent the Assiniboines, were well armed, but poor in horses. The Kutenais, Shoshones and Flatheads were rich in horses, but poorly armed.

Once they were armed and mounted, the Blackfoot formed strategic alliances with a couple of small tribes, the Sarcees and the Gros Ventre, who posed no threat to them. But to others, Blackfoot war parties became roving emissaries of terror. They chased the Kutenais, Shoshones and Flatheads off the plains and over the mountains. By the early nineteenth century, they controlled the territory stretching almost from the North Saskatchewan River in present-day central Alberta, south to the upper Missouri in the modern state of Montana, from the Rocky Mountains in the west to the contemporary Alberta–Saskatchewan border in the east.

Indians from enemy tribes were unwelcome in Blackfoot country. So were most whites, and they learned to stay out. The Hudson's Bay Co. and the rival Northwest Company operated competing trading posts along the North Saskatchewan prior to the 1821 merger. But they did not send their employees into Blackfoot country to trade, nor did they ever establish permanent posts there. Instead, they allowed the Blackfoot to bring fresh, dried and processed buffalo meat to them. This arrangement led to minimal contact and generally cordial relations for several decades.

But for many years, the Blackfoot harboured a deep hatred of the Americans, and their encounters with the Long Knives usually ended in violence. The hostilities began with the earliest contact between the two groups. Meriwether Lewis and William Clark were the first Americans to travel through Blackfoot country, and they did so on their historic voyage of discovery, which was commissioned by President Thomas Jefferson, and which took them up the Missouri, over the Rockies, down to the Pacific and back. The explorers and a party of forty to fifty soldiers and civilians left St. Louis in May 1804.

In mid-July 1806, on the return trip down the Missouri, Lewis and three of his men left the great waterway to search for the headwaters of the Marias River, a major tributary. There, Lewis expected to find the continental divide that separated the waters that flowed east to Hudson Bay, and south to the Gulf of Mexico. He planned to find and plot this height of land because it marked the divide between American and British territory. Instead, he encountered eight Piegan warriors, all teenage boys or young men.

The two parties spent an amiable night together. But in the morning, the youthful warriors tried to steal a gun and drive off the horses of the Americans. Lewis shot a man in the stomach. He survived, but one of his companions, a youth named He-that-looks-at-the-Calf, was stabbed in the chest by one of Lewis's men and died instantly. That encounter set the course of Blackfoot-American relations for the next twenty-five years.

From then on, Blackfoot war parties relentlessly attacked individual American trappers who attempted to exploit the fur-rich creeks and streams of their upper Missouri territory. These skirmishes left many dead on both sides. The Blackfoot were equally hostile toward three American fur companies, which established posts on the Missouri, and they drove them out by killing their employees, and in some cases plundering their furs and trade goods. John Jacob Astor's American Fur Company finally succeeded where the others had failed. In 1828, the company established Fort Union at the confluence of the Missouri and Yellowstone Rivers, just beyond the limits of Blackfoot country.

Two years later, this firm managed to make peace with the Piegans by offering them Canadian-style trade, in which company employees remained at their posts and allowed the Piegans to bring furs and buffalo robes to them. In the fall of 1831, the company built the first successful post—Fort Piegan at the mouth of the Marias River—on lands controlled by the Blackfoot. The following year, this establishment was moved a few miles upriver and renamed Fort McKenzie in honour of the man who ran it—Kenneth McKenzie, a Scot and former Hudson's Bay employee.

The American Fur Company had made a significant breakthrough, which is clear from a remark found in the journals of Prince Maximilian of Wied, a wealthy German explorer and scientist who travelled from St. Louis to Fort McKenzie and back as a guest of the company in 1832–33. "They [the Blackfoot] are always dangerous to white men who are hunting singly in the mountains, especially to beaver hunters, and kill them whenever they fall into their hands; hence the armed troops of the traders keep up a constant war with them. It is said that in the year 1832, they shot fifty-eight whites and, a couple of years before that time, above eighty."

Gradually, Blackfoot animosity toward the Americans faded. From the early 1830s until the mid-1840s, they murdered only four traders, and business continued despite these incidents. However, a conflict occurred in January and February 1844 that closed the trade for two years. The trouble began when American Fur Company employees at Fort McKenzie refused to admit a war party. The Blackfoot responded by killing a pig. The traders pursued the warriors who, in turn, ambushed the whites and killed one of them.

The Americans took revenge a few weeks later when a Piegan band of men, women and children arrived to trade. They fired a cannon filled with musket balls at the unsuspecting party assembled outside the gates. Several Indians died instantly and others were injured. The traders then rushed out of the post, killed the wounded, chased off the survivors and scalped the dead, about thirty people in all. The enraged Blackfoot retaliated by spreading terror along a 650-mile stretch of the upper Missouri, from Fort Union to the Rocky Mountains.

The Blackfoot and the Americans made peace in 1846 because their trade in buffalo hides had become too large and lucrative to be closed permanently. The hides were used in the eastern United States to make overcoats, as well as winter robes for sleighs and carriages. In return, the Blackfoot could purchase manufactured goods from several European countries, as well as colourful beads, bells and ornaments from the Caribbean.

The trade with the Americans on the Missouri and the Hudson's Bay Co. on the North Saskatchewan brought many benefits. It also brought alcohol into the lives of the Blackfoot. When a band arrived, the traders often distributed generous amounts of liquor, which could lead to a day or two of debauchery before the bartering and haggling and exchange of goods began. Prince Maximilian witnessed several of these sessions at Fort McKenzie in mid-August 1833 when there were about eight hundred Bloods and Piegans camped at the post.

"They traded their furs for whiskey and clamoured for it incessantly," he wrote in his journal. "Many came singing and dancing and offered their wives and daughters in exchange for whiskey. Others brought horses, beavers and other skins, and we saw indescribable scenes. The young as well as the old got something to drink, and even very small children here and there could neither stand nor walk."

Alcohol, or "white man's water," as the Blackfoot called it, was a scourge, and all attempts to control it failed. As long as there were Americans on the Missouri and British traders on the North Saskatchewan, and as long as there was competition between them, they would ignore or circumvent the edicts issued by politicians or bureaucrats in distant Washington or by company directors in even more distant London prohibiting the sale of alcohol to the natives.

Despite the debilitating effects of whisky, the trade in buffalo meat, pemmican and hides provided tangible benefits. The Blackfoot acquired the weapons they needed to become a power on the northwestern plains. They had risen to power in the latter half of the eighteenth century, and they consolidated their position in the first half of the nineteenth. In the 1830s and 1840s, when Crowfoot was a boy and then a teenage warrior, his people and their allies were the unquestioned masters and sole inhabitants of thousands of square miles of territory from the upper Missouri almost to the North Saskatchewan.

Such was the status of the Blackfoot nation in 1850, when Crowfoot reached his twentieth birthday and gave up the roving, adventurous life of a warrior to take a wife, start a family and acquire possessions. He was a strikingly handsome young man, taller than most, with piercing eyes, prominent cheekbones, an aquiline nose and thin lips. He had the countenance of a commander, and the temperament to go with it. Guns and horses had made the Blackfoot a warlike people, and Crowfoot had compiled an impressive war record. White demand for buffalo meat and hides also made the Blackfoot a prosperous people. And over the next two decades, Crowfoot became a very prosperous man by Blackfoot standards.

He began this phase of his life modestly enough, with a small herd of horses acquired during raids on enemy camps. He married his first wife, Sisoyaki, or Cutting Woman, when he was in his early twenties and they began their life together in an ordinary lodge, which would have been spacious and comfortable and made of about twelve buffalo hides. But over the next few years, Crowfoot built his herd through astute trades and sound breeding. As his herd grew, so did his household, because horses were the basis of wealth among his people. Horses made many things possible. The Blackfoot, and other plains Indians, could travel greater distances than ever before. They could hunt more effectively, move their camps faster and haul more goods. A man could trade a horse for almost anything he wanted, a handsome overcoat, a colourful necklace, even a pretty woman.

Crowfoot eventually owned a herd of four hundred horses and became master of a very large household. He was still in his twenties when he took his second and third wives—Nipis-tai-aki, or Cloth Woman, and Ayis-tsi, or Packs on Her Back. Over the course of his life, he had ten wives, although he usually had no more than three or four at one time. Many wealthy and powerful men had several wives, a practice that was purely pragmatic. In any Blackfoot camp, there were widows and other unattached women because so many men died prematurely in warfare. As a man with more than one wife, Crowfoot was merely following the customs of his tribe.

His wealth in horses allowed him to do something that few, if any, of his peers could do: he employed half a dozen men, including his younger brother, Iron Shield, and a half-brother named Big Fish, to tend his herd and hunt for his household. He wisely split his horses into several groups while grazing the animals and had his men guard them twenty-four hours a day. Hence Crowfoot rarely lost horses to raiders from enemy tribes like the Cree.

His lodges were another sign of his wealth and status. He maintained one average-sized tepee for his hired hands. He, his wives, his mother and his children—he had twelve, although only four survived to adulthood—lived in one unusually large tepee made of thirty hides. It was was too heavy for one horse and had to be transported by two pack animals when the Biters were on the move. It had two entrances and two fires—one used only for lighting ceremonial pipes and burning fragrant prairie herbs.

It is unclear how many years Crowfoot spent acquiring his horses, his other property and his large household. For the Blackfoot storytellers who preserved the accounts of these events, when and where were of less significance than what a man did, and what those actions said about his abilities and his character. Nevertheless, he was almost certainly affluent and successful by the late 1850s when significant changes occurred in the leadership of the Blackfoot tribe. There was, within the space of seven years, a passing of the patriarchs.

In about 1858, a chief named Old Swan, head of the Bad Guns band, died and was replaced by a nephew, Big Swan. Two years later, Old Sun of the All Medicine Men died. His son, who bore the same name, succeeded him. The transition in both cases was quick and orderly, but the complexion of the leadership had changed sharply. The two old men had maintained harmonious relations with the white traders, and to some extent with neighbouring tribes. Both new leaders were hostile toward white men. Big Swan was a physically huge man with a ferocious temperament and Old Sun the younger had once killed and scalped a trader on the Missouri. He also carried the scalp of a young blond-haired girl, a trophy from a raid on a wagon train, an attack that led to the slaughter of every white person present.

In 1865, the third of the elderly, peaceful and respected leaders died. He was Three Suns, head chief of the Biters. The natural heir was the son of the old chief. He, too, was called Three Suns, and he possessed many of the qualities necessary to be a leader. But there was another eminently capable and popular candidate among the men of the Biters band. His name was Isapo-Muxika, and that made the issue of succession more complicated than it had been for the Bad Guns or the All Medicine Men.

Like most plains Indians, a Blackfoot band could choose a new leader in one of two ways. When the dying chief had a capable, trusted and popular son or nephew, the choice was automatic. But when there were doubts about the heir apparent, or when there was another clearly superior individual available, the people might spurn a chief's son and accept someone else as leader. They would attempt to reach a consensus through private deliberations among family and friends. Sometimes they were unable to agree, and the band would split. This is what happened to the Biters. Close to thirty families remained loyal to Three Suns, many of them related to him. Twenty-one families followed Crowfoot and became known as the Big Pipes band, and later the Moccasins.

Crowfoot had been a chief only a short while when he fought one of his most famous battles and saved Three Suns and his band from being annihilated by a Cree war party. The battle began on the night of December 4, 1865, and continued until almost noon the following day. Three Suns was camped on the Battle River, so named because Cree and Blackfoot had clashed along that waterway so many times over the years, and he had as his guest Father Albert Lacombe, who worked with both nations.

According to the account provided by Father Lacombe, everyone was sleeping soundly, wrapped snugly in buffalo robes with their feet to the fire. Suddenly the chief leapt to his feet and screamed, "*Assinaw! Assinaw!*" The Crees. The Crees. Outside, it was as black as tar. There were no stars and no moon, only flashes of gunfire to illuminate the night. But the air was filled with the horrific sounds of war: the screams of attackers, later estimated to be six hundred to eight hundred-strong; the frenzied barking of the dogs; the whinnying of terrified horses; the pleas of the wounded; and the sobs of dying men and women.

The Crees, bolstered by Assiniboine allies, repeatedly charged into the camp and threatened to overrun it. Each time, Three Suns and his tiny force of defenders, numbering about eighty, managed to turn them back. Throughout it all, Father Lacombe raced about the camp, shouting encouragement to the Blackfoot. At one point, he found himself face to face with a warrior he couldn't recognize in the dark. "Who are you?" asked the priest.

"Crowfoot," the man replied. He and his band were camped several miles downstream. When they were awakened by the sound of gunfire, he led his warriors to the fight. They launched a withering assault on the Crees, drove them out and forced them to seek shelter behind a nearby hill.

At dawn, the enemies were entrenched and fog descended over them. They fired only periodically. Father Lacombe took advantage of a lull to try to end the conflict. He strode gallantly into the no-man's land between the combatants, brandishing his crucifix and holding aloft a white flag, and shouting, "Here, you Crees. Kamiyo-atchakwee speaks." But the gunfired resumed, and the priest sustained a flesh wound when a musket ball grazed his forehead. This ignited the Blackfoot, who erupted from their sheltered position and drove the Cree from the battlefield.

The fight had been long and the damage horrendous. Twelve members of Three Suns' band had died, fifteen were wounded and two children had been abducted. The horses, some three hundred in all, had been stolen. Half the lodges had been shredded and most of the pemmican was missing. Three Suns had been hit by a musket ball that shattered his leg. But for all they had suffered, Three Suns and his followers would long be grateful to Crowfoot, whose timely arrival and courageous performance—"He fought like a bear," Father Lacombe told white audiences for years to come—had saved the day.

As he became a more established chief, Crowfoot served his people in many other ways. He was a member of the new generation of leaders. He had his faults. He drank occasionally. He had a hot temper and a tendency to erupt when provoked, or when he had been drinking. But his strengths outweighed his shortcomings and he became a popular chief. He had been a great warrior in his youth and he became an exceptional provider. The poor and the elderly in his camp never had to beg for food after a successful hunt because Crowfoot ensured that his men distributed buffalo meat to the needy. Nor did the elderly and the infirm have to worry about travelling from camp to camp when the band moved. Crowfoot always had a horse for them.

The old people began to call him *manistokos*—father of his people. In those days, he had a small following and a reputation that did not extend much beyond his own tribe. But in the years ahead—when he led his people on the dreadful journey from freedom into subservience—his wisdom and eloquence would impress all who came to know him. And Bloods, Blackfoot and Piegan alike would come to call him Our Great Father.

P*itikwahanapiwiyin*

Poundmaker
Born about 1842

NIGHT AFTER NIGHT,
during that winter he spent in the Blackfoot camp, the tall,
slender, youthful-looking Cree man sat close to Crowfoot in
the great lodge of the warrior chief. Sat with his long, braided
locks cascading down his back and over his chest, almost to the
ground. Sat and talked, or played his drum with quick, agile
hands. He always kept his instrument close by, and he usually
began to play as the afternoon waned and evening fell quickly
on the camp. His light, rhythmic, barely audible drumbeat
served as an invitation to the Blackfoot players, who came with
their drums, rattles and songs. They joined this lean, stately
looking Cree, who was like a son to Crowfoot, and together

they chanted and sang and wove dense musical tapestries that filled the lodge and flowed through the camp as children finished their games, hunters and horsemen and scouts returned from the plains, the prized ponies and the day's kill were brought in, the stews and soups simmered over fires.

He and his fellow players broke for the evening meal, which was often long and leisurely, and lasted well beyond nightfall. Afterward, he smoked with Crowfoot and the men who had dined with him. He listened to the talk around the fire, and through listening he learned their language. He became fluent in Blackfoot and well-versed in the history and myths of a people whom he had known only as an enemy to be feared and avoided since he was old enough to understand anything about the world around him. He became familiar with the stories about the leading men of the Blackfoot Confederacy—the shamans, the chiefs and the warriors. He heard the rousing tales of their battles with neighbouring tribes—the Kutenais and Flatheads in the southwest, the Shoshones and Crows in the south, the Assiniboines in the east, and his own Cree people, who lived to the east and the north.

Often, after the evening had ended and the guests had left, when Crowfoot's wives and children were asleep, when the fires in the lodges had burned low and all was quiet except for the restless west wind, the chief and his Cree friend talked into the night about the past and the future of their peoples. They talked about promoting peace between them. And they talked about their own lives. Crowfoot had gone to war against the Cree many times when he was younger and had killed and scalped at least one Cree warrior. The knife he had driven into that young man's chest, inflicting a fatal wound, remained one of his cherished possessions.

Crowfoot had once hated the Cree, and the youthful warriors

in his band still regarded them as the enemy. They were baffled by this strange and unprecedented action on the part of their leader—taking a Cree into his household and calling him "my son"—and they resented the man's presence in their camp. Sometimes, after they had been drinking, for this was in the days when whisky traders from south of the 49th parallel had moved into the land of the Blackfoot, the warriors prowled outside Crowfoot's lodge and talked about murdering his Cree guest. Sometimes, after their heads had cleared, they talked among themselves of killing him surreptitiously, if an opportunity arose. They didn't dare question Crowfoot directly. Instead, they talked behind his back. He was behaving foolishly, the warriors said. He had no business befriending a member of an enemy tribe.

Others, who were more temperate in their outlook and disposition, reminded these youths that Crowfoot was recovering from the tragic loss of a beloved son, who had been killed in a skirmish with the Cree. He had shown that he still possessed a warrior's fire and fury, for upon learning of his son's death, he had dispatched four scouts who quickly found a Cree camp. Crowfoot himself led the war party that attacked this enemy band and killed one of its members. But vengeance had not driven the sorrow from his heart or the darkness from his mind. He had lost his eldest son, whom he had been grooming to be his successor. He could not transfer those aspirations to his two surviving boys because one was unable to speak, and the other was losing his sight. For a man as successful as Crowfoot, the disappointment was deep and slow to abate.

Then, during a lull in the interminable wars that had convulsed the northern plains for decades, something entirely unexpected had occurred. The Cree and the Blackfoot were at peace, and Crowfoot took advantage of the truce to visit a Cree camp. While there, one of his wives encountered a man who bore a remarkable resemblance to the great chief's dead son. The woman insisted that Crowfoot meet this man, and he, too, was struck by the similarities. The young man's name was Pitikwahanapiwiyin, or Poundmaker. As Crowfoot gazed into his eyes, a strange thought passed through his mind: perhaps his son had simply gone away for awhile and mysteriously returned. The Blackfoot chief had reacted to this strange encounter by doing something unexpected. He had invited Poundmaker to visit his camp. He had made him a member of his household. He had given him a Blackfoot name, Makoyi-koh-kin, or Wolf Thin Legs. And he had begun to know and love him like a son.

They had spent many hours together during the quiet of the night, stretched out in the lodge of the Blackfoot chief, enjoying the warmth of soft, thick buffalo robes and soothing, slow-burning fires, and they had talked until they were lulled to sleep by the deep, peaceful breathing of Crowfoot's slumbering wives and children. During their nocturnal chats, they came to respect and admire one another. In the dead of a prairie winter, amid howling storms and days so cold that the air crackled, they developed a friendship as strong as that between any father and son.

Crowfoot began to refer to Poundmaker as his son. He was charmed by his Cree friend, and so were many of the older men of the band, particularly the head men whom the chief relied upon for advice. These were men who had fought their own battles against the Cree, men who had lost sons and brothers and friends in conflicts with this enemy tribe. They were intrigued by the resemblance between Poundmaker and Crowfoot's dead son and they were impressed with his character. They saw that he possessed many of the qualities they looked for in a leader. They admired the courage he had demonstrated by coming to live for a winter among the enemies of his people. They liked the composure he had dispayed in dealing with the resentment and hostility of the Blackfoot warriors. They were pleased that he was a skilful hunter. And they were captivated by his nimble drumming, his sharp mind, his natural eloquence and his talent for telling a story.

Some nights he entertained them with Cree tales of strange beasts and unusual occurrences. He told the story of Spirit's Lake, a body of water his Blackfoot listeners were familiar with, and how it came to acquire that name. "One time, not a great many years ago, there were large bands of Crees, Stoneys and Saulteaux camped at the narrows in this lake. It was not very long after the ice had taken, and there was not much snow. They were all on the lake, and they saw a pair of red horns standing up through the ice. Two young girls took an axe to go and cut off the horns to make combs of them, but the old people told them not to touch them. They would not listen, and attempted to cut off the horns. I do not know whether they cut off the horns, but just then the spirit of the great animal moved, and all the ice in the lake broke up, and the two foolish girls and a great many families drowned, though all had run for shore as soon as they saw that the girls were determined to cut off the horns. Since then, the lake has been called Spirit's Lake."

The lake was the source of another story that Poundmaker liked to tell, and it was about a big otter. "There is a large island in Spirit's Lake," he told his Blackfoot audience one night, "and one time a lot of men were going to hunt for bears on this island. They made a raft of logs, and ten men got on it to go to the island. They were poling the raft along and suddenly they saw the water moving all around the raft, and felt something knocking underneath it. They were frightened, and would have poled back to the shore again, but a big otter put his paws on the raft, and one of the Indians, who had dreamed about it before, killed the otter with his knife. They towed the monster ashore, and found that he only lacked less than a hand's breadth of being three fathoms long."

And once, after he had been among the Blackfoot long enough to have earned their trust and respect, he told the tale of the great grizzly. "One time, a very large party of Cree warriors were going for a raid upon your people, and meeting a great grizzly bear, they killed him. But when he was killed, they found him so large that they thought he must be a spirit. He measured over seven hands' breadth across the top of the head and he was proportionately large elsewhere. They did not skin him or cut him up, but set him upon his feet again. They put scarlet cloth about his neck and strings of beads on his head, and gave him tobacco and trinkets. They lit their pipes and blew smoke in his face, and allowed him to smoke their pipes in turn. They spread fine skins and cloths before him, and prayed to him to give them good luck. And he did give them good luck, for in that raid they did not lose a horse or a man, though they killed many Blackfoot, and captured more than three hundred ponies."

The tale he told most often, during that winter among the Blackfoot, was the story of his own life. He had told it first to Crowfoot, of course, shortly after he arrived. It had taken several evenings because he was then in his early thirties and his life had been full of twists and turns. He had an older brother named Yellow Mud Blanket and a younger sister, Chinesese. His father had died when he was just a boy, and his mother had remarried and had children by her second husband. Then she too had died. Poundmaker had found a home with another family, as had his siblings. He had survived childhood and the horse-stealing raids and skirmishes with enemies that were a standard part of the lives of most Cree and Blackfoot adolescents. Afterward, he married. He was a very capable provider and soon took a second wife. Shortly before he left to spend the winter among the Blackfoot, Poundmaker learned that one of his wives was pregnant.

Crowfoot had listened attentively as Poundmaker related the story of his life, and he had asked many questions. How many times have you been to war? Have you fought against my people? And under what circumstances? Have you ever killed a man? Sometimes the Blackfoot chief would be silent a long time as he contemplated an answer or crafted another question. And sometimes they slept before Crowfoot put his next query, so the conversation had to be continued on a subsequent evening.

As Crowfoot relayed bits and pieces of Poundmaker's story to the band councillors, they began to seek out the young man to hear things first-hand. They had a tremendous curiosity about him and his people because most of them knew little about the Cree except that they were the enemy. Tell us about your leading chiefs, they would say. And your shamans, are they powerful? How many horses do you own? How many wives do you have? Was your father a warrior?

He answered their questions in his dignified and eloquent way, and in the frequent recountings of his life story he was always patient. He invariably started at the beginning, with the story of his father, Sikakwayan.

A STONEY INDIAN BY BIRTH, whose name meant Skunk Skin in his native tongue, Sikakwayan had left his own people as a young man. He settled among a division of the Plains Cree known as the House People, who acquired their name because they inhabited the forests and plains around Fort Carlton, sometimes known as Carlton House, on the North Saskatchewan River, seventy-five kilometres north of present-day Saskatoon.

The forests in the vicinity of this Hudson's Bay trading post were not as dense and shaggy as those found farther downstream, nor were the plains as raw and open as the prairie to the south. The countryside around Carlton was a pleasant mix of woods and grasslands—prairie with a gentle roll to it, with spruce and poplar groves sprinkled here and there, giving the area "more the appearance of a park" than a wilderness, according to one contemporary observer, the Toronto painter Paul Kane, who travelled through the country in the late 1840s, when Poundmaker was just a boy, and recorded his impressions in a book called *Wanderings of an Artist Among the Indians of North America*.

Sikakwayan, according to some accounts, was originally a member of a Stoney band that lived near the confluence of the Battle and North Saskatchewan Rivers, no more than two or three days southwest of Carlton by canoe. Others say his people lived much farther away, along the upper reaches of the Saskatchewan in the foothills of the Rocky Mountains. These Stoneys roamed that heavily wooded, extremely hilly terrain that lay between Blackfoot country and the mountains, surviving on elk, deer, moose and buffalo.

Many Stoney bands lived in close proximity to the Plains Cree but they remained a distinct people with their own language. The most distinguishing feature of the Stoneys was their hair. "It is seldom cut," the Northwest Company trader Alexander Henry wrote prior to his death in 1814, "but as it grows is twisted into small locks or tails, about the thickness of a finger. Combs are never used; what loose hair falls is twisted into those tails, and frequently false hair is added. Many wear numerous tails trailing to the gound; but it is customary to twist this immense flow of hair into a coil on top of the head, broad below and tapering above like a sugar loaf nine inches high."

Despite their differences, the Stoneys and Crees had been allies for many generations. The Stoneys were a branch of the Assiniboine nation, a people whose name was derived from an Ojibwa term for cooking with stones. The Assiniboine were known for heating stones in a fire and depositing them into a pouch, often the stomach of a large animal, which was filled with water and morsels of meat. The stones would heat the water and slowly cook the meat. The Assiniboine had once been part of the Sioux but had broken away from that nation, according to some accounts, when a personal dispute over a woman, perhaps involving two families or clans, escalated into a tribal conflict. These events occurred sometime in the early 1600s, when the Sioux and Assiniboine were woodlands people occupying territory southwest of Lake Superior, near the headwaters of the Mississippi River.

After the rupture, the Assiniboine are believed to have moved north and settled around Lake of the Woods. The first written reference to them as a separate people occurred in a document written in 1640 by a Jesuit missionary and they were mentioned again by a Jesuit in 1658, this time living near a large body of water now known as Lake Nipigon, north of Lake Superior. The Assiniboine became allies of the Cree after their break with the Sioux, and both tribes subsequently migrated west, largely through their participation in the fur trade. They reached the prairies before the end of the seven-teenth century and settled in the Saskatchewan and Assiniboine River valleys.

Crees and Stoneys had similar histories and common enemies —the Sioux and the Blackfoot. They often lived side by side and frequently intermarried, all of which made it perfectly acceptable for a man like Sikakwayan to leave his band and join the House People. When Sikakwayan went to live with these Cree people and under what circumstances is not known. But once he was there, he married a woman of Cree and French-Canadian descent whose name has not been preserved. She had a brother named Mistawasis, or Big Child, who later became one of the leading chiefs of the House People. Indeed, his name appears first among the forty-six Cree and Metis leaders who signed Treaty Number Six, negotiated at Forts Carlton and Pitt in September 1876, thereby relinquishing their people's title to approximately 120,000 square miles of territory.

Big Child's sister was said to be Sikakwayan's fourth wife, meaning that he had to be a prosperous man who could pro-vide for a large household. In fact, Sikakwayan was one of those individuals the whole band relied upon at times for food. He was a buffalo caller, a man who possessed both an intimate knowledge of the ways of the herds and the spiritual powers necessary to lure the beasts into immense circular traps known as pounds. And Sikakwayan likely acquired his abilities from his Stoney forefathers, who were renowned for their use of these devices. "It is supposed," Alexander Henry wrote, "that these people are the most expert and dextrous nation of the plains in constructing pounds and driving buffalo into them."

The use of pounds was an ancient practice among the plains Indians and one laden with rituals and beliefs. A pound was a

circular corral, usually about thirty yards across, that was constructed out of a thicket. Trees were cut down and the under-
brush cleared, and all of this debris was piled and woven
together to form walls anywhere from eight to fifteen feet
high. A mature tree, used for ceremonial purposes, was left
standing in the centre of the corral. "On this they hang offerings to propitiate the Great Spirit to direct the herds toward
it," wrote the painter Kane, who saw pounds in use. "A man is
also placed in the tree with a medicine pipe-stem in his hand,
which he waves continually, chanting a sort of prayer to the
Great Spirit, the burden of which is that the buffaloes may be
numerous and fat."

The entrance, which generally faced east and was about
twenty feet wide, was built between two trees that were left
standing to form a set of uprights. A log was strapped horizon-
tally, like a crossbeam, between the trees at the same height as
the walls of the pound. Then a ramp consisting of small logs
was built up to meet the beam. Along each side of the entrance
ramp and extending about a hundred yards beyond it, fences
were built of piled logs and brush that opened up like a funnel.
These fences had a sharp curve in them at the approach to the
ramp so that a herd of stampeding buffalo charging into the
lane formed by the fences would not see the pound and the
trouble ahead until they had reached the foot of the ramp, at
which point it was too late to stop or change direction. Beyond
the fences, the men of a band piled heaps of brush at intervals
of thirty yards or so for several miles. These mounds served as
blinds to conceal men called beaters who would leap up at
appropriate moments to frighten the buffalo and keep them
advancing toward the pound.

Pounds were used primarily by those bands that had access
to abundant supplies of wood and lived on lands that sustained

large numbers of buffalo. The House People, and most other divisions of the Plains Cree, had both. Herds of staggering dimensions grazed in Cree country in the days when Sikakwayan acquired his reputation as a poundmaker, which is evident from the following lines taken from *Wanderings of an Artist*. It is an account of a trip that Kane and several companions made by horseback along the North Saskatchewan from Fort Pitt to Edmonton House in September 1846:

"I left the fort on horseback, accompanied by Mr. Rowand, Mr. Rundell, an Indian boy and a fresh hunter; on reaching the river we crossed in a boat, and swam our horses by the bridle. We left this establishment in true voyageur style, unburthened with food of any kind, and, although contemplating a journey of 200 miles, trusting solely to our guns, having not even a grain of salt. After leaving the boat, we saddled our horses, and had not proceeded more than ten miles, when we fell in with immense numbers of buffaloes.

"During the whole of the three days that it took to reach Edmonton House, we saw nothing else but these animals covering the plains as far as the eye could reach, and so numerous were they, that at times they impeded our progress, filling the air with dust almost to suffocation.We killed one whenever we required a supply of food, selecting the fattest of the cows, taking only the tongues and boss, or hump, for our present meal, and not burdening ourselves unnecessarily with more."

Such herds usually dispersed as winter approached, and smaller groups numbering up to a few thousand animals sought the shelter of river bottoms and wooded areas. The poundmaker, and the young men who assisted him, preyed upon these lesser herds. And it took a person with special gifts to lead the buffalo to a pound, which could be ten to fifteen miles away. "The poundmaker was in a class by himself," wrote

Robert Jefferson, who was married to Pitikwahanapiwiyin's half-sister and spent half a century among the Cree, primarily as a farm instructor after they had settled on reserves. "He was a professional. He could guide the buffalo in any direction he pleased. The spirits of the buffalo communed with him in his dreams, and were at his command when he needed them. In no other way can the unsophisticated Indian explain the facility with which a herd of buffalo was seduced to its destruction."

Jefferson, who wrote of pounds and poundmakers in his book *Fifty Years on the Saskatchewan*, went on to say: "Indians who could be relied on to bring the buffalo within range of the hidden beaters were few. Many tried it; some could do it occasionally. Wonderful tales are told of this or that man who could make the buffalo follow a song to their destruction."

Wonderful tales were no doubt told of Sikakwayan, and Jefferson undoubtedly heard them, since he had married into the great poundmaker's family. But he never thought to write them down for such tales were, as he put it in his book, "generally too wonderful for belief." All that remains is a name: Piti-kwa-han-apiwiyin, or Poundmaker. Such was Sikakwayan's renown as a maker of pounds that he was allowed to bestow this name upon one of his sons. Sikakwayan likely died before he could teach his boys how to build a pound and call the buffalo. But the youthful Poundmaker would have observed the rituals that accompanied such an undertaking because they were performed in the poundmaker's lodge, which was always erected adjacent to the gate to the corral.

When the people were in need of food or a herd had been located, the poundmaker invited several young men, possibly apprentices, to participate in the rituals. He began by burning sweetgrass to cleanse the air, and then held up a pipe to invite his spirit helpers to come and smoke with him. He asked these powers to help make the hunt a success, and then he gave the young men berries to eat and instructed them to blow on eagle bone whistles. To complete the rituals, the poundmaker placed a buffalo skull and cloth offerings near the runway. Then he sent the young men off to bring in the buffalo, which was often a marathon exercise requiring unusual patience.

The men might spend the better part of a day or most of the night stretched out on the frozen ground or in the snow near the herd, protected from the cold only by their leather garments and buffalo robes. They would slap the robes on the ground until the noise caught the attention of the animals and caused them to move away. The men would creep up on the herd and repeat the process. This went on until the buffalo had wandered in between the outlying heaps of brush.

At that point, band members concealed behind the piles triggered a stampede to the pound, a part of the hunt nicely described by Jefferson. "An Indian jumps up from his hiding place, waves his blanket and the herd shies off to the other side cannoning, as it were, from one side to the other, till they enter the brush lane. They are scared into hurrying on and the further they get the more incessant becomes the hue-and-cry, till their efforts to escape assume the proportions of a stampede. Behind the brush lanes too, people are stationed to prevent the frightened animals from breaking through the fences and to shoo them into the pound. Over the inclined threshold into the enclosure they go. A dancing crowd of Indians with waving blankets and shouts, blocks the entrance way, and the frantic herd mills round and round until shot down by the hungry foes that encompass them. Dead and dying are pitted together in a writhing mass, till the knife ends the butchery."

As the son of a poundmaker, Pitikwahanapiwiyin would have enjoyed a comfortable, even privileged childhood. He would have witnessed the rituals, inhaled the sweetgrass and heard his father's songs and incantations. He would have felt the thunder of a thousand panting, panic-stricken buffalo charging to their deaths. He would have sensed the pride his father took in his work, and the respect he had earned among the Cree bands around Fort Carlton. His father was a shaman who could commune with the spirit of the buffalo. When the buffalo were plentiful, his abilities as a maker of pounds would have ensured that his family and fellow band members were well fed, clothed and housed. Buffalo meat dominated their diet. The hides were used for clothing, for bedding, for robes and as coverings for tepees. Spoons and ladles were fashioned from buffalo horns and hooves. The teeth were used to make necklaces. The paunch, the first and largest of a buffalo's stomachs, was employed as a water jug. The hair could be braided into rope, the sinews into threads and bowstrings. The skin of the tongue was rough enough to be used as a comb. Cartilage from the head was boiled to produce glue. When there was no wood available, dried buffalo dung produced a fine fire.

With a skilled poundmaker in its midst, a band often killed far more buffalo than its members could possibly consume, according to contemporary observers like Kane. "I have myself seen a pound so filled up with their dead carcasses that I could scarcely imagine how the enclosure could have contained them while living," he wrote. "It is not unusual to drive in so many that their aggregate bulk forces down the barriers. There are thousands of them annually killed in this manner; but not one in twenty is used in any way by the Indians, so that thousands are left to rot where they fall. I heard of a pound, too far out of my direct road to visit, formed entirely of the bones of dead buffaloes that had been killed in a former pound on the same spot, piled up in a circle similarly to the logs above described."

Kane encountered a band of Crees who had driven three herds into the same pound within the space of ten or twelve days. He was, in fact, present to witness the third of these kills in September 1846 while travelling along the North Saskatchewan from Fort Carlton to Fort Pitt. At the time, Sikakwayan was one of the foremost poundmakers in the district, and it is possible that the painter and the poundmaker met.

By the time Kane travelled down the North Saskatchewan on his way back to Toronto, Sikakwayan was probably dead. The date of his death and the cause are not known, but he is believed to have died when Poundmaker and his siblings were youngsters. Their mother married again, but she died before her children reached adulthood. Within the compact world of a Plains Cree band, children who had lost their parents were generally well cared for. Many members of the community were related by blood or marriage so there were always aunts and uncles to take in orphans. Furthermore, generosity was a cultural trait of the Cree. The strong and the healthy were expected to assist the poor, the elderly and the misfortunate.

Once Poundmaker reached adolescence, he had to begin making his own way in the world. His goals were undoubtedly similar to those of other energetic and ambitious Cree youths: to acquire horses and status, and to marry well. The few sketchy accounts of Poundmaker's early years describe him as a popular member of his band, in part because he was naturally outgoing and gregarious, but also because he was a proficient hunter who was generous toward the needy. He is said to have possessed some of his father's skill at leading buffalo into a pound, and he was adept at tracking and bringing down smaller game.

The surest way to win the respect and recognition of both peers and elders was to display courage in battle and to compile an impressive war record. Nothing is known of Poundmaker's performance on the battlefield, which is undoubtedly a reflection of his character. Indeed, his brother-in-law Robert Jefferson wrote that "Poundmaker had never distinguished himself as a warrior but had acquired what reputation he possessed from his ability as a negotiator." Jefferson went on to say that "he called himself a peacemaker."

Poundmaker finally got the opportunity to become a peacemaker in the early 1870s. He was then a young man of thirty-one or thirty-two. He was personable, generous, and the head of a growing household. His first wife was named Little Beaver and she is said to have encouraged him to marry her sister, Grass Woman, a common enough practice among the plains Indians. Usually, a man married his wife's sister because she had been widowed and had no other means of support. Sometimes, a woman whose husband was a decent man and a capable provider was willing to share her good fortune with a female sibling, and this appears to be what happened in Poundmaker's case.

In any event, he was a man with two wives, and about to become a father for the first time, by Little Beaver, when he met the renowned Blackfoot leader Isapo-Muxika who invited him to visit his camp. Poundmaker accepted, of course, and his time with Crowfoot proved to be a turning point in his life. Before this, he had gone to war, stolen horses, learned to hunt and become expert in the medicines of his people. These accomplishments undoubtedly would have made him a prominent young man among his people. But his experience with the Blackfoot propelled him into the ranks of the leaderhip of the Plains Cree.

Poundmaker accepted Crowfoot's invitation because he undoubtedly saw it as an opportunity to pursue something he had long dreamed of: peace between his people and the Black-foot. He had had his fill of warfare. He was tired of seeing young men—sons, brothers and friends, nephews, cousins and acquaintances—riding off to war and failing to return. He had no more stomach for the tears and wailing of grief-stricken women—of mothers who had lost sons, wives who had lost husbands, and sisters who had lost brothers. Every family had lost somebody or knew a family who had.

But Poundmaker was wise enough to know that he could not embark on a peace initiative on his own. He knew that he could never venture unprotected into Blackfoot country unless a leader of the stature of Crowfoot extended his hand in friend-ship. He knew all this because the murder of a famous peace-maker and Cree chief named Maskepatoon, or Broken Arm, was still fresh on everyone's mind, even though the crime had been committed several years earlier.

Maskepatoon had promoted peace between the Cree and the Blackfoot for more than a decade before his death and even arranged several short-lived truces. He had frequently displayed extraordinary courage. At least twice in the late 1850s, he had walked into a Blackfoot camp unannounced, bearing only a peace pipe, and told the startled inhabitants that they could talk peace or kill him on the spot. Both times, he and the Blackfoot leaders concluded a peace treaty, and Maskepatoon returned to his people with good news and horses, which the Blackfoot had given him as gifts. But in the early spring of 1869, while a group of Crees and Assiniboines were camped south of the Red Deer River, well within Black-foot country, the celebrated peacemaker and several others met a horrible end. The circumstances surrounding Maskepatoon's death were recorded by a friend, the Methodist missionary John McDougall.

"It turned out that the Crees and Blackfoot were in proximity, having been forced there by the movements of the buffalo," McDougall wrote, "and the Blackfeet made proposals of peace which Maskepatoon answered favourably, and himself and his son with a small party set out to arrange and ratify the compact. As he approached the camp of the Blackfeet, the latter came out to meet him with loud acclaim, and seemed very friendly, and the whole crowd on both sides sat down to quietly converse, and, as far as Maskepatoon was concerned, to smoke the pipe of peace. But while this function was going on, at a signal given by one of the Blackfeet, the massacre of the old chief and his people began, and very soon all were killed by this consummate treachery."

By the time Poundmaker turned to peacemaking, the worst of the Indian wars on the Canadian prairies were over. Cree and Blackfoot faced much more formidable adversaries and foes than enemy war parties. New epidemics had swept the plains. Whisky traders from south of the medicine line—the U.S. border—were pouring into Blackfoot country. And more whites were arriving from eastern Canada. Nevertheless, the decades of conflict had left a residue of hatred and hostility between the two dominant tribes of the northern plains. Small-scale raids and skirmishes were still occurring, which had led to the death of Crowfoot's son. Peacemaking remained a dangerous enterprise, one that required steady nerves and unusual courage. Several years after his time among the Blackfoot, Poundmaker described his experiences to a visiting journalist, W.H. Williams, a correspondent with the *Toronto Globe*.

"Poundmaker's experiences among the Blackfoot would, if carefully drawn out of him, make an interesting book, but his allusions to them were very brief, as though he was averse to telling what he had done," Williams wrote in his book *Manitoba and the North-West: Journal of a Trip from Toronto to the Rocky Mountains.* "In his boyish days he often went among the Black-feet, but it was always to murder their people and steal their ponies. When he grew to be a man, he conceived the idea of making peace between the two nations, and then it was that he carried his life in his hand so often that 'it made his body shrink' when he thought of it afterward.

"He spent one whole winter among the Blackfeet, and though he had but little dread of them when they were sober, he had everything to fear from them when they were drunk, and they had liquor in their lodges nearly all that winter. Many and many a night had he slept in their lodges with his big Remington revolver at full-cock in his right hand, and many a time when he was thus alone, far away even from his friend Crowfoot, and when the Blackfeet supposed him to be sleeping soundly, had he heard them carrying on whispered debate as to whether they should kill him or not."

Poundmaker left Crowfoot's camp at winter's end, as the Blackfoot were leaving the sheltered valley bottoms of the Red Deer or one of its tributaries, and moving south to their tradi-tional summer hunting ground out on the prairie. He rode north to find his own people, who were in the midst of making the same move. It was spring, and the prairies sprang to life with startling quickness. The snow melted. The rivers flowed. The crocuses blossomed. Gophers, badgers and bears resurfaced after their long sleep. The wind carried the musty smells of disintegrating ice and oozing mud. It bore the first faint hum of the insects that would soon torment men and beasts alike, and it danced to the jubilant refrain of the meadowlark.

This was the season of anticipation and excitement on the plains, the time when a young man's mind might turn to thoughts of chasing buffalo and stealing ponies, and Poundmaker was filled with a sense of elation as he rode north, through the northern limits of Blackfoot country, past landmarks like the Neutral Hills and the Eagle Hills, and back to the land of the Cree. He travelled quickly, for Crowfoot had sent him away on a fine horse and had given him several spirited and handsome ponies as an additional sign of their friendship.

Still, he was on the trail several days, hardly pausing to eat or sleep, before he reached a Cree camp, and could enjoy a hot meal, and the warmth of a fire. He stopped overnight and told the story of his winter among the Blackfoot, of his friendship with Crowfoot, and how they had come to be as close as father and son. When he had concluded the account of his adventure, he delivered the message that Crowfoot had asked him to carry back to his people. He stood before them—a tall, slender, stately man with hair that flowed down his back and past his waist—and he spoke with all the passion and eloquence he could muster because he heartily endorsed Crowfoot's message himself.

Poundmaker told them that his friend, the renowned warrior and enemy chief, wished to extend the truce that had been in place the previous autumn when he had visited the Cree, a visit that had marked the beginning of their friendship. He wished to bring an end to the horse-stealing raids and the warfare that had taken the lives of so many young men of both nations over the years. Let there be peace between the people of these two nations, Crowfoot had said. Let Cree and Blackfoot live like brothers from this day forward. Let them share the diminishing bounty of these plains. Let them conserve their numbers and their strength, for white men will soon arrive in great numbers. They will covet these lands and try to take them from the Indians. So, let there be peace.

Poundmaker visited other camps along the Battle River and

along both branches of the Saskatchewan that spring. Wherever he went, he told his story and he repeated Crowfoot's message, until at last he reached his own band and rode triumphantly into the circle of tepees. His wives were overjoyed to see him, and Little Beaver presented him with their child. Chiefs, elders and warriors came out to greet him, to hear his story and to admire his horses. Poundmaker had been transformed. His unusual strengths and abilities had been recognized by Crowfoot, who loved him like a son. His friendship with Crowfoot, and his new wealth in horses, had elevated him in the eyes of his family and fellow band members. His name was becoming known even among more distant divisions of the Plains Cree. And, a short time after his return, he became a minor chief, a trusted adviser to an older, more experienced leader named Red Pheasant.

But events in the near future—in the form of cataclysmic change—would further enhance his reputation and status. He would become one of the foremost leaders of the Cree people who made their home on the great plains. He would become known to the white world, and many who met him would be deeply impressed. Poundmaker could speak like few of his brethren. He possessed all the grace, eloquence and power of a natural orator. He could sway opinions and move men. But the Indian nations of the plains were facing an inundation of whites—members of an alien race that coveted their lands and could back their demands with superior numbers and technology. Poundmaker's eloquence could not alter the historic forces and changes unleashed upon his people. His days as leader, therefore, were destined to be brief, turbulent and, finally, tragic.

PART

TWO

F*reedom's*
End

The Theft of the
Iron Stone *and the Trouble*
That Followed, 1866 to 1884

PEOPLE HAD BEEN VISITING
the Iron Stone for as long as anyone could remember, certainly
since the days when a man could lift it. That was long ago,
before the stone had started to grow. Now, it was too big and
too heavy for any man to lift. The stone had changed over the
years, but it hadn't lost any of its special properties. It was still
smooth and shiny, and harder than the metal in a knife. It
could protect those who visited and paid homage. It could
shield them from sickness and hunger and many other calamities that might befall a man and his family. It could give a
warrior strength and bring a hunter luck.

The Creator had placed the Iron Stone at the summit of a

prominent hill overlooking lands frequented by many Cree and Blackfoot bands. To them, it was a sacred monument dedicated to Old Man Buffalo, the spirit that protected and guided the herds. People from both nations visited the stone to pray and make offerings. They left behind old moccasins and arrows, strips of bright, colourful cloth and numerous other objects. And in the spring, after the herds had re-assembled and the first hunt had taken place, holy men would make a pilgrimage to the Iron Stone and leave tasty morsels of meat for Old Man Buffalo.

So, even if a man could lift the stone, why would he want to? And what would ever possess someone to remove it from the hilltop where it had rested for longer than anyone could remember? And who would do such a thing? These were the questions that raced through Cree and Blackfoot camps that summer the stone went missing. Word of the theft spread quickly. The offence had occurred during the season when people were on the move, when hunters who had wives, children and aging parents to provide for were pursuing buffalo, and the younger males, the warriors and would-be warriors, were out looking for horses to steal or making war on one another.

When people heard the news, their reaction was almost always the same. Missing, they said incredulously. Stolen, they added, with disbelief etched on their faces. Yes, stolen, someone would respond. The news travelled by word of mouth. And it travelled fast. Soon, everyone knew who had done it: a Methodist clergyman posted at Victoria Mission on the North Saskatchewan, midway between Fort Pitt and Edmonton House. The man in charge of the mission was George McDougall, who hailed from Kingston in what was then Canada West. McDougall had arrived in the North-West ablaze with Christian zeal.

"War, murder, gambling, polygamy and demon-worship are all producing their natural effects," McDougall wrote to a Methodist colleague in Toronto in 1869, "and if civil law and Gospel light are not speedily brought to the rescue of these tribes, they will perish from the earth." McDougall spent many years among the Indians, and his son John carried on the work. He became his father's biographer, and he portrayed him as a driven man. "All within his range and capability must be done for the rescuing of these peoples from the barbarism, and shiftlessness, and ignorance and superstition of centuries and the removing of *debris* that lay thick upon them," the younger McDougall wrote.

His father looked upon Indian veneration of the Iron Stone as a manifestation of ignorance, superstition and demon worship, so he had the 380-pound, triangular-shaped stone, which was actually a small meteorite, hoisted onto a cart and hauled a hundred miles north to the Victoria mission whence it was shipped to Winnipeg and, eventually, to a Methodist college in Toronto, while out on the prairie, in Cree and Blackfoot camps, toothless old men with creased and weatherbeaten faces pounded buffalo hide drums and shook coyote skull rattles. They sang melancholy songs and foresaw disastrous consequences flowing from the theft of the Iron Stone. Some said, There will be war. Others said, There will be pestilence. Still others warned, All the buffalo will soon be gone.

And all these things came to pass. War, disease and starvation seared and ravaged the people, leaving them dead, wounded or scarred. Other troubles, things the shamans could not foresee, hit one after another. American whisky traders and wolf poisoners poured into once impenetrable Blackfoot country. Mounted police in red tunics marched west across the prairie, imposing law and order. White men arrived in Cree and Blackfoot camps, representatives of the assertive new Dominion of Canada, and they urged the Indians to surrender their lands and sign treaties. Then the buffalo became so scarce that the people had no choice but to give up their old ways and settle on reserves, where they endured indignities and humiliation until their patience was long gone, their pride battered and their anger turned to rage and, finally, in the spring of 1885, they erupted.

BACK IN THE SUMMER of 1866, when McDougall's men desecrated the shrine to Old Man Buffalo, the Cree and the Blackfoot had no reason to suspect that calamity and misfortune lay just beyond the horizon. Both tribes were formidable and permanently at war. But perhaps the shamans had seen that the motive and nature of the warfare had changed. Perhaps they had seen that the battles were becoming bigger, and the costs horrendous. The final years of the Cree–Blackfoot struggle for supremacy on the northern prairie were distinguished by bloodshed and casualties on a scale hitherto unknown.

The first of these battles occurred at the Red Ochre Hills on the South Saskatchewan River in March 1866. The Hudson's Bay trader Isaac Cowie visited the site five years later and camped on the prairie overlooking the ravine where a slaughter of Blackfoot warriors had taken place. "It was still full of the grim skeletons," Cowie wrote in *The Company of Adventurers*, "and I followed from the mouth of that death trap, for miles up the flat bottom lands of the South Saskatchewan valley, a trail of bleached bones of the Blackfeet who had fallen, in panic-stricken retreat, to the fury of the pursuing Crees."

Those Crees, along with some allies whom Cowie identified only as Swan River Indians, had likely travelled west from the Qu'Appelle Valley or south from the Touchwood Hills to hunt buffalo. The Blackfoot sent out a party of warriors six hundred strong to push the interlopers out. Blackfoot war parties usually travelled on horseback, but these warriors walked east, following the South Saskatchewan River valley, which was largely free of snow, until they came to a ravine where two old Cree women were gathering firewood. The Blackfoot murdered the women, then clamoured noisily up the still snowbound ravine toward two Cree lodges pitched above them on the edge of the prairie. They envisioned a quick victory over the inhabitants of the tepees, but were unaware that the larger Cree hunting party was camped in the nearby Red Ochre Hills.

"All were eager to get there," Cowie wrote, "and they crowded into the deep and melting snow on each side of the track. Stumbling and falling, the powder in the pans of their flintlocks got wet also. Meanwhile, the Crees in camp, hearing the volley echoing through the ravine, had taken alarm, and [their] warriors rushed to the brink commanding a full view of the ravine, now filled with a helpless crowd of enemies. That was a black morning for the Blackfeet as, floundering in the snowdrifts and unable to use their guns, the well-armed Crees lined its brink on each side and slaughtered them as they were wont to slay herds of impounded buffalo."

The Cree no doubt rejoiced afterward because rarely, if ever, had they defeated the Blackfoot so decisively. But they would never again enjoy such a triumph. Future battles brought the Cree sorrow rather than joy. This was certainly true of a skirmish in July 1868 near the Cypress Hills, those imposing hulks that tower hundreds of feet above the surrounding prairie and stretch for miles. These hills were neutral ground and a source of wonder to all the native peoples who frequented the lands around them. That summer, several bands of Cree, Saulteaux and Assiniboine, numbering about 350 lodges and 3,500 people, had camped about twenty miles north of the hills on turf long held by the Blackfoot. They were there because the buffalo were almost completely absent from their own territory in and around the Qu'Appelle Valley.

Cowie travelled out from Fort Qu'Appelle for the summer trade, bringing with him cartloads of ammunition, powder, tea, sugar and other goods. When he had come within a mile of the site, Cowie later wrote, "a hundred horsemen sallied out to meet us and escort us into their beleaguered encampment for it was surrounded by hovering bands of Blackfeet." The place was smouldering with tension. Supplies were low. Members of some of the bands detested each other. Then there was the relentless scrutiny. "Ever since the camp crossed the frontiers," Cowie wrote, "the Blackfeet in large numbers hovered around it as an army of observation, prepared to take advantage of any opportunity of successful attack."

That opportunity occurred when sixty young men set off on foot for the Cypress Hills, or *me nach tah kak* as the Cree called them. They went to collect the gum-like sap of pine trees, but on the return journey, a Blackfoot war party, mounted on swift, well-trained ponies, caught these youths exposed and unprotected on a plain. "The Blackfeet circled round the fated band, out of range generally, but with occasional swoops near enough to shoot under their ponies' necks, while they lay on the far side of their mounts, protected and concealed from the Crees. What feats of valor these performed have never been told, for not one of the sixty escaped to tell the tale. They were found by a party, sent out the next day, lying all dead on the plain, scalped and with their bodies as full of Blackfeet arrows as a porcupine is full of quills."

The families whose sons had been killed and scalped knew

what had led to this latest massacre. One father told Cowie that the white man's endless demand for pemmican was destroying the herds and forcing his people to travel farther afield, into the land of their enemies, in search of food. The Cree had lived harmoniously for two centuries with white traders and explorers. They had allowed them into their lands and participated in the fur trade. The relationship had been mutually beneficial. But not any more. Not after the theft of the Iron Stone. Not with the decline of the buffalo. And certainly not with the news that raced through Cree and Blackfoot country in the summer of 1869: the Hudson's Bay Co. had sold their lands to someone called the government of Canada.

As the missionary George McDougall put it in a letter to his superiors in Toronto: "Six years ago the sight of a pale face in a Cree camp was a cause of rejoicing; now the very opposite is the fact. In the winter of 1867–68 these Indians suffered great destitution, and the whole cause is attributed to the whites. Recent events have added much to their previous dissatisfaction. In all past time they have regarded the honourable Company as the highest representative of the Queen. Now a rumour reaches them that a power greater than that Company will soon be here to treat with them for their lands. Injudicious parties have informed them that their old neighbors have received a large sum for these lands, and the Indian is not so ignorant but to enquire to whom has he ever ceded his hunting grounds."

RUMOURS ABOUT THE SALE swept the prairie like a whirlwind, sowing confusion and anxiety. All through the winter of 1869–70, Hudson's Bay men tried to appease the Indians. They travelled from camp to camp with interpreters who read a proclamation, issued by the governor-general of Canada, explaining the principles by which the Dominion intended to govern the North-West. This document also stated that the Canadian government hoped for a peaceful transfer of the territory. Edmonton House received the last available printed copy and the factor there had his men produce handwritten copies so the proclamation could be read even farther afield. The Bay men and their interpreters read and re-read the proclamation. They explained it over and over.

But their efforts failed to alleviate the unrest. It percolated all winter. Then spring arrived and so did a fresh round of rumours. The Indians heard there had been a Metis uprising at Red River, under the leadership of Louis Riel, that the rebels had executed a white man, and that the government of Canada was sending troops west to suppress the rebellion. Tension and discontent mounted in many native camps, but nowhere more so than at Fort Qu'Appelle. Metis families who had wintered on the prairie began arriving daily and the rabble-rousers among them wanted to attack and pillage this Hudson's Bay post.

"News of the troubles in Red River swiftly reached Qu'Appelle in every form of distortion and contortion," according to Cowie, who was stationed there, "and as it was further spread by rumour all over the plains, produced a state of such unrest and excitement that the business of hunting came almost to a stop. Family after family of Metis came in to hear the latest news and take part in discussing it, and to be at hand to participate in any action taken in sympathy with, or imitation of their fellows in Red River."

The turmoil lasted for weeks. The Hudson's Bay men, hopelessly outnumbered by the Cree and Metis, appealed for calm. The Metis had enough men and firepower to ransack the post, seize its stores of weapons and ammunition, and declare themselves rulers of the Qu'Appelle country. And the Cree were caught in the middle. They had no interest in supporting the Metis, yet were increasingly distrustful of the company. But as spring turned to summer, this political crisis was swept aside by a genuine catastrophe unfolding elsewhere on the prairie.

Omikiwin, the disease of the scabs, as the Cree called smallpox, had appeared among the Blackfoot the previous autumn. It waged silent but deadly war on that ferocious nation all winter and many people remembered what the shamans had predicted after the Methodists stole the Iron Stone. They had foreseen war, pestilence and hunger. Now, the second of the prophecies had come true, and the people were filled with terror and rage.

THE EPIDEMIC, LIKE OTHERS before it, had arrived via the Missouri River. It crossed the tribal divide in late spring or early summer of 1870. A Cree raiding party rode into a Blackfoot camp that was deserted except for the dead and the dying, and the Cree warriors carted off weapons, clothing and other goods—all contaminated with the smallpox virus. Then the disease cut a swath of destruction through Cree country.

Scores died around every trading post and mission: one hundred at Fort Pitt; two hundred at the French mission of St. Albert, ten miles north of Edmonton; three hundred at Edmonton. Fear of catching the disease drove some people to commit suicide by drowning. Others fled to avoid being infected and died of starvation. White travellers in Blackfoot country found dozens of dead, abandoned and unburied. The Blackfoot were enraged that this catastrophe had devastated their nation, and some vented their fury by stealing or killing farm animals at the Methodist mission at Victoria. They even attempted to spread the disease to the whites by leaving infected blankets and clothing in white settlements, and rubbing their infected hands on doors and gates.

The saddest story from this summer of sorrow involved a young woman driven to despair by the horror and devastation of smallpox. Her tale was told for years afterward and was eventually published by Joe Dion in his book *My Tribe the Crees*. "We were told a story of a small party of Crees trying desperately to avoid coming in contact with the sick until at last they came across a village of tepees. As they were moving swiftly along, they noticed a beautiful young woman emerging from a large tent in the middle of the circle. The girl stood in the doorway and in a loud, clear voice she told them that she was the only survivor of the village. Then she sang one of her favorite ballads, ending with the word *ahwiya*, an expression of extreme pain. 'How I used to love that song when we were all alive,' she lamented as she retreated into the tepee. Some of the folks wanted to take her along but the elders would hear nothing of the kind. They were too concerned about trying to save their own hides.

"A halt was called not far from the ghost village and that night two young men decided to return and bring the unfortunate woman back with them. They reasoned that if they brought her a change of clothing she could not bring the disease with her. The two men, arriving at the death camp, went and stood at the door of the tepee where the girl had been seen. When they did not get any response to their call, they ventured within and there found the poor girl, her feet almost touching the ground. She had hanged herself."

BY LATE SUMMER OR early fall, the epidemic had subsided. As the Cree began putting their lives back together, the Qu'Appelle chiefs concluded that Blackfoot losses had greatly exceeded their own. They convinced their brethren on the North Saskatchewan that an opportune moment had arrived. It was time for an all-out attack on their old enemies, time to break the back of the Blackfoot nation, and to secure for their own people access to the dwindling herds of buffalo. And so a large war party of six hundred to eight hundred warriors assembled, under the leadership of Big Bear and Little Pine from the Saskatchewan, and Piapot and Little Mountain from the Qu'Appelle.

The chiefs led their warriors up the South Saskatchewan River to its source, the confluence of the Bow and Oldman Rivers. From there, they proceeded up the valley of the Oldman to a point about eighteen miles northeast of the present-day city of Lethbridge. They had by this time reached the heart of Blackfoot country, a feat that would have been unthinkable a few years earlier. But, at this juncture, dissension split the war party. Piapot had a dream that seemed to be full of foreboding. A war council was held to discuss this premonition, and the Young Dogs leader made a speech that concluded with the following remarks:

"My children, I had a dream last night. I saw a buffalo bull with iron horns goring, stamping and killing us. We were unable to destroy it. After long meditation, I have come to the conclusion that we must abandon this venture, and return home. Otherwise, misfortune awaits us."

But another chief opposed him. "My children," this man shouted in response, "don't believe in a dream. Advance and capture the Blackfoot nation, women and children. The smallpox killed off most of their fighters, so we won't be opposed by any great number."

The council failed to achieve a consensus, so Piapot turned back, taking with him a number of warriors. The chiefs who stayed dispatched scouts to locate the Blackfoot. The advance men quickly found a small Blood camp on the Belly River, not far from where it drained into the Oldman. The Cree leaders decided to attack after dark. Upon arriving, they pounced swiftly, announcing themselves with wild spine-tingling war whoops, slashing their way into the buffalo hide lodges, and knifing and scalping whomever they found inside.

Blood warriors sprang to the defence of their homes and families while fleet-footed runners sprinted into the night to seek reinforcements. Blackfoot camps were spread along a twenty-mile stretch of the Oldman, and several Piegan bands, which had been chased out of their usual hunting grounds below the forty-ninth parallel, were camped a few miles to the south on the St. Mary River. However, the Cree scouts had failed to locate these camps—a dreadful mistake that became apparent at dawn. "Warriors from Blackfoot camps, north and south, could be seen approaching, on horseback, in twos and threes, over hills and knolls, chanting their war songs in joyful anticipation of battle," according to an account compiled in 1956 by the Blood writer Mike Mountain Horse. "The Cree braves, noticing these horsemen, cried out to the others: 'Look at them coming over every hill. We are outnumbered. Let us retreat.' "

The Cree sought refuge in a coulee three hundred to four hundred feet wide that dropped sharply from the prairie to the banks of the Belly, several hundred feet below. The Bloods, Blackfoot and Piegans took up a position in an adjacent coulee. With a ridge ranging in width from seventy-five to two hundred feet between them, the enemy forces blasted away at each other for most of the morning, a standoff that left about a dozen Blackfoot and an undetermined number of Cree dead.

The tide turned after a contingent of Blackfoot took control of a butte above the Cree and were able to fire from this position. They flushed their foes out of their stronghold and drove them toward the river.

"Pursuers and pursued rushed headlong, horses and men tumbling over each other, the men fighting and struggling for dear life, until the bank was reached and the fight became a butchery," according to George A. Kennedy, a North-West Mounted Police doctor who prepared his account of the battle for a Lethbridge, Alberta, newspaper in April 1890. "The Crees plunged into the current, and moved across in a solid mass, while the Blackfeet stood on the brink and shot them down like sheep.

"The slaughter did not end at the river. The Blackfeet followed the Crees across, and being joined by a large contingent of their brethren, who had crossed higher up, the butchery went on, and at one spot where the Crees made a sort of stand, about fifty of them were killed. Finally, the Crees reached a clump of trees . . . and, having abandoned most of their horses, took refuge there, and made a last stand."

By the time the Blackfoot stopped shooting, three hundred to four hundred enemy warriors were dead. A few members of the Cree war party, precisely how many is unknown, survived the slaughter. They walked almost 250 miles back to their homeland in late autumn and found their nation in disarray.

THE SMALLPOX EPIDEMIC AND the campaign against the Blackfoot had disrupted the summer buffalo hunt, leaving the Cree desperately short of pemmican and dried meat as winter descended. Furthermore, the herds did not come to the North Saskatchewan, and the people remembered the third prophecy of their shamans: all the buffalo will soon be gone. Fifteen bands were forced to spend the winter hunting on the prairie rather than in the Saskatchewan River valley, where there was shelter from the winds and firewood to keep the lodges warm. The bands assembled in one camp well south of the Battle River to hunt buffalo, and this caught the attention of the Hudson's Bay men, who feared the Indians were plotting against them.

"[The natives] began to counsel among themselves," John McDougall recalled in the biography of his father, "and presently, word was brought to Edmonton that the Indians were gathering for a war of extermination on the whites. They laid the blame for all their calamity upon [us]." The younger McDougall visited the camp on behalf of his father and the company to defuse any potential trouble that might be brewing. He called the leaders together to remind them that the Hudson's Bay Co. and the missionaries remained their friends. The Cree chief Sweetgrass spoke for his people, and his words revealed that the whites had completely misunderstood the actions of the natives.

"We are thankful that our friends in the north have not forgotten us," Sweetgrass told the white missionary. "In sorrow and in hunger and with many hardships we have gathered here, where we have grass and timber, and, since we came, buffalo in the distance, few, though still sufficient to keep us alive. We have grumbled at hunger and disease and long travel through many storms and cold. Our hearts have been hard, and we have had bitter thoughts and doubtless said many foolish and bad words. Your coming has done us good; it has stayed evil and turned our thoughts to better things. We feel today we are not alone."

The Cree bands of the North Saskatchewan had come

together for survival, not war. They had, in fact, sent offerings of tobacco to the Blackfoot that winter—a sign of their desire for peace. And their old enemies had accepted, for disease and whisky had all but eliminated their ability to wage war.

THE BLACKFOOT HAD BEEN able to purchase alcohol for decades during their annual or semi-annual trading sessions at the Hudson's Bay posts along the North Saskatchewan and the American establishments on the upper Missouri. Liquor became much more accessible after 1869, however, when John J. Healy and Alfred B. Hamilton, two enterprising Americans from Fort Benton on the Missouri River, tried a new approach to the Indian trade.

They took their goods north and conducted business within Blackfoot territory. After a six-month foray, they returned with enough buffalo robes to net $50,000 for themselves and their backers. Profits of that magnitude caused a stir in Fort Benton, a frontier commercial centre where a few established business-men and merchants were making fortunes, and countless spec-ulators, desperadoes and restless Civil War veterans drifted into town seeking theirs. In this milieu, Healy and Hamilton started a stampede into Blackfoot country.

Itinerant traders hauled the usual mix of goods north—foodstuffs, tools and personal goods. But liquor produced the quickest, fattest profits, and the lust for those returns created the whisky trade. Unscrupulous traders sold dreadful concoc-tions. One popular brand contained whisky, along with chew-ing tobacco, red pepper, ginger and molasses, all diluted with water and heated to increase the potency.

Initially, the trading took place in Blackfoot camps, but after a few of their kind were robbed and murdered, the American interlopers began building the notorious whisky posts, and more than two dozen spread like a blight across what is now southern Alberta and Saskatchewan. They had colourful names—Fort Whoop-Up, Slideout, Standoff, Robbers Roost and Whisky Gap—and the territory they occupied became known as Whoop-Up Country. The majority of these establishments were crudely built, the exception being Healy and Hamilton's Fort Whoop-Up, the most famous of them all, which stood in the Oldman River valley, near present-day Lethbridge. The rectangular fort was constructed of squared timber, the buildings had earthen roofs to make them fireproof and two brass cannons were placed in corner bastions to defend the inhabitants, if necessary.

Whoop-Up was built to last. But the whisky trade was too corrupt and depraved to survive for long. This illicit commerce turned a vast tract of territory, once the sole domain of the Blackfoot, into the most lawless and dangerous part of the entire western frontier. In 1871 alone, drunken brawls among Indians led to eighty-eight murders, according to Colonel Patrick Robertson-Ross, a Canadian officer who reported on conditions in the North-West for the Dominion government. By the summer of 1872, Ross observed, the traders were doing business outside the walls of Fort Edmonton and sneered at a Hudson's Bay officer who tried to stop them. "They coolly replied that they knew very well that what they were doing was contrary to the law of both countries, but as there was no force there to prevent them, *they would do just as they pleased,*" the colonel wrote.

These men treated their clients with even more contempt. They kept the booze flowing until the Indians had traded away their robes, horses, weapons and even their women. They kept trading, that is, until the people had nothing left to exchange.

"It was painful to see the state of poverty to which they had been reduced," wrote the Catholic priest Constantine Scollen after spending the summer of 1874 among the Blackfoot. "Formerly, they were the most opulent Indians in the country. Now they were clothed in rags, without horses and without guns."

The whisky traders opened Blackfoot country to another, more odious class of men—the wolf poisoners. Small parties of these crude, unkempt frontiersmen spent the winter on the prairie making enemies almost everywhere they went. Their method of operation was simple: they would shoot a buffalo, sprinkle strychnine on the carcass, and allow wolves to feed on it. Afterward, the wolfers skinned the dead animals and sold the hides in Fort Benton. Indian dogs also died after inadvertently feeding off the baited carcasses, so enraging their masters that they took to murdering the wolfers at every opportunity.

Dead wolves, dead dogs, dead Indians: these were the unexpected and unhappy by-products of the whisky trade. And nobody seemed to care because greed ruled Whoop-Up country. It blinded the free traders and the merchant princes of Fort Benton who bankrolled them: Isaac G. Baker, Thomas C. Power and William G. Conrad, among others. But many people on the Canadian side of the forty-ninth parallel were offended and angry. Missionaries, explorers and employees of the Hudson's Bay Company were appalled by the depravity they observed and demanded a response from the Canadian government. And they soon got it.

On April 28, 1873, as the Benton merchants were looking forward to another year of exorbitant profits, Sir John A. Macdonald rose in the House of Commons, in far off Ottawa, and introduced a bill "Respecting the Administration of Justice and for the Establishment of a Police Force in the North-West

Territories." Macdonald's bill led to the creation of the North-West Mounted Police.

But more than fourteen months elapsed before the government had determined the structure of the force, before officers were appointed, before recruits were hired, trained and outfitted, and before the three-hundred-man force, dressed in red tunics, black pants and leather boots, left Fort Dufferin, Manitoba, on July 8, 1874, and began an eight-hundred-mile ride to Whoop-Up country at the foot of the Rocky Mountains. And all the while, through another full cycle of the seasons and then some, whisky flowed, wolves were slaughtered and Indians drank their way to poverty.

The era of the whisky trader and the wolf poisoner reached its bloody nadir on a Sunday morning in early May 1873. A few days after Macdonald introduced his bill and long before the mounted police marched west, a pack of drunken wolfers became embroiled in a deadly gunfight against a party of intoxicated Assiniboine warriors on Battle Creek, a small waterway that flowed south out of the Cypress Hills. These wolfers, about a dozen in all, and a mix of Americans, English Canadians and French Canadians, came north from Fort Benton to recover horses stolen a few weeks earlier by Assiniboine warriors. They followed the trail of the thieves until it went cold a few miles from Battle Creek, where competing whisky posts stood a mere two hundred yards apart.

The atmosphere here was thick with tension and hostility. A starving and impoverished band of Assiniboines was camped nearby and had threatened to destroy the establishment operated by trader Moses Solomon. Another group of Indians had recently stolen thirty horses from the rival post owned by Abel Farwell. Then the wolfers arrived, dirty and short-tempered, after a hard ride north. They fully expected to find their horses and became dejected when they learned that no one had seen them. They stayed on to enjoy a few days of Farwell's liquor-laden hospitality and awoke one morning to discover another horse missing.

Toward noon, the enraged and by then drunken wolfers barged into the Assiniboine camp, brandishing rifles and revolvers, and demanding the return of the horse. Farwell tried to play the mediator but failed, and the confrontation quickly escalated. Women and children fled. Assiniboine warriors threw off their robes. Someone fired a shot. And the fight was on. It lasted for hours. The wolfers were armed with repeating rifles that could fire seven to eight shots a minute whereas the Indians could get off only one shot every forty-five seconds or so with their old muzzle loaders.

Given the differences in weaponry, the outcome was hardly surprising. One wolfer and twenty Assiniboines died that day. When the fight was over, the triumphant wolfers vented the last of their fury by committing atrocities. They abducted and raped several Assiniboine women. They decapitated the chief, Little Soldier, and impaled his head on a pike. They finished the day by burning the tattered lodges and paltry possessions of this threadbare Assiniboine band.

The Cypress Hills Massacre, as it became known, caused an uproar in central Canada and a diplomatic row between the United States and Great Britain. It turned the perpetrators into fugitives, eight of whom were eventually arrested and tried in Helena, Montana, and Winnipeg, Manitoba, although none were convicted. And it sent the whisky trade into an irreversible tailspin. By the time the North-West Mounted Police reached Whoop-Up country in the fall of 1874, most of the traders had deserted their whisky posts and fled south. The force quickly suppressed the remnants of this wretched enterprise, and the grateful Blackfoot felt as though a scourge had been lifted from their land.

As Crowfoot later put it, "If the police had not come to the country, where would we all be now? Bad men and whisky were killing us so fast that very few, indeed, of us would have been left today. The police have protected us as the feathers of the bird protect it from the frosts of the winter."

IN THE DIFFICULT YEARS ahead, the mounted police would frequently prevent the anger and exasperation of natives and whites from escalating into violence. And the potential for confrontations grew as civilization spread west, as the first towns sprang to life on the North Saskatchewan—Prince Albert in 1866, the Metis community of St. Laurent in 1871 and Battleford in 1874—and as the white population shot up from a thousand in 1870 to almost seven thousand by 1881. Newcomers of all sorts arrived—settlers, merchants and newspaper publishers—or simply passed through the country: surveyors who delineated the border between Canada and the United States; workmen who strung a telegraph line from Winnipeg to Fort Edmonton; and more surveyors who plotted a road for the prairie portion of Canada's transcontinental railway.

All of these things occurred before the Plains Cree or the Blackfoot had signed treaties extinguishing their title to the land. As early as April 1871, Sweetgrass, one of the leading Cree chiefs of the North Saskatchewan River, petitioned A.G. Archibald, lieutenant-governor of the territories, for a treaty, as well as cattle, tools and agricultural implements to ease the transition to a new way of life. But over five years elapsed before the Dominion government got around to negotiating.

Between 1871 and 1875, commissioners appointed by Ottawa

negotiated five treaties with Ojibway, Cree, Saulteaux and Assiniboine Indians whose ancestral homelands stretched from the western end of Lake Superior all the way to the Cypress Hills. Finally, in the fall of 1875, the lieutenant-governor of the day, Alexander Morris, asked the Reverend George McDougall to deliver a message to the Cree bands who lived around Forts Carlton and Pitt on the Saskatchewan. McDougall visited twenty-two camps to announce that the government wished to make a treaty with them the following summer. At one large encampment, he addressed Mistawasis, a leading chief of the Carlton district, Beardy of the Willow Cree, and several Assiniboine head men. Sweetgrass was absent, but his son and most of his councillors were present. All of these men were delighted with the news.

"That is just it," Mistawasis said. "That is all we wanted."

"If I had heard these words spoken by the Great Queen," Beardy said, "I could not have believed them with more implicit faith than I do now."

There was one dissenting voice and it belonged to Big Bear. The Methodist missionary had known the Cree chief for years. In his report to Lieutenant-Governor Morris, McDougall dismissed him as a "troublesome fellow" from Jackfish Lake. He was the leader of a small band, a man of no consequence and an outsider. Big Bear was an Ojibwa, a member of that tribe of conjurers and mischief-makers. But there he was, trying to take over a Cree council.

"We want none of the Queen's presents," Big Bear told McDougall. "When we set a fox-trap, we scatter pieces of meat all around. But when the fox gets into the trap, we knock him on the head. Let your chiefs come like men, and talk to us."

Big Bear sensed that traps and dangers lay ahead, and perhaps he remembered his youthful vision in which white men arrived in droves and pushed the Indians off their lands. But Lieutenant-Governor Morris, who arrived at Fort Carlton in mid-August 1876 to negotiate with the Crees, envisioned a bright, harmonious future for both races.

"I cast my eyes to the East down to the great lakes and I see a broad road leading from there to the Red River," Morris said at one point during the negotiations. "I see it stretching on to Ellice, I see it branching there, the one leading to Qu'Appelle and Cypress Hills, the other by Pelly to Carlton. I see the Queen's Councillors taking the Indians by the hand saying we are brothers, we will lift you up, we will teach you. All along that road I see Indians gathering, I see gardens growing and houses building; at the same time I see them enjoying their hunting and fishing as before."

Morris and his deputies, a retired Hudson's Bay factor named William J. Christie and Manitoba agriculture minister James McKay, met with the Crees of Fort Carlton on August 18, 1876. The governor's tent was erected on a knoll about one and a half miles from the fort, facing the Indian camp of some 250 lodges and 2,500 people about four hundred yards away. The Indians approached Morris and his deputies, beating drums, firing their guns, singing, dancing and circling on horses. After a ceremonial display of friendship and formal introductions, the commissioner spent the entire day explaining the purpose of the treaties and the Queen's desire to treat the Indians fairly.

On the second day, Morris outlined the Queen's offer to her Cree subjects: reserves based on 640 acres of land—one square mile—for every family of five; schools where numbers warranted; a ban on the sale of alcohol; hoes, spades and scythes for each family; a plough and two harrows for every ten families; oxen to pull the ploughs; one bull and four cows per band; seeds for growing grain and vegetables; tools for building homes. There would be $1,500 worth of ammunition and twine yearly; $5 per year for every man, woman and child, payable to the head of the family; $25 annually to each chief and $15 per head man; and new coats every three years for the chiefs and councillors. And there were signing bonuses: $25, silver medals and flags for the chiefs; $15 for their head men; and $12 per individual.

Morris may have been an honourable man who envisioned a future of prosperity and racial harmony. But he underestimated the challenges facing the Crees and their fear of the future. He offered them a few acres each in exchange for 120,000 square miles of land. Some of the older, more prominent chiefs, notably Mistawasis and Atahkakoop, were prepared to accept the offer as tendered. They knew that the position of their people was becoming untenable and that many other bands from Lake Superior to Cypress Hills had taken the same deal. But several younger Cree chiefs objected, and Poundmaker spoke for them. "The governor mentions how much land is given to us," Poundmaker said. "He says 640 acres, one square mile for each family, he will give us. This is our land! It isn't a piece of pemmican to be cut off and given in little pieces back to us. It is ours and we will take what we want."

He and the others recognized, as Morris clearly didn't, that their people would need more than farm implements and carpenter's tools because they did not know how to till the soil or grow crops or build homes. "When I commence to settle on the lands to make a living for myself and my children," Poundmaker told Morris, "I beg of you to assist me in every way possible—when I am at a loss how to proceed I want the advice and assistance of the Government; the children yet unborn, I wish you to treat them in like manner as they advance in civilization like the white man."

This demand put Morris in a tight spot. He had no mandate to promise open-ended assistance of the kind the Indians wanted, but got around the problem by enriching the offer of tools, agricultural supplies and farm animals, and by agreeing to what might be called a disaster relief clause. It stipulated that the government would, in the event of "any pestilence or a general famine," provide assistance sufficient "to relieve the Indians from the calamity that shall have befallen them."

With that, the negotiations at Carlton were finished, and the commissioners moved on to Fort Pitt, where Sweetgrass and a number of lesser chiefs accepted the treaty without argument or modification. Once again, Big Bear provided the lone voice of dissent. He had come in to speak for several Cree and Assiniboine bands who were hunting on the plains, and he arrived late. His fellow chiefs, many of them now Christians and swayed by the missionaries, urged him to sign as well. But he would have none of it.

"Stop, stop, my friends," Big Bear pleaded to his fellow chiefs. "I have never seen the Governor before. When I see him I will make a request that he will save me from what I most dread, that is: the rope to be about my neck, it was not given to us by the Great Spirit that the red man or white man should shed each other's blood."

This statement was poorly translated and subsequently misinterpreted, according to Big Bear's biographer Hugh Dempsey. He was speaking figuratively about the impact of giving up his freedom to roam and settling on a small piece of land like a reserve. To Big Bear, this would be equivalent to being choked by a rope and would ultimately lead to bloodshed. Morris thought the Cree chief was speaking literally about his fear of being hung if he murdered someone, and he delivered a lecture on capital punishment and how it would be applied equally to Indians and white men, if necessary.

So the two men parted, with a chasm of misunderstanding between them. Big Bear went back to his camp, fearful and aggrieved, and determined to resist having any ropes placed around his neck. Morris returned to Winnipeg, his work complete, his political masters grumbling that he had been too generous with the Cree, and his term as lieutenant-governor of the North-West Territories over. A new man, David Laird, took his place, and it fell to him to negotiate an accord with the Blackfoot, the only major tribe left between the western end of Lake Superior and the foot of the Rocky Mountains that hadn't signed a treaty.

THE BLACKFOOT WERE MOST anxious to settle with the Dominion of Canada. The Catholic priest Constantine Scollen, who had spent many years among them, submitted a pre-treaty report to the government on their character and condition. "They have been utterly demoralized as a people," Father Scollen wrote, adding that this was due to smallpox and the whisky trade. "They have an awful dread of the future."

Laird and Lieutenant-Colonel James F. Macleod of the North-West Mounted Police met the Blackfoot at two o'clock in the afternoon, on September 17, 1877, on the banks of the Bow River, about fifty miles downstream from the nascent settlement of Fort Calgary. The Blackfoot leadership chose the site, a place of unusual beauty called *soyohpoiwko*, which meant "ridge under water." It was an important place to the Blackfoot for they had been coming here for generations to cross the quick, cold Bow.

The Canadian party set up camp on the south side of the river, in a valley bottom about three miles long by one wide, with plenty of timber along the Bow and feed for the horses. The Indians—Blackfoot, Bloods, Piegans, Sarcees and Stoneys —camped on both sides of the river and some pitched their tepees on the prairie overlooking the valley. All told, there were about a thousand lodges, thousands of horses, and traders from north and south peddling their wares.

"It was a stirring and picturesque scene," according to one mounted police officer, Inspector Cecil Denny. There were "great bands of grazing horses, the mounted warriors threading their way among them, and, as far as the eye could reach, the white Indian lodges glimmering along the river bottom. By night, the valley echoed to the dismal howling of the camp curs, and from sun to sun the drums boomed in the tents. Dancing, feasting, conjuring, incantations over the sick, prayers for success in the hunt or in war, all went to form a panorama of wild life vastly novel and entertaining, and seen but once. Never before had such a concourse of Indians assembled on Canada's western plains."

After some vigorous debate within their councils, the Blackfoot accepted the treaty without demanding any substantive changes. Crowfoot's willingness to sign swayed most of the leading chiefs, and the few who remained opposed quickly fell into line. "The plains are large and wide," he said in his acceptance speech to Laird. "We are the children of the plains, it is our home and the buffalo has been our food always. I hope you look upon the Blackfeet, Bloods and Sarcees as your children now, and that you will be indulgent and charitable to them.

They all expect me to speak now for them, and I trust the Great Spirit will put into their breasts to be a good people—into the minds of the men, women and children, and their future generations. The advice given me and my people has proved to be very good. I am satisfied. I will sign the treaty."

And he did, there in the governor's council tent, on the banks of the Bow River, on September 22, 1877. He took pen in hand, perhaps for the first time, and etched a big, bold X beside the words CHAPO-MEXICO, the government's rendering of his name, Isapo-Muxika. From that day forward, life changed for Crowfoot and his people. In the winter of 1877–78, which was as strange a season as anyone could remember, they became refugees chasing the last fleeting herds, like thousands of other children of the plains.

THERE WERE NO BUFFALO in the wooded valley bottoms north of the Red Deer River, Crowfoot's traditional wintering grounds. Nor was there any snow. It was mild and dry. Fires blackened the land, and smoke filled the skies. Crowfoot and some two thousand followers sought refuge on the edge of the Great Sand Hills. There were Crees and Assiniboines camped south of them, and they, too, were far removed from their normal winter camps. And still farther south, from the Cypress Hills to the border, there were several thousand fugitive Sioux who had fled to Canada with the famous Sitting Bull after the Battle of the Little Big Horn in June 1876. All of these Indians were homeless and hungry, and things only got worse.

By the spring of 1879, people were starving. People who had lived on the buffalo—the monarch of the plains—were eating anything they could kill: rabbits and gophers, mice and moles, porcupines and badgers. They slaughtered their dogs, and then they boiled moccasins and rawhide for nourishment. For nearly two years, Crowfoot kept his people at the Blackfoot Crossing, where he had signed the treaty and where he intended to take his reserve, while other Canadian Indians crossed the border into Montana in search of buffalo.

Adversity forced the Blackfoot to join the exodus in late 1879. A thousand desperate Crees had arrived at the Bow that summer and set up camp near Crowfoot's people. But there were no buffalo for either tribe. American hide hunters had deliberately set prairie fires for hundreds of miles along the Canada–U.S. border to prevent the herds from coming north. Crowfoot finally decided to go to Montana after a meeting with the freshly appointed Indian commissioner for the North-West Territories, Edgar Dewdney.

"I advised them strongly to go," Dewdney said later in a private letter, "and gave them some provisions to take them off. They continued to follow the buffalo further and further south until they reached the main herd and there they remained. . . . I consider their remaining away saved the Govt. $100,000 at least."

They were gone for almost two years. Crowfoot first took his people to the Bearpaw Mountains on the Milk River, before moving south to spend the winter of 1879–80 on the Missouri near the Little Rocky Mountains. Big Bear arrived a short time later with his large camp of three hundred lodges, and these old enemies, the Blackfoot and the Cree, spent the winter side by side. In the fall of 1880, the scarcity of buffalo forced Crowfoot to uproot his people again. This time he led them south to a new camp on the Musselshell River, a tributary of the Missouri.

Their final months in exile were marked by one calamity after another. The Blackfoot had arrived in Montana with hundreds of horses but most were stolen by rival bands during their stay there. Whisky traders appeared again to prey on the Indians and create havoc within their camps. Drunken warriors ignored the chiefs and elders and traded their last robes, their best horses and even their women for another bottle. Hungry natives killed an estimated three thousand cattle in the winter of 1880–81, or five per cent of the Montana herd, and ranchers retaliated by killing Indians. In the spring, epidemics of mumps and measles brought sickness and death to the camps.

By late May, five hundred despondent people had left Crowfoot's camp on foot to begin the four hundred-mile trek back to their former homeland. A short time later, the chief himself decided to return. He and his followers walked to the Missouri, on to the Milk River and on to the international border, which existed only in the minds and on the maps of the white man. They reached Fort Walsh, a mounted police post in the heart of the Cypress Hills, then swung west and walked across the prairie, a ragged, hungry, exhausted line of refugees that stretched for miles.

They had left most of their possessions behind at their camps on the Musselshell, and now they were forced to leave the dead—mostly children and old people—along a trail watered with the sorrow of the Blackfoot. They arrived at Fort Macleod on the Oldman River after a six-week journey and there they saw the future. Their impoverished brethren were clustered around the fort, surviving on rations—a pound of beef and half a pound of flour per person—distributed daily by the redcoats or Indian Department employees.

Crowfoot did not stop there, however, but led his followers north a hundred miles to the Blackfoot Crossing, where they had signed the treaty four years earlier and where they would now take a reserve. He arrived with 1,064 people. One thousand

Blackfoot had died since 1879. With their numbers reduced, their country gone and the buffalo nearly extinct, the power of the Blackfoot had evaporated, and with it went their freedom, their autonomy and their will to resist white civilization.

THE WILL TO RESIST HAD not been snuffed out entirely among the native peoples of the North-West. It survived in the minds and hearts of several thousand renegade Crees camped near Fort Walsh. They were gaunt and hungry and surviving on NWMP rations. They were clothed in rags and living in dilapidated tepees. Most had accepted the treaties, but were not prepared to go meekly to reserves, nor would they quietly take up new lives as farmers. "They are the most worthless and troublesome Indians we have," Dewdney wrote to one of his superiors, the Superintendent-General of Indian Affairs, in January 1882.

Their leaders were Piapot, Lucky Man and Little Pine, and in late April of that year Big Bear arrived from the United States with about three hundred people. They were the last Indian refugees hunting buffalo in Montana, and the U.S. Army had dispatched cavalry and artillery units armed with bayonets, rifles and cannon to chase the Cree home. Big Bear was the most independent chief and the shrewdest native politician on the Canadian prairie, but to the mounted police and the federal Indian agents he was just a rabble-rouser.

He had yet to sign the treaty. He had repeatedly demanded that the agreement be renegotiated, and the terms improved, something Sir John A. Macdonald, who was both prime minister and minister of Indian Affairs, had categorically rejected. Now Big Bear and his troublesome brood were back, and the Canadian government was ready for them. The government controlled the food supply in the North-West. Hence, food, as opposed to military might, became the weapon that would force Big Bear and the other recalcitrant chiefs north and on to reserves. Mounted police officers met Big Bear upon his return and laid out the government's policy: he could sign the treaty or his people would starve. Furthermore, the police force banished him and his followers to Cypress Lake—thirty miles from Fort Walsh—where they were expected to fish for their survival.

But Big Bear held out as spring turned to summer, summer to fall, and fall to winter. In mid-October, a police administrative officer and a physician named Augustus Jukes toured the Cree camps, and both were shocked by the conditions. "Few of their lodges are of Buffalo hide, the majority being of cotton only, and many of these in the most rotten and dilapitated condition," Jukes wrote in a letter to Dewdney. "Their clothing for the most part was miserable and scanty in the extreme. I saw little children at this inclement season, snow having fallen, who had scarcely rags to cover them. Of food they possessed little or none; some were represented to me as absolutely starving and their appearance confirmed the report. It would indeed be difficult to exaggerate their extreme wretchedness and need."

Big Bear and his fellow chiefs believed their people had been cheated. The government of Canada had taken their lands for a pittance, much less than the £300,000 that the Hudson's Bay Co. had received in 1869 for relinquishing its claims to the North-West, and the company had never owned the land in the first place. They knew that their brethren who had settled on reserves received inadequate rations and were often hungry, and that the government had failed to provide the seeds, livestock and farm implements the reserve Indians needed to become successful farmers.

They also knew that the government could ignore their complaints and grievances if each chief spoke only for his own band, and if each band lived on its own reserve. But if several bands were to take reserves adjacent to each other, and if those Indians were to speak with one voice, then maybe the government would listen. This was the goal of Big Bear and the other recalcitrant chiefs. They wanted to create an Indian territory in the Cypress Hills.

But the police and the Indian agents would not discuss the idea. They were mere functionaries in the field. They followed the policies set in distant Ottawa by Macdonald and his deputy minister, Lawrence Vankoughnet. And these two wanted the Indians settled north of the railway, out of the path of settlers who would soon be pouring into the country. They wanted to preserve these lands for the newcomers, and they would not relent even if the Crees went to bed hungry every night and shivered in their rags and rotting tepees as the snow piled up, and the cold deepened.

An outraged mother finally broke the stalemate between the chiefs and the government. Her name was never recorded, but she was the wife of a man named French Eater, and the daughter of Big Bear. She had ten children of her own, and many nieces and nephews, all of them starving. Her brother Twin Wolverine had five children, and a second brother Imasees had two sons and two daughters. Her older sister, Nowakich, had five children. French Eater's wife was not prepared to let the children die of starvation, so she broke with her father and took the treaty in order to obtain rations. Within days, 133 members of Big Bear's band, including his sons Twin Wolverine and Imasees and daughter Nowakich, had defected.

Big Bear could resist no longer. On December 8, 1882, he

walked from his tepee to the office of the Indian agent Allan McDonald at Fort Walsh. He stood opposite McDonald with the few men on those wide plains who were prepared to stand with him that day: Piapot, Lucky Man, Little Pine and several family members. And he unburdened himself. He raged at this minion of the government of Canada and all the other whites who had starved his people into submission and turned his own sons and daughters against him.

His speech was not recorded but it was likely similar to the message he delivered a few months later to an Indian agent in Battleford, then the territorial capital. A journalist from the *Saskatchewan Herald* recorded parts of Big Bear's harangue as it was translated. "Long before the advent of the palefaces, this vast land was the hunting ground of my people," he said on that occasion. "This land was then the hunting ground of the Plains and the Woods Crees, my fathers. It was then teeming with buffalo and we were happy. This fair land from the Cumberland Hills to the Rockies and northward to Great Green Lake, the River of the Beavers, and the shores of Lac la Biche, and south and westward toward the setting sun is now the land of the white man—the land of the stranger. Our big game is no more. You now own our millions of acres—according to treaty papers—as long as grass grows on the prairies or water runs in our big rivers. We have no food. We live not like the white man, nor are we like the Indians who live on fowl and fish. True, we are promised great things but they seem far off and we cannot live and wait. Alas, we cannot work. We are tired. Feed us until we recoup our wasted bodies and then speak of labor. We are hungry."

Big Bear went on to explain that his people were children of the plains. The Great Spirit had given them these lands, and covered them with buffalo so the people would have food and clothing and coverings for their lodges. Now that the Great Mother owned the land, and now that the buffalo were gone, the Great Mother had an obligation to provide for her children. But that obligation had not been fulfilled and the people were famished.

Big Bear spoke for four hours on that December day in 1882 and would have kept going, but his son-in-law Lone Man and one of his boys pleaded with him to take the treaty before it was too late. With great reluctance, Big Bear took the pen and marked an X on two documents signifying his acceptance of Treaty Six. Big Bear had been forced to sign away his freedom. But no government could ever break his will.

THE WINTER PASSED. Spring arrived. And the Cree holdouts were still camped near Fort Walsh. They were still trying, through peaceful resistance, to force the government to renegotiate their treaties. But by then, the police and the Indian agents were determined to end this defiance. In late May 1883, they announced that they were closing Fort Walsh and moving the mounted police detachment to Maple Creek, on the transcontinental railway line. The Cypress Hills post had become, in the words of Commissioner Acheson G. Irvine, nothing more than "a temptation to straggling bands of lazy Indians whose desire was to loaf about the post, and when in a destitute condition, make demands for assistance from the government."

The police tore down the buildings and gave the Indians two alternatives: go to the reserves that had been selected for them, or stay behind and face certain starvation. At that, the protest crumbled. Piapot and his followers left for their reserve near Indian Head, forty-two miles east of Regina. By the end of June, Big Bear, Lucky Man, Little Pine and their people,

550 in all and most of them on foot, had begun a twenty-one-day trek to the North Saskatchewan River valley, accompanied by an Indian agent, Thomas Quinn, and fifteen mounted police.

The authorities intended to take them to Fort Pitt, and from there to reserves that had been selected for them. But Big Bear had his own agenda. He insisted that he and his followers would visit Poundmaker at his reserve, forty-five miles west of the forks of the Battle and North Saskatchewan Rivers. And he had a new grievance against the government. Federal agents had contravened the terms of the treaty by assigning him a reserve near Frog Lake, about fifteen miles northwest of Fort Pitt, rather than allowing him to choose his own site. He refused to go to Frog Lake. He and his people spent the fall, as well as the winter of 1883–84, on the Poundmaker reserve while Little Pine was granted a reserve adjacent to Poundmaker's. Again, Big Bear and his followers paid a high price for their defiance: a winter without rations, and days spent scouring the land for any morsel of flesh that might sustain a man and his family.

Yet even as they suffered, Big Bear's people couldn't help but notice that their brethren who had complied with the treaties and settled on the reserves several years earlier were scarcely better off. Misery ruled the Cree camps of the North Saskatchewan, the Touchwood Hills, the Qu'Appelle Valley that winter. And it didn't stop there. All the children of the plains—Blackfoot, Sarcees and Assiniboines included—were cold, hungry and sick.

Rations had been reduced everywhere, and the orders to cut back had come from Sir John A. Macdonald and his deputy, Vankoughnet. Canada was in a recession. Business was down and so were government revenues. Budget surpluses had become budget deficits. Departmental expenditures were being slashed, and Vankoughnet, a diligent and parsimonious civil servant, could trim a budget as well as any of his colleagues. Furthermore, he was convinced that some of his Indian agents had been too liberal when it came to dispensing rations.

Vankoughnet had toured the North-West in the fall of 1883 and, upon returning to the capital, wrote to Macdonald recommending a cut of $140,000—fifteen per cent of his budget, which he deemed to be "needless expenditure." Agents and clerks were dismissed, and those who remained were put on a short leash. They were given new and tighter regulations to follow, and Ottawa had to approve any departure from the rules. The government also introduced a new policy on rations: they would be distributed only to the aged, the infirm and those who worked. Departmental employees stationed in the North-West, from Dewdney down to the local agents, objected vigorously. They had felt Indian hostility first hand and they feared this policy could lead to violence. Some resigned in protest, but to no effect.

Events quickly proved the agents right. In February 1884, twenty-five armed Saulteaux and Cree confronted the agent on their reserve at Crooked Lake, about a hundred miles east of Regina and demanded food. The agent stuck to the government's no-work, no-rations policy and refused the starving men. They nearly beat him to death before ransacking the rations house. A mounted police inspector and ten officers tried to make arrests but were stopped by heavily armed Indians holed up in a dance lodge, who were prepared to die in a blaze of bullets rather than sink into oblivion as wasted, weakened shadows of men. The mounted police held their fire and negotiated for over a week before the desperate Saulteaux and Cree surrendered.

HUNGER BRED DISCONTENT and resentment in every Indian camp that winter. But Poundmaker's reserve became the epicentre of the turbulence, and Big Bear led the agitation. He was determined to make one more attempt to secure better terms for his people. He was convinced the white man would listen only if the Indians could speak with a united voice. Hence, he decided to hold a thirst dance and a grand council in the summer of 1884. He sent runners off in all directions bearing invitations to the leading chiefs of the Cree and Blackfoot. And his efforts yielded results. By early June, more than two thousand Indians were camped on Poundmaker's reserve. By the time they had departed, Indian-white relations on the North Saskatchewan had taken a terrible turn. The government's no-work, no-rations policy had almost provoked an Indian war.

The gathering began as a social event. Old friends became reacquainted. They shared stories about their new lives on the reserves and the hardships that had befallen them. They reminisced about the freedom and excitement of the nomadic lives they had left behind. And they listened to the captivating tales of the storytellers. Hunters extolled the thrill of the chase and the great feasts that followed. Warriors told of the tingle in their spines as they stole into Blackfoot camps at dawn and rode away on prized ponies. They relived the danger and glory of war and, for the first time in months, their eyes glowed from something other than hunger.

All this talk stirred the passions of young men who had so recently been warriors. Some were ready to crush the whites in the tiny settlement of Battleford, forty-five miles to the east. Others wanted to unleash their fury on the mounted police. But the chiefs wanted peace, even though they filled mornings and afternoons with political harangues against the new order that had reduced their people to subservience. They would renegotiate rather than fight, and Big Bear would speak for them. He would carry their message to Indian Commissioner Dewdney in Regina, the new territorial capital, and he would take it from there to Ottawa. He would present their case to this man named Canadian government. Big Bear would demand more food, better treatment and the fulfilment of the promises made in the treaties.

Having settled on a plan, the chiefs prepared for the thirst dance. Big Bear, a religious man who had sponsored many of these ceremonies, fasted and went without sleep the night before the dance began. He discarded his clothing, coated himself in clay dust, and prayed to the Great Spirit. The following morning, he joined the young men who were building a large, circular lodge for the three-day dance. First, they cut an appropriate tree to serve as a centrepole. They cut down others and erected them around the centrepole to form the outer walls of the lodge. They enclosed the structure with heaps of brush and branches, and old lodge coverings. Soon, the rhythmic throb of Indian drums filled the prairie sky while dancers in animal skins and feathered headdresses chanted power songs that had once carried them into battle.

The drummers and dancers went all night, and into the day, just as they had in former times when the thirst dance was a celebration of summer, and plenty, and life. In those days, the drummers pounded their skins with joy, and the dancers danced with glee. But there was no joy, and precious little glee at Big Bear's thirst dance of June 1884. Nevertheless, the drummers and dancers pushed themselves to exhaustion, bringing to a boil their hatred of the new order.

So trouble was inevitable when a small contingent of police

officers interrupted the dance to arrest two brothers—sons of the prominent chief Lucky Man. One of the brothers had whacked an Indian agent across the arm with an axe handle a day earlier after the agent refused to give them rations. The officers pushed their way into the dance lodge but were unable to locate the suspects amid the swirl of painted faces, and the chiefs refused to surrender them. Big Bear prevented a violent confrontation by promising to deliver the men when the dance was over.

The police withdrew to the rations house on Poundmaker's reserve. They worked feverishly overnight to fortify the structure and brought in volunteers from Battleford to help defend it. The following day at noon, Big Bear and Poundmaker arrived. They offered themselves in place of the two brothers. But the police wanted their men, and they rode toward a huge mob of Indians, assembled a few hundred yards away, to make the arrests. As the officers approached, Lucky Man convinced one of his sons, Man Who Speaks Our Language, to step forward and explain how the assault had occurred. However, the police were not interested. They seized the man and dragged him forcibly toward the rations house.

At that, the Indians exploded. They charged on horseback, whooping and howling. They bumped and jostled the officers, and stripped many of them of their guns. Big Bear attempted to stop the mêlée, shouting "Peace, peace." Meanwhile, Poundmaker wielded his ceremonial war club, an axe with three knives driven through it, and threatened to kill one of the officers. But the Indians would not fire the first shot: to do so would have been cowardly and deplorable. Instead, they hoped to provoke the police into opening fire. But the officers kept their composure, and eventually reached the rations house where Superintendent Leif Crozier then had a stroke of inspiration. He ordered his men to begin handing out food, and so the crisis passed, without bloodshed or casualties.

AFTER THE SCUFFLE between the Cree and the police, Big Bear knew he had no hope of meeting Dewdney or travelling to Ottawa. But the resistance he had led for so long began to grow. In late July 1884, he participated in a meeting of twelve chiefs from the Carlton area, most of whom had a history of cooperating with the Canadian authorities. Now they, too, were disillusioned with the government and its treatment of their people. And in the fall, the chiefs along the North Saskatchewan launched a major diplomatic campaign. They began organizing a grand council of all Plains Cree leaders for the summer of 1885, the objective being to force the government to renegotiate their treaties.

The Canadian government, meanwhile, remained wedded to the status quo and more determined than ever to crush the Cree resistance. The "no-work, no-rations" policy stayed in place. Prime Minister Macdonald ordered the recruitment of a hundred new mounted police officers, confiding in a letter to an associate that "I do not apprehend myself any rising, but with these warnings it would be criminal negligence not to take every precaution." Dewdney, by now lieutenant-governor of the territories, as well as Indian commissioner, hired a mixed-blood interpreter named Peter Ballendine to spy on the Cree leaders by visiting their camps and gathering information about preparations for the grand council. And he concocted an insidious plan to smash the Cree diplomatic initiative by having the police arrest Big Bear, Piapot, Little Pine and other leaders in the spring of 1885. He would then have them charged with inciting insurrection.

Uncertainty prevailed in the North-West as fall turned to winter and a new year began. At the very least, the Plains Cree and their adversaries in the Canadian government were headed for a political confrontation. But rebellion was also a possibility. Settlers in the vast but sparsely populated territory talked fearfully of an Indian uprising, and some eastern Canadian newspapers were predicting violence. It was more than idle speculation.

Two wild cards had surfaced to make the political situation even more volatile. The Metis of the South Saskatchewan were fed up with the distant and indifferent government of Canada, which for years had ignored their pleas and petitions for recognition of land claims along the river and its tributaries. Finally, in the spring of 1884, they had sent a delegation south to bring Louis Riel back from exile in Montana to lead their cause. Riel provided the spark that set the country ablaze. Furthermore, he gave the Canadian authorities the pretext they needed to crush the Plains Cree, once and for all.

National Archives of Canada c2424

D*ays of Defiance*
and Resistance
The Troubles of '85

THE CHRISTMAS OF 1884
came and went quietly in the tiny frontier town of Battleford,
which had stood for a decade on the south shore of the Battle
River, where it drained into the North Saskatchewan. The
highlight of the season, as in previous years, was the mounted
police ball, held December 26 in the officers' barracks at Fort
Battleford, overlooking the town from a prominent hill about
half a mile away. The barracks was gaily decorated, the food
plentiful and the police band's music so lively that the men and
women of the town danced all evening.

New Year's Day normally brought the holiday season to a
lively, colourful conclusion. But this time around, the festivities

were subdued, as P.G. Laurie, editor of the weekly *Saskatchewan Herald*, noted in the first edition of 1885. "The Indians have always been in the habit of paying their compliments to their white brethren by calling on them on New Year's day," Laurie observed. "This year, however, they all stayed on their reserves, and even those who are living about town paid no visits."

Laurie drew no inferences from this break with tradition on the part of the Crees and Stoneys who lived on seven reserves around the town. And that was understandable. In the previous edition of the *Herald*, he had chided the news correspondents of the east who persisted in writing of the North-West Territories "as if they were on the eve of a rebellion, and so frightening the more timid or ill-informed of those who contemplate emigrating to them." Laurie had concluded by assuring the townspeople, "There is not the slightest ground for any apprehension."

The territories did, indeed, seem tranquil in those early days of 1885. The Metis of the South Saskatchewan celebrated the New Year by holding an enormous banquet for Louis Riel. Two hundred people packed the home of Baptiste Boyer, a prosperous member of the community, to eat, dance and toast the man who had returned from exile in Montana to press their grievances against the Canadian government. They demonstrated their affection for Riel by presenting a letter that evening declaring him "the true father of the French populations inhabiting the vast territories of the Northwest."

The Metis, who were the most likely source of trouble in the North-West, had put their agitation on hold temporarily. They were awaiting a response to a petition submitted to the federal government on December 16, 1884. This document, drafted by Riel over a period of several months, made numerous demands, including land grants for the Metis, title to lands already held, responsible government and provincial status for the territories.

By the end of January, the Metis had their answer and, from their perspective, it was completely inadequate. The Macdonald government did not address any of their grievances but, instead, decided to establish the three-member Half-Breed Land Claims Commission with a mandate to do nothing more than determine who might be eligible for land grants. This decision resurrected the Metis agitation. It re-ignited their anger. And it set off a chain of events that culminated, eight weeks later, in armed rebellion.

For anyone familiar with the North-West in early 1885, there was one other potential source of trouble: Big Bear's band. Big Bear had led the movement to renegotiate the treaties. His large following included many warriors who hated the way of life that had been imposed on them and longed to make war on the white man. Furthermore, they had endured a hard winter. Big Bear still had not settled, so his people had camped on the shores of Frog Lake, about thirty miles north-west of Fort Pitt, on the reserve of another Cree band.

A brief item in the March 13 edition of the *Saskatchewan Herald* hinted at the toll of an especially cold winter. "Disease has all but exterminated their horses, leaving them without the means of moving about as freely as of old, and the old procrastinator seizes on this as another excuse for not settling down because he has not horses where with to move. This is, of course, a mere pretence. Big Bear has always an excuse for not going on to a reserve."

But one week later, on March 20, the *Herald* notified its readers that the chief and his followers had chosen a site at Dog Rump Creek, about twenty-five miles west of Frog Lake. "Big Bear has at last yielded his point and selected his reserve and will move to it at once," Laurie wrote before snidely dismissing the chief's tactics as "schemes that were meant to secure free rations without work."

Big Bear was through fighting. He was worn out. He and a few others—Piapot, Lucky Man and Little Pine—had led the Cree resistance until those who had settled on reserves and cooperated with the whites—leaders like Poundmaker, Mistawasis and Atahkakoop—became disillusioned with the Canadian authorities and their broken promises. But Big Bear had paid a high personal price. He had alienated his sons Twin Wolverine and Imasees. And he had nearly destroyed his band.

Many of his followers had no stomach for political struggle, for an endless fight against impossible odds. They simply wanted a home and whatever assistance the government might provide to help them start new lives. They had hoped Big Bear would choose a reserve after the long march north from the Cypress Hills in the summer of 1883. And they became sullen and resentful when he stalled yet again in the fall of 1884, using any small disagreement with the Canadian authorities as a reason to avoid selecting a site. They rallied around Imasees, who wanted a land base, and who was, for all intents and purposes, running the band.

The camp included another faction. It was made up of warlike young men who still dreamed of riding the plains and ridding them of whites. They rallied around Wandering Spirit, Big Bear's militant war chief. In the winter of 1884–85, Wandering Spirit acquired a potent ally—the spellbinding Little Poplar, a renegade Cree who had rolled in from Montana preaching defiance and spoiling for a confrontation.

Big Bear had lost the will and the ability to govern. Half of his band wanted to settle down and try to survive. The others wanted blood and vengeance. Yet the old chief had paid little or no attention to either faction. Instead, he spent most of that winter in the bush north of Frog Lake hunting muskrat. He let others take over the fight with the Canadian authorities. He let them organize the grand council of plains Indian chiefs planned for the summer of 1885. And he had shown little interest in the political storm brewing in the Metis communities of the South Saskatchewan. He just wanted to live quietly and try to scratch out a living.

But things had advanced too far for that to happen. "The combination of cold weather, destitution, hunger, Little Poplar's provocative harangues and impatience with Big Bear created a seething undercurrent of unrest," Dempsey wrote. "On the surface all seemed calm, as men chopped wood, women cooked bannock and bacon, and a few people ventured out to hunt; but, in fact, the camp was like a hungry, sleeping grizzly, needing only a small provocation to send it raging through the countryside."

The Fight at Duck Lake
March 26

PRIOR TO LEAVING FORT CARLTON and marching east to Duck Lake, Superintendent Leif Crozier ordered his men, about a hundred all told, a mix of mounted police and volunteers, to hold their fire. Riel issued similar instructions to his forces. Neither man wanted to be responsible for starting a war. But on both sides, there were men itching to take aim and fire. Too much had happened in the previous two weeks to expect these poorly trained, loosely disciplined forces to restrain themselves.

The trouble began when Riel's rhetoric became hard and menacing, when he began urging the Metis to demand their rights. The mounted police responded on March 13 by sending a detachment of twenty-six officers and a seven-pound cannon from Battleford to Fort Carlton, the old Hudson's Bay post. This move stirred up the Metis communities of the South Saskatchewan, and several days later a rumour circulated that five hundred officers were headed north from Regina to arrest Riel.

In fact, only a hundred officers, under the command of NWMP Commissioner Acheson Irvine, had set out across the frozen, snow-covered prairie. They began the 210-mile trek from Regina to Prince Albert on March 18—the day the rebellion began. The mere fact that the police had moved was all the provocation the Metis needed to take up arms against the Canadian state. Within twenty-four hours, the rebels had cut the telegraph wires linking Prince Albert to the outside world. They had arrested almost a dozen people, including an Indian agent and his interpreter, two men who had been repairing the telegraph line, several merchants and a Metis who remained loyal to Canada. They sacked three stores in Batoche, the rebel capital, and carted off the arms and ammunition.

The following afternoon, most of the Metis from the South Saskatchewan attended a church service in Batoche. It was the feast of St. Joseph, their patron saint. Afterward, Riel rose to address the congregation. He declared that the time was right to challenge the authority of the government of Canada. He announced the formation of his provisional government and he promised "a war of extermination upon all those who have shown themselves hostile to our rights."

The Metis had already taken control of their own territory, which stretched for less than fifty miles along the east side of the South Saskatchewan, and was only a few miles wide. For the next week, a precarious calm prevailed as the rebels and their Canadian adversaries tried to figure out their next move. The Metis council sent emissaries to Fort Carlton demanding that Crozier surrender the post to them. Crozier sent his own representatives to Batoche urging the leaders of the rebellion to give themselves up and promising not to arrest anyone else. Neither proposal was even discussed. This state of uncertainty ended on the evening of March 24 when Riel and his councillors decided to take the tiny settlement of Duck Lake the following day.

This village, which took its name from a nearby lake, was located about halfway between Batoche and Fort Carlton. There were both whites and Metis living in the community, and on the western shore of the lake was the reserve of the Willow Cree, under chief Beardy, who wanted nothing to do with Riel and his uprising, although some of his warriors had joined the rebels. Riel's military commander, the fearless and formidable Gabriel Dumont, took the village without a fight on the afternoon of March 25 with only a small contingent of the best Metis fighters. Riel arrived a short time later with the rest of his men, about three hundred in all. The rebel forces now controlled the trails to both Fort Carlton and Prince Albert. More important, the stage was set for the first armed conflict of the rebellion.

Prior to sunrise the next morning, Superintendent Crozier, who was unaware that the Metis had taken Duck Lake, sent out eight horse-drawn sleds, eighteen men and an advance guard of four officers to collect provisions from a store in the community owned by a white man named Hillyard Mitchell. But the Metis intercepted the police party about two miles from their destination and forced them to turn back. When word of this action reached Carlton, the zealous volunteers insisted on a confrontation. Crozier, against his better judgement, relented. At ten o'clock that morning, a force numbering fifty-two police officers and forty-three volunteers left for Duck Lake.

Crozier and his men stopped briefly to confer with chief Beardy, then continued. They had just reached the northern boundary of the reserve when they spotted a Metis patrol of about twenty-five horsemen. The police drew their wagons across the road while the volunteers sought protection in a grove of trees. The rebels split in two. They took shelter in heavy brush to the right of the trail and a shallow gully. Some took up a position behind a building that allowed them to fire unobstructed on the volunteers. Then, unexpectedly, an elderly Cree named Assiyiwin and another man, Dumont's brother Isidore, came walking down the trail waving a white flag. Crozier and his interpreter, a mixed-blood named Joseph McKay, went out to meet them.

"Who are you?" the police superintendent asked.

"Crees and half-breeds," replied one of the men. "What do you want?"

"Nothing," Crozier replied. "We only came to see what was wrong. You had better go back."

Instead, Assiyiwin, who was nearly blind, lunged for McKay's rifle, and a struggle followed.

"Don't shoot each other," Isidore Dumont shouted. "We want to find a way to work this out peacefully. We don't want anyone killed."

Those were his last words. McKay drew his pistol and fired two shots. One hit Assiyiwin in the stomach, mortally wounding him. The other struck Isidore Dumont in the head, killing him on the spot. At that, gunfire erupted on all sides.

As the battle raged, Riel charged to and fro behind the Metis line, brandishing a large crucifix and screaming "God is with you, men, God is with you" while bullets whizzed by his head. And many of his men came away from the battle at Duck Lake believing God was on their side. Four of their brethren died, but Riel was unscathed. Gabriel Dumont had been grazed by a bullet, but was unhurt. And they had thrashed the Canadians. The volunteers, who had been so eager to teach the Metis a lesson, suffered the heaviest losses, with nine dead and several seriously wounded. Three police officers also lost their lives before Crozier, seeing a slaughter coming, ordered his men to retreat, leaving most of the wounded behind.

The defeat stunned the Canadians. "It is with a heavy heart that I take up my pen this evening to record the doings of this most eventful day," wrote a correspondent for the *Saskatchewan Herald*. "Little did any of us think, as we drove out of Fort Carlton this morning, amidst the hearty cheers of our comrades, that the cold hand of death would be laid upon any of us ere the sun had set."

Heeding the Call of Country
Late March–Early April

IN THE SPRING OF 1885, the Canadian public and its scanty armed forces were unprepared for a war within their own borders. Newspapers had carried reports of the growing Metis unrest in the Saskatchewan country but an armed uprising seemed a distant possibility. On March 22, however, the Dominion government quietly began preparing to mobilize. Dewdney sent an alarming telegram to Prime Minister

Macdonald, who ordered Major-General Frederick Middleton, commander of the Canadian militia, to leave for the North-West. Middleton, fifty-nine, was a short, portly former British officer with a ruddy complexion and a swirling, silver moustache that looked like a set of drop-down handlebars. He had fought valiantly in New Zealand and India, but was new to Canada, having arrived only nine months earlier to take a position that was intended to see him through to a secure and quiet retirement.

The general took the train from Ottawa to Toronto, stopping long enough to advise Lieutenant-Colonel William Otter, a forty-two-year-old career soldier and commander of the local infantry school, to be prepared for a call to arms. He then travelled by rail through the United States, reaching Winnipeg on the morning of March 27, just as news of the defeat at Duck Lake hit the city of 22,000. Middleton immediately wired Adolphe Caron, the defence minister, with instructions to send the country's best militia units west.

Later that day, he boarded a Canadian Pacific train, along with members of the 90th Rifles, Winnipeg's volunteer battalion, and rode to Qu'Appelle Station, the stop closest to the rebel capital of Batoche. Then began the real work. Drilling citizen soldiers who had never fired a gun. Studying a country he'd never seen. Developing a plan

Saskatchewan Archives Board R-A5070

to suppress a rebellion. And, once the rest of his troops arrived, moving them over prairie trails during spring thaw.

Back in Ottawa, Caron had moved with admirable dispatch, issuing mobilization orders on March 27 to the Queen's Own Rifles, the 10th Royal Grenadiers and the Mont Royal Rifles of Montreal. The following day, orders went to the 9th Voltigeurs of Quebec City and several rural militias from counties east of Toronto, who were instructed to assemble in Cobourg and to form the Midland Battalion.

Men in all these places responded with amazing alacrity. In Toronto, they were lined up outside the drill hall by 8:30 A.M. on Saturday, March 28, and by noon the Queen's Own and the Grenadiers had each filled their 250 spots. The two battalions could have left that afternoon—trains were waiting and the troops were eager to board them—but Otter wisely waited till Monday to give his raw but robust recruits time to gather essentials like woollen blankets, warm hats and sturdy boots.

Toronto was transformed that weekend "from a quiet civilian city... into a burgh having all the appearances of a garrison town," the *Daily Mail* reported. The military fervour culminated March 30 in the dazzling spectacle of troops marching through city streets—led by battalion bands playing "Auld Lang Syne" and "The Little Girl I Left Behind," and roused by the cheers of their fellow citizens. Ten thousand people gathered around Union Station, and thousands more lined York and King Streets. They stood on verandas, waved from windows and watched from rooftops. "Round after round of cheers burst forth and women waved handkerchiefs," the next day's *Daily Mail* reported. "But amid that wildly excited multitude, there were many eyes that, blinded by tears, could not see the troops as they filed past."

The tears were shed by women watching sons, husbands

and brothers march away to war. Their men, called to serve so suddenly and unexpectedly, were not professional soldiers. They were clerks, factory hands and shopkeepers, who happened to belong to the city's volunteer battalions. For this, they received smart-looking uniforms and acquired considerable prestige. They learned to march with military precision, they learned to handle weapons and they picked up the fundamentals of soldiering, skills that few, if any, of these proud, young men had ever tested on the battlefield.

At five minutes past noon, under a cold and heavy drizzle, the first four-car train pulled out of Union Station carrying the Queen's Own Rifles, and twenty minutes later the next left with the Royal Grenadiers. One final cheer rose from the crowd. The bands played "God Save the Queen." And, as the *Daily Mail* reported, "in a few moments only a long stream of smoke above indicated the presence and passage of Toronto's citizen soldiers."

Stirring scenes occurred in Cobourg and Belleville, Kingston and Ottawa, Montreal and Quebec City, wherever ordinary working men left their homes, families and jobs to enlist. They boarded trains that carried them north, through the towns and villages and handsome farms of southern Ontario, and into the primeval shield with its endless rock and water and forest. And then they went west, across the top of Lake Superior. For many of the soldiers, this proved to be the most trying part of their military service.

There were four gaps totalling eighty-nine miles in that stretch of the line. Where the rails ended, the troops rode in horse-drawn sleds, trudged through deep snow, and walked across frozen bays. Traversing the bays was an ordeal that left some of the men sunburnt, frostbitten and snowblind. And where the rails were in place, the men rode on open flatcars, huddled in coats and blankets that did little to shield them from piercing winds and bone-numbing nights, when the mercury dropped to minus thirty Fahrenheit and the stars sparkled like icy diamonds.

The first of these chafed and wind-strafed troops, the Queen's Own Rifles and the Royal Grenadiers, reached Winnipeg April 5, and within three weeks 2,500 more had completed this excruciating rite of passage. Under Middleton's plan of attack, they were split into three columns. The first moved north from Qu'Appelle Station, led by the general, to crush the Metis at Batoche. The second set out from Swift Current, under Otter, and was supposed to come down the South Saskatchewan by steamboat to attack Batoche from the west. The third ventured north from Calgary, commanded by Major-General Thomas Bland Strange, a former British officer who owned a large cattle ranch south of that raw, new prairie town.

M*assacre at Frog Lake*
April 2

BIG BEAR HAD JUST returned from the bush with a modest harvest of furs, muskrat mainly, that would fetch a few dollars for him at the local Hudson's Bay post. He was happy to be back at his camp and he was eager for the news. After all, he had finally selected a reserve, and with the arrival of spring it would be surveyed and his people could begin breaking land and planting crops. But Big Bear had barely set his things down when a messenger arrived at his door: "The Sioux Speaker wishes to see you at once."

The messenger was referring to Thomas Quinn, the Indian

sub-agent for Frog Lake, a settlement that had sprung up to serve several reserves in the district northwest of Fort Pitt. It consisted of a smattering of homes and stores, a Catholic church and rectory, a blacksmith shop and a sawmill, a small mounted police detachment and fewer than two dozen white and Metis residents. Quinn was a mixed blood of Sioux descent, who spoke Cree fluently and was married to a woman from Big Bear's band. But despite his native heritage, he was often rigid and overbearing with the Indians. As a result, many despised him.

"Big Bear," he said when the old chief arrived at his office, "I sent for you as soon as I heard you were back. Thanks for your prompt response. I was in Onion Lake yesterday whence I travelled all night. The Indians out there are in a restless mood. There is serious trouble in the east. The half-breeds and Indians are fighting whites at several points. I want you to use all your influence to maintain peace among the people here. I want you to send for Kehiwin, the chief at Long Lake, immediately so that we will have plenty of help in case trouble should come our way."

"Yes, Dragon fly," replied Big Bear, using the nickname the Indians had given Quinn. "You know I have always tried to keep my people contented and at peace. You know also that times have changed. My word as chief does not carry the weight it had of old; however, I will do what I can."

This conversation occurred on April 1, or Big Lie Day, as the Crees called April Fool's. It was an occasion for merriment, and some of Big Bear's warriors had played a trick on William Cameron, the twenty-three-year-old Hudson's Bay store clerk. Wandering Spirit, the war chief, and Miserable Man sent one of their brethren to the store to say that Quinn wanted to see Cameron immediately at the home of John Delaney, the farm instructor. When Cameron arrived, Wandering Spirit yelled,

Saskatcewan Archives Board R-A27292

"Big lie day" and everyone had a good laugh. Several of the warriors, including Wandering Spirit, remained at the settlement until well into the evening, and harmony prevailed.

But later, back at their camp, the mood among the warriors changed. They held a war dance that went on all night. Somewhere amid the drumming, the dancing and the singing, a murderous intent arose among these ragged, displaced, angry men. It surfaced first in Wandering Spirit. "Quiet," he called out at one point. "Tomorrow, I am going to eat two-legged meat. So what do you think?"

There was no response. Wandering Spirit sat down and the dance resumed. A short while later, he spoke again. This time, he challenged his followers. "Tomorrow, I am going to eat two-legged meat. If you don't want to join me, then go home and put on your wives' dresses."

The war chief's challenge worked. When the dance ended,

Wandering Spirit and his men stole through the still, silent bush with painted faces and weapons in hand, and arrived at the settlement shortly before sunrise. Their first stop was Quinn's house. Several warriors entered the dwelling, awakening the agent, his wife and their baby. "Man Speaking Sioux, come down," Wandering Spirit shouted. Big Bear's son-in-law, Lone Man, who had accompanied the warriors, dashed upstairs and urged Quinn to stay were he was. But the agent confronted the intruders. They immediately seized him and his family and marched them off to Delaney's home.

Meanwhile, some of the warriors began rounding up the rest of the settlers. Others went to the Hudson's Bay store, helping themselves to merchandise and demanding ammunition from Cameron, who had been roused by the disturbance. The clerk gave them what little he had. Then Big Bear arrived and ordered his followers to stop the looting. "Don't touch anything in the company's place," he said. "If there's anything you need, ask Cameron for it."

By this time, most of the settlers had been forced from their homes and taken to Delaney's. From there, everyone moved to the church, a tiny structure measuring about twenty feet by twenty feet and constructed of poplar logs. It was Holy Thursday, and the two Roman Catholic priests, Adelard Fafard and Felix Marchand, were determined to hold an early-morning service. Several Indians, including Big Bear, stood at the back of the church during the mass and Wandering Spirit knelt on one knee in the centre aisle, with a Winchester rifle in one hand and a lynx-skin war bonnet on his head. Others, who had uncovered a stock of sacramental wine, barged in and out of the church, shouting, laughing, banging their drums and showing signs of drunkenness. As the disruptions escalated, Father Fafard ended the mass.

For another hour or so, the warriors looted and harassed the whites. Then the Crees decided to take the settlers to their camp as prisoners. Wandering Spirit ordered Quinn to leave first. "You have a hard head," the war chief told the agent. "When you say 'No' you mean no and stick to it. Now, if you love your life you will do as I say: Go to our camp."

"Why should I go there?" Quinn asked.

"Go," said Wandering Spirit.

"I will stay here," replied Quinn.

"I tell you, go," the warrior snapped. But Quinn stood his ground. And Wandering Spirit shot him in the head.

Some of the prisoners had begun walking to the Cree camp when the first shots were fired. Seeing what had happened, William Gilchrist, an employee at the sawmill, and George Dill, an independent merchant, panicked and ran. At that, warriors gave chase and murdered both men. Charlie Gouin, a mixed-blood carpenter, was shot in the shoulder, then died of a gunshot wound to the chest as he tried to dive into a building, and John Williscraft, another sawmill worker, pleaded for his life but was gunned down when he turned to run.

John Gowanlock and his wife, Mary, also started to leave the settlement for the Indian camp. He was the next victim. Gowanlock collapsed into the arms of his wife when the bullet hit and she fell to the ground with him. "I laid upon him, resting my face on his, and his breath was scarcely gone when I was forced away by an Indian," she later recalled. "I did not seem to know what it all meant, and I went through it dazed and stunned, with only the power of my limbs left to me to follow the Indian, as he dragged me after him."

A terrified Delaney and his wife, Theresa, witnessed the murders of Williscraft and Gowanlock. A moment later, the farm instructor staggered away from his wife and gasped, "I am shot." Theresa Delaney dropped to the ground to comfort her husband, who was seriously wounded, and Father Fafard knelt beside them and prayed. Undeterred, a Cree warrior named Bare Neck pulled the trigger again. "I thought this shot was meant for me," Mrs. Delaney said, "and I laid my head upon my husband and waited. It seemed an age, but it was for my poor husband and he never spoke afterwards. Almost immediately another Indian ran up and ordered me away."

With the women removed, Wandering Spirit shot and wounded Father Fafard and a second Cree, Round the Sky, finished him off. Father Marchand was the last of nine men to die that morning. He was shot in the neck as he knelt in prayer. The Frog Lake Massacre, as it came to be known, was over in a matter of minutes. It was the work of a few men driven by alcohol and rage. Afterward, the warriors were in control of Big Bear's camp, which had grown to about two hundred lodges with the arrival of Kehiwin and three other bands of Bush Cree who had been summoned by Quinn. Along with these additions, there were the prisoners—Mary Gowanlock, Theresa Delaney, William Cameron and several Metis. But one resident of the settlement, Quinn's nephew Henry, had escaped unnoticed and fled to Fort Pitt with news of the massacre.

Big Bear had run down the road screaming at his warriors to stop. But they had paid no attention. They continued to ignore him as they debated their next move. They also brushed aside the objections of the Bush Cree, many of whom were appalled by the killings and wanted no part of any war against the whites. Indeed, the councils that followed the massacre nearly led to violence between the two groups of Crees. At one point, a chief named Seekaskootch confronted Wandering Spirit and said, "It is a shame to see how you have butchered those innocent white people down there, but you cannot scare me."

But whatever their fears and reservations, the Bush Cree dared not defy Big Bear's warriors by attempting to leave the camp. So Wandering Spirit and his councillors had their way. They would move east. They would plunder Fort Pitt. They would go to Battleford to be reunited with their brethren in that district. Then they would join what they imagined to be a general uprising aimed at sweeping the white man from the prairie.

But first they celebrated the slaughter of whites at Frog Lake. They ordered their followers to take as much food as possible from the settlement and had them round up all the cattle in the district—about four hundred head. Three days after the massacre, several Indians, led by Big Bear's councillor Four Sky Thunder, returned to the settlement to burn some of the buildings, including the church where the bodies of the two priests, along with those of Delaney and Gowanlock, had been laid in the basement. It is said that as the church burned, the smoke took the form of a man, then changed to a horse, and this was seen as a sign of bad luck. Nevertheless, the victors danced and feasted for another week and lived as they had in the days of freedom. Then they began marching toward Fort Pitt.

The Fall of Fort Pitt
April 15

BIG BEAR HAD LED HIS people in to Fort Pitt many times: coming out of the bush in the spring, sleds laden with the winter's harvest, furs to be traded for powder and shot, axes and teapots and myriad other wonderful and useful goods; and returning in the fall, coming in off the prairie, travois loaded with buffalo robes and pemmican, provisions for the Hudson's Bay Co.'s northern brigades that worked the vast river, lake and bush country beyond the Saskatchewan. In those days, when the buffalo were plentiful, when the land belonged to the Indians and when they were a free people, Big Bear always rode or marched at the front of the column, sending his high-spirited young men ahead to fire their guns and announce their arrival.

Now he was old and weatherbeaten. He walked at the back of the column with the women and children, the elderly and the infirm. Wandering Spirit was in charge and he had brought the young men of the camp to a boil with his message about a broader Indian campaign that had already taken control of Calgary, Edmonton and Qu'Appelle, torn up the railway and burned Fort Carlton. They would join the campaign and help rid the plains of this cursed race of men who had subdued, confined and humiliated them.

They reached Pitt late in the afternoon on April 14, after a thirty-mile march, and the Hudson's Bay factor, William McLean, witnessed their arrival. The warriors, he later recalled, "fully two hundred and fifty strong and all mounted, made their appearance on a ridge north of and about two thousand yards back from the fort." The Crees sent messengers to the fort, who conferred outside its walls for about an hour with McLean. They informed him that they wanted police to evacuate the post and warned that, if the officers resisted, everyone would be at risk.

This made for a tense night at Pitt. Twenty-five mounted police were stationed there, under the command of Inspector Francis Dickens, the incompetent and alcoholic son of the famous British novelist, and over forty civilian men, women and children. They knew that the warriors camped on the ridge had massacred civilians at Frog Lake. They knew that Pitt could not be defended since it was surrounded by ramshackle fences that could easily be torn down or surmounted. And they did not have enough horses to escape.

The following morning, McLean and an interpreter went to the Cree camp on the ridge and tried to persuade them not to attack. But Wandering Spirit was in a belligerent mood. He loaded his gun, placed a hand on McLean's shoulder and said, "That will do. You have said enough. We do not want to hear anything about the Government and if you want to live, do as I tell you." The war chief let McLean know what he had in mind for the police who were holed up in the fort. "They will not be long there; we will . . . kill them all as if they were young ducks, but we want you to get your wife and children out of the way of danger."

In the midst of this meeting, two officers from the fort, constables Clarence Loasby and David Cowan, along with their guide, Henry Quinn, committed an inexplicable blunder. Dickens had sent them out the previous day to look for Big Bear's camp, contrary to McLean's advice, and they inadvertently rode into the Indian camp as they returned to Pitt. Cree warriors mistakenly believed they were being attacked and opened fire. Cowan was hit in the heart as he and his companions tried to gallop their horses toward the fort. Loasby was shot in the leg and the left side, but managed to crawl to safety under covering fire from his fellow officers who had come out of the fort. Quinn, who had escaped with his life at Frog Lake, managed to get away again.

When the shooting subsided, Big Bear and McLean frantically tried to negotiate a peaceful surrender of the fort. Both were determined to prevent a bloodbath, and they convinced Wandering Spirit to allow the police to leave Pitt, provided everyone else surrendered to the Indians. They gave the officers two hours to clear out, then extended the deadline an hour. As heavy snow began to fall, the police emerged, carrying the wounded Loasby. They boarded a leaky scow, while McLean's wife waited nearby with some of her nine children, acting as a shield to ensure that the Cree warriors did not attack. Then the police officers began their journey to Battleford down the ice-clogged North Saskatchewan.

Fort Pitt had fallen to Wandering Spirit and his warriors. They spent the next day looting and ransacking the place. Once they had taken what they could, they set fire to the fort, let it burn to the ground, and returned to Frog Lake.

The Siege of Battleford
March 30–April 23

HOMES HAD BEEN BURNED, stores looted, livestock stolen and settlers murdered. But the Cree, Stoney and Metis marauders did not lay a finger on P.G. Laurie's printing presses. Laurie had published a standard four-page edition of the *Herald* on March 27, including a brief account of the fight at Duck Lake. But for the next three Fridays, his presses were silent. Then on April 23, a Thursday, the *Herald* returned and the entire front page was given over to an ordeal that the publisher, and most of his readers, had endured together: the siege of Battleford.

News of the Metis victory at Duck Lake left the residents of Battleford, and the farmers in the neighbouring countryside, fearful for their safety. There were seven reserves around Battleford, including those of Poundmaker and Little Pine, two of the most discontented chiefs among the Plains Cree, and many whites in the district shuddered at the thought of Indians taking up arms and going to war.

The Indians had learned of Duck Lake as quickly as the townspeople. Metis messengers had spread the word of their triumph, hoping it would encourage the Indians to join the uprising. But the Crees did not rush to the side of the Metis. Instead, they saw the rebellion as an opportunity to push their own grievances. With this in mind, Poundmaker, Little Pine and a third chief named Strike-him-on-the-back, along with a large entourage of young men, set out for Battleford on March 28. Word of their imminent arrival prompted many people to flee their homes and seek protection in the rickety mounted police post.

The following day, two of the town's prominent citizens, Judge Charles Rouleau and A.T. Berthiaume, overseer of public works, left with their families for Swift Current, ostensibly to demand immediate relief from the Canadian troops assembling there. Late that same afternoon, the townspeople learned that the Indians were camped at a farm seven miles west of town. At that, panic swept Battleford. Almost everyone fled to the barracks. Once the farm families from the outlying districts had arrived, five hundred men, women and children were crammed into a fort where some fifty officers normally resided.

Poundmaker and his contingent arrived on the morning of March 30, hoping for a meeting with the Indian agent, John Rae. "Poundmaker sent a message to Mr. Rae," Laurie later reported, "to the effect that the Indians had heard of a fight between the Police and the Half-breeds, and that as soon as the police had done with these they would turn on the Indians; and they only wanted an assurance from Mr. Rae that it was not so, and the gift of some tea and tobacco and they would return to their reserves."

But Rae, who was fearful of the natives at the best of times and who had landed his job largely because he was the prime minister's cousin, refused to meet them. The local Hudson's Bay factor, William McKay, did so instead, along with the mixed-blood interpreter Peter Ballendine, who had acted as Dewdney's spy the previous winter. McKay offered the Indians enough food to quell their hunger but nothing else. He was not prepared to give them the blankets, ammunition and other goods they wanted. Nor was he going to discuss their grievances. That was the job of the Indian agent. Having done what he could, McKay returned to the fort.

The Crees waited all afternoon for Rae to appear. As the time passed, they became perplexed. They could not understand why the whites, normally so pushy and domineering, had fled without a shot being fired. And when the sun started to go down, the Indians found themselves alone in a deserted town where there were well-stocked stores and comfortable homes. They were, by then, cold and hungry. The temptation to help themselves grew among some of these young men and, a short time later, the looting began. "The evening and night were spent in carting away goods of all kinds from the shops of the Hudson's Bay Company and Mahaffy & Clinskill, and raiding and destroying private homes," Laurie reported. "The devilish ingenuity displayed in the destruction of things that were of no use to them would put to the blush a city mob."

When the sun rose the following morning, the town was quiet. The Crees had left. But the terrified townsfolk were not going anywhere. In fact, settlers from the surrounding district sought refuge at the post, bringing with them chilling accounts of native marauders roaming the countryside, ransacking homes, stealing livestock and committing cold-blooded murder. They told of the killing of James Payne, the farm instructor on one of the Stoney reserves, twenty miles south of Battleford in the Eagle Hills, and the gruesome murder of rancher Barney Tremont, who lived alone a few miles south of the town.

The whites, feeling besieged and isolated, transmitted desperate pleas by telegraph for military relief, along with vivid accounts of the misdeeds of the Indians, some of which were published in eastern Canadian newspapers and served to inflame public opinion. These missives, along with news of the Frog Lake massacre, forced Middleton to alter his plans of attack. Originally, he had ordered Otter's column to travel north from Swift Current to Batoche to participate in one crushing assault on the Metis. But given the political pressures, Middleton reluctantly ordered Otter to relieve Battleford.

For several days after the departure of Poundmaker and his followers, Indians occasionally returned to Battleford, although the whites could not tell whether they were Crees or Stoneys. And during a lull, two men left the fort to collect the body of Tremont, who had been a solitary individual with a virulent hatred of Indians, which he had demonstrated on occasion by driving them off his property.

"The body presented a horrible appearance and gave evidence of the depths of fiendishness that marked his murderers," Laurie later wrote in the *Herald*. "Not satisfied with shooting him twice from behind while he was greasing his wagon, the fiends inflicted two frightful gashes on his head just above his right ear, fired a bullet through his head after he was dead, the gun being held so close to his head so as to burn the skin; and firing an iron-shod arrow into his breast as he lay stretched in death. He died with his wagon wrench in his hand, showing how he had been employed when the fatal first shot was fired."

The quiet around Battleford ended on the night of Saturday, April 4, when a large group of Indians burned a store and pillaged several homes. Four days later, on Wednesday, April 8, more homes were looted, and the following week the Indians lit a number of prairie fires until a swath of land twenty miles long was ablaze. Nothing else happened until April 22, when a sniper killed a young Battleford resident named Frank Smart, who was out on night patrol. And in one last act of defiance, the Indians ransacked and burned Judge Rouleau's large, comfortable home on the afternoon of April 23.

For all the damage they did, the Crees and Stoneys never intended to attack the town or its inhabitants, according to Robert Jefferson, Poundmaker's brother-in-law and the farm instructor on his reserve. Jefferson spent the month of April 1885 in the huge Indian camp of almost fifteen hundred people that had assembled on Poundmaker's reserve. "During the whole of the outbreak," Jefferson later wrote, "there was no organised attempt at besieging the barracks: indeed there was not enough Indians to do it. Great consternation prevailed in the white camp but it rose altogether from the preconceived idea of Indian warfare and the barbarities that accompanied it."

The siege finally ended late on April 23 when a messenger arrived with word that Otter's column of 470 Canadian soldiers, accompanied by 50 mounted police under the command of Superintendent William Herchmer, was just a few miles south of Battleford. Laurie rushed to get out an edition of his paper, demanding that the Indians pay for their actions. "The Government and the people of Canada have been deceived as to the civilization of these wild tribes," he wrote in his editorial. "They have shown themselves incapable of gratitude; their apparent tractability was cunning; their civilization but a cloak to hide their hellish plans. They have thrown down the gauntlet, and now that it has been taken up the issue must be pressed until the fullest justice has been done."

S *tandoff at Fish Creek*
April 24

MIDDLETON'S MEN SLEPT soundly on the night of the twenty-third. They had marched eighteen miles that day— from Clarke's Crossing on the South Saskatchewan River north toward Batoche, the Metis headquarters. The general and his troops had spent the better part of six days at the crossing, ferrying horses, wagons, supplies and two of their four field guns across the river, which was about a thousand yards wide at that point. Afterward, Middleton had split his column of almost a thousand men. Lieutenant-Colonel C.E. Montizambert, an artillery officer, led just over four hundred men down the west side of the river. The balance continued on the east side under Middleton, with the two contingents using flags to signal messages during the day, and lanterns at night.

The weather had warmed up, and the men were tanned and fit. For many of them, the painful memories of the miserable trip across the top of Lake Superior had faded, and so had their fears of the enemy. The enthusiastic amateurs from the settled and tranquil east had arrived in the North-West braced for encounters with stealthy foes, Metis snipers who might harass them as they marched north over flat, treeless prairie, or wild Indians who might emerge from a bush or the evening shadows and slit a man's throat if he strayed too far from his comrades.

Some of the recruits had brought their own knives and hand-
guns to protect themselves from such attacks. But they had now
marched close to two hundred miles, from Fort Qu'Appelle
almost to Batoche, and they had seen nothing more than the
occasional enemy scout.

After a peaceful night, the troops awoke before sunrise on
the twenty-fourth expecting another tedious day. Batoche lay
thirty-five miles north, and Middleton had his men moving by
6:30 A.M. They followed a well-established trail that ran from
Clarke's Crossing to the Metis capital. A troop of mounted
scouts, commanded by Major Charles Boulton, scoured the
countryside ahead. Middleton and his officers rode behind
them, followed by the soldiers two to three miles back. The
three hundred Winnipeggers of the 90th Battalion marched
out of the camp whistling in unison, since singing was not per-
mitted, and one soldier later wrote to his wife saying wagers
had been made that "the troops would return to Winnipeg
without discharging a rifle save at a gopher or a goose."

Little did these happy-go-lucky young men know that 150
Metis and Indians were waiting for them a few miles ahead in
Tourond's Coulee. The trail to Batoche skirted this broad,
wooded ravine before dropping into the valley and crossing
Fish Creek, a tributary of the South Saskatchewan. Gabriel
Dumont had deployed his forces just below the lip of the
prairie and planned to lure the unsuspecting Canadians off the
trail and into their midst, where they would be slaughtered like
buffalo in a pound, as he later put it.

With his men hiding in bushes, lurking behind rocks and
crouching in rifle pits, Dumont and a few of his fighters rode
off, hoping to lead the Canadians into an ambush. But some of
the Metis fired prematurely on Boulton's scouts, who returned
the fire, then pursued their foes until they disappeared into the

coulee. The scouts gave up the chase, threw themselves to the ground, and the battle had begun. Middleton arrived a few minutes later and deployed his men to the left and right of the rebels. It was mid-morning and, as the correspondent for the Toronto *Daily Mail* wrote, "a hot combat ensued. The whistle of bullets and the balls from the enemy shotguns rattled in all directions."

Rifles crackled and blazed for an hour, until a steady rain began to fall and took the sizzle out of the fight. Mist and smoke enveloped the field. Visibility became poor, the firing sporadic. The Canadian infantrymen were pinned to a cold and sodden battlefield, unable to advance or even get up for fear of being picked off by Metis sharpshooters. Middleton ordered the artillery into action, and the roar of the field guns frightened many of the rebels. But everything the big weapons hurled at the Metis and their Indian allies sailed harmlessly overhead, shredding the trees behind them and killing fifty-five horses. By early afternoon Middleton realized that, even with four times as many men and far more firepower, he wasn't going to dislodge the enemy without heavy casualties.

The battle was not going glowingly for Dumont, either. His forces were short of ammunition, and some of the more undisciplined men, having never fought a protracted battle before, began drifting away when they'd had enough. Dumont tried to divert the Canadian forces by setting the prairie on fire to the east of them, but Middleton was not taken in. The longer the battle lasted, the less tenable the Metis position became. Three companies of Royal Grenadiers had re-crossed the South Saskatchewan and were advancing from the west. By the end of the afternoon, they could have trapped the Metis.

But that didn't happen. Middleton called it a day rather than trying to win a decisive victory at horrendous cost to his own men. The Canadian guns fell silent. He had lost six men during the fight, four more would die from their wounds and forty-five were injured. Meanwhile, Dumont was down to fifty-four men. Four of his fighters had died on the battlefield, one was mortally wounded and the rest had abandoned the fight.

Neither side had won or lost any territory, so technically the clash at Fish Creek was a standoff. But psychologically, the Metis were winners that day. First, there was Dumont's defiant departure. He mounted his horse and waved his rifle as he galloped away, while the glum and bedraggled Canadians watched from a battlefield strewn with the dead and wounded. Then there were the thoughts of two observers, recorded while the sound of gunfire and the smell of smoke were still fresh on their minds. "Dumont exhibited the qualities of a light infantry soldier to perfection," wrote the *Daily Mail's* correspondent, "seeking every sort of shelter with a sure instinct and enabling his men to shoot without being shot which, after all, is the highest art of war."

The Canadians, meanwhile, had clearly been stung. "None of us are ever likely to forget the dark night of the 24th," wrote Middleton's chief of staff Lord Melgund, "close to the deep ravine, still holding for all we knew, a concealed enemy, and with us nothing but raw troops, totally unaccustomed to night work, and hampered by wounded men. We thought we had come out for a picnic, and it was impossible to help feeling that war's hardships are doubly cruel to the civilian soldier."

The Battle at Cut Knife Hill
May 2

ALL THE MAKINGS OF A fiasco were there from the moment Otter and his men marched into Battleford to a stirring welcome and ended the siege that never should have happened. First, there were the white townsfolk and settlers who wanted revenge. There were the soldiers who were itching for a taste of battle. There was Otter—the earnest, inexperienced but ambitious commanding officer. Finally, there was the attitude of the soldiers and their commander. One and all were wildly overconfident. They were dead certain that all they had to do was march west from Battleford, and the Indians would run.

Marching west to confront the Crees and their Stoney allies was never part of Otter's mandate. Middleton initially ordered him on April 11 "to get to Battleford as quick as possible." His task was to relieve the citizens of the town and he had achieved this simply by showing up. The Indians had fled. The beleaguered citizens were perfectly safe. But Otter's men quickly became bored. On April 26, he wired Dewdney, rather than his commanding officer, seeking approval to go on the offensive. "I would propose taking part of my force at once to punish Poundmaker leaving 100 men to garrison Battleford. Great depradations committed. Immediate decisive action necessary. What do you think?"

"Think you cannot act too energetically or Indians will gather in large number," the lieutenant-governor wired back enthusiastically from Regina. "Herchmer knows country to Poundmaker's reserve. Sand Hills most dangerous country to march through. Be sure to secure good reliable scouts." Middleton sent a telegram the same day. It read: "You had better remain at Battleford until you can ascertain more about Pound-maker's fort and the kind of country he is in."

Dewdney's reply was all that Otter needed to hear. As he planned his assault, he continued to wire Middleton to coax out of him unconditional approval. He never received it. Never-theless, at noon, on Friday, May 1, Otter issued his marching orders and by 4 P.M. a force of 325 men left Battleford to the hearty cheers of the citizenry. Officially, the purpose of the mission was reconnaissance, to patrol the country in force. But his real objective was to crush the native resistance with one quick blow and restore order to the countryside.

According to Laurie's report in the May 4 *Herald*, the scouts departed first, followed by a troop of mounted police officers. Behind them stretched a train of forty-eight wagons bearing, first, the artillery pieces, two seven-pound, muzzle-loading cannons borrowed from the NWMP, and one of the two Ameri-can Gatling guns Middleton had purchased prior to leaving Ottawa. One company from the Toronto School of Infantry rode in the wagons behind the field guns, followed by the Governor-General's Foot Guards, the Queen's Own Rifles, the provisions and the Battleford Rifles, a hastily assembled volun-teer regiment.

It was an impressive spectacle to a populace so recently cowed and terrorized. But most of the men who rode west that afternoon had never felt the heat of enemy fire. Otter was almost as green as his troops even though he was a full-time soldier who was in charge of Toronto's infantry school. His battle-field experience consisted of one skirmish in the Niagara Penin-sula nineteen years earlier when the Queen's Own Rifles, of which he was then a member, had fled for their lives after an attack by eight hundred Civil War veterans bent on invading Canada as part of the Fenian movement for Irish independence.

Yet Otter and his men hastened west, up the valley of the Battle River. The train stopped early in the evening, having covered about half the distance to Poundmaker's reserve. The troops ate dinner and waited till dark. Then they pressed on under moonlight. Otter was planning a surprise attack at dawn on the Indian camp, which mixed-blood scouts had found a few days earlier on the east bank of Cut Knife Creek, a few miles south of where this marshy and meandering stream joins the Battle River.

The Canadians arrived about 4 A.M. on May 2. But Otter's well-crafted plans fell apart immediately. The Indians had moved and seemed to have gone west. The colonel ordered his troops to cross the creek and advance to the summit of a broad, gently rising hill with sides scoured by deep, heavily wooded ravines. They were to stop there for breakfast. The wagons rolled over the soft, sandy creek bed one by one, then moved slowly across two hundred yards of scruffy marshland to the foot of the hill. Unbeknownst to the Canadian troops, the Indian camp stood on the other side of the hill and an old man named Jacob with Long Tangled Hair had observed their approach.

"He saw the scouts ahead lining out the trail from the last camp," Robert Jefferson later wrote. "He saw mounted men following and he saw wagons, wagons, wagons, filled with soldiers, winding towards him. From where he stood he was visible to the whole camp, so that his alarms and demonstrations quickly roused the sleepers and, when the first soldiers came to the summit of the rise, they saw the Indians—like ants disturbed in their hill—streaming in all directions away from their tents."

The lead Canadians encountered a small force of armed natives and the two sides traded gunfire. The soldiers quickly unleashed their artillery and the Gatling gun on the village, shredding many of the empty tepees. Meanwhile, Cree and Stoney warriors infiltrated the ravines and opened fire, which stopped the advance of the Canadians. As the battle erupted, Jefferson sought out Poundmaker's tent. "He was just performing his toilet, and appeared in no way perturbed by the unexpected attack," the farm instructor recalled. "He donned the fur cap he always wore and proceeded to invest himself in what looked like a patchwork quilt. In my ignorance, I ventured to ask him what it was. Poundmaker's expression at once made me realise how flippant and hasty was my question. With great dignity he informed me that it was his war cloak: that it rendered its wearer invisible to an enemy. Then he got up and stalked out of the tent without another word."

As the political leader of the camp, Poundmaker did not fight in the battle. Instead, he watched it with the women, the children and the elderly from the summit of the actual Cut Knife Hill, which was about one and a half to two miles away. The war chief, a man named Fine Day of the Strike-him-on-the-back band, scattered squads of four to five men throughout the ravines and used a mirror to signal orders to them. They popped up here and there, firing first from the left, then the right, and pinning the Canadians to the exposed summit of the hill.

Fine Day's clever tactics sowed fear and confusion among the Canadians, who were convinced they were fighting five hundred hidden Indians when, in fact, there were only about fifty. And the superior Canadian firepower made no difference in the outcome. The Gatling gun, for all its thunder, spewed bullets harmlessly overhead. Both cannons broke down. Worst of all, by late morning, the Indians had almost surrounded Otter and his men.

"What ever he had come for had not been accomplished," Jefferson wrote. "His men were wasting ammunition, shooting by guesswork at imaginary Indians. Every minute he stayed increased the perils of his situation. He gave the order to retreat." Eight Canadians died that day, one of whom had to be abandoned on the battlefield, and fourteen were wounded. It could have been much worse. Cree and Stoney warriors mounted their horses and prepared to pursue the Canadians as they withdrew from the battlefield. But Poundmaker stopped them. "They have come here to fight us and we have fought them," he told the warriors. "Now let them go."

The Battle of Batoche
May 9 to 12

MIDDLETON'S MEN WERE restless. They were tired of delays, deliberations and days wasted. They had been stalled at Fish Creek for nearly two weeks, waiting idly for steamboats, which were supposed to come down the South Saskatchewan from Swift Current to deliver supplies and take the wounded away. But as April turned to May, the men were in no mood to be patient while the general grappled with legitimate logistical problems, and his private doubts and fears, for Middleton's confidence had been badly shaken by his first encounter with the enemy.

The men, officers and foot soldiers alike, had begun to question their commander's judgement and character. The foremost critic was Lieutenant-Colonel Arthur Williams, the popular head of the Midland Battalion, which consisted of regiments raised in nearly a dozen small central Ontario communities

from Bowmanville to Kingston, and stacked with staunchly
Protestant farmboys spoiling for a showdown with Riel's French
Catholic followers. Williams, the ambitious son of a wealthy
businessman who fought in Nelson's campaign against Napol-
eon, had grown up on his father's Port Hope estate and later
lost much of the family fortune on misguided business ventures.
He was more successful at politics, winning seats in the provincial legislature and the House of Commons, but he had put his
political career on hold to pursue his dream of achieving glory
on the battlefield.

With the arrival of one of the steamboats, the *Northcote*,
Middleton issued orders to move. On May 7, the column of
850 men and 150 wagons advanced about six miles, ransacking
deserted houses, killing livestock and burning Gabriel
Dumont's home to the ground along the way. The following
day, the troops made camp about nine miles south of Batoche.

The capital of the Metis nation was a humble village of a
few homes, a few stores, a Catholic church, a rectory and a
cemetery. It stood on a rectangular swath of tableland about
half a mile wide and a mile long, defined on the south, the west
and the north by the meandering South Saskatchewan. To the
east there was bush and open prairie, about 150 feet above the
river. At least three trails ran from the prairie down to the village, each passing through heavily wooded slopes.

As modest as their capital was, the Metis and their Indian
allies had prepared very solid defences. They had dug three
lines of rifle pits, which were concealed in the brush-covered
slopes between the prairie and the tableland. These pits were
about waist deep and had been reinforced by earthen mounds
and heavy logs piled across the front. They were strong enough
to withstand anything but a direct hit from an artillery shell.

Middleton devised a simple plan of attack. The *Northcote*,

fortified with wood from Dumont's barn and sacks of grain, would cruise down the South Saskatchewan past Batoche just as the general launched an assault from the high ground south of the village. Ideally, the rebels would abandon their rifle pits to fire on the *Northcote* and allow Middleton to take Batoche quickly and painlessly. Middleton decided to put the plan into effect on May 9, and by 5:30 A.M. that day his troops were marching toward the village.

However, they failed to keep pace with the steamer, and the *Northcote* got to Batoche at 8 A.M., an hour or so ahead of the ground forces. Dumont, who hoped to capture the vessel and make prisoners of the soldiers onboard, ordered his men to lower a ferry cable across the river. But they placed it too high and only managed to shear off the smokestacks. The soldiers and the rebels fired furiously at each other for a few minutes without inflicting any serious damage on each other.

By the time Middleton launched his attack, the *Northcote* had drifted past Batoche and the Metis had returned to their positions. All morning, the cannons bellowed and lurched, hurling smoke, thunder and destruction at the Metis capital. The shells shredded several buildings, and the infantrymen filled the air with lead. But for all their firepower, the Canadians could not shake their hidden enemy. They were shooting blindly again, just as they had been at Fish Creek and Cut Knife Hill. And again, the Canadians fought from high, exposed ground. If they stood, or attempted to advance, they risked becoming easy targets for rebel marksmen in well-protected rifle pits. By mid-afternoon, Middleton realized the futility of prolonging the fight and, after consulting his senior officers, ordered the troops to withdraw. They established a new camp about one mile south of the battleground, aligning the wagons around the exterior and digging trenches to protect themselves.

It had been another exasperating day. The Canadians had gained no ground. They had taken no prisoners. They had barely seen the enemy. Yet two of their comrades had died, and ten were wounded. As the correspondent for the *Toronto Daily Mail* observed in his dispatch from the battlefield: "The firing on our part has to be done at the puffs of smoke from their guns, or at spots where we suppose the enemy to be. The rebel rifle pits lie right before us but it is impossible for us to capture them without hideous slaughter."

The next two days proved to be almost as frustrating for the Canadians. On the morning of May 10, most of the troops dug trenches around the camp to strengthen their defences. Middleton sent his artillery back to the battlefield to shell the village, accompanied by the Grenadiers, who provided support and cover. They remained there all day, keeping their casualties—one dead and five wounded—to a minimum, but achieving nothing of significance. Middleton also sent Captain John French and a few of his scouts to the open prairie east of Batoche to assess the potential for an attack from that direction.

The general dithered again on the third day. He sent the artillery to its now familiar ground, accompanied by the infantry units, to shell houses on the other side of the South Saskatchewan, and his troops again sustained light casualties. Meanwhile, Middleton, his senior officers, and a healthy contingent of mounted troops, Gatling gun in tow, set out to examine the open prairie that the scouts had discovered the previous day. When they reached the edge of the bush, the general ordered his men to cross the clearing. They didn't get far before the Metis opened fired from their rifle pits at the edge of the valley. The Canadians promptly retreated and returned the fire. A short, hot skirmish occurred, but there were no casualties on either side.

With the general occupied elsewhere, Williams decided to test the resolve of the men in the rifle pits. He and some of his troops charged a line near the church. The Indian defenders abandoned their position at the sight of the oncoming soldiers, allowing the Midlanders to swoop down and cart off pick-axes, shovels, pots, kettles and blankets. They were the heroes of the day, and their actions sharpened the discontent among Middleton's men. The Canadian soldiers were not interested in a lengthy siege. They wanted to crush the rebellion with a quick, decisive blow, and the Midlanders had shown that charging the enemy positions was the way to do it.

Middleton, who disdained most of the Canadian officers and doubted the fighting abilities of their men, was not about to order a charge. However, he did plan an aggressive attack for the fourth day of the battle, May 12. He and the mounted troops would launch an assault from the prairie to the east with a nine-pound cannon. The sound of the big gun would be the signal for the remaining artillery and infantry to attack from the south.

But the battle plan fell apart because a strong west wind carried the sound away from the general's main force. The commanding officer, Lieutenant-Colonel Bowen Van Straubnezie, could not hear the cannon and failed to send the troops into the fight. A furious Middleton returned for the noon meal and publicly tongue-lashed his officers. He also ordered them to advance as far as they could after lunch.

The general was still dining when the battle resumed in the afternoon. Before he had finished, he heard wild cheering from the battlefield and returned to find that the whole line, a mile in length, had charged the enemy positions. The Midlanders, who were on the left, went first. The Grenadiers broke next, and the men of the 90th completed the charge.

The Canadian troops raced downhill toward the rebels concealed in the bush, dropping to the ground before enemy fire, then resuming their advance. "The rebels stoutly contested every pit," the *Daily Mail* correspondent wrote, "but ultimately broke and fled northeast into other pits."

After punching through the front lines, the Canadian troops quickly reached the settlement of Batoche, occupied the buildings and freed the prisoners held by the Metis. A few determined rebels fired on the Canadians from rifle pits near the village itself, but they quickly gave up and fled when the cannon and Gatling gun were turned on them. By the end of the day, Middleton and his men controlled Batoche.

A dozen rebels died during the Battle of Batoche, all of them on the final day. Most of those who survived the onslaught surrendered to the Canadian forces and became prisoners. The rest fled with Riel and Dumont. On May 13, Middleton sent one of the prisoners after them with a note urging them to give up. Riel did so, deciding he would take his chances in a Canadian court of law. But Dumont rode into exile in the United States. The resistance was effectively over.

The Surrender of Poundmaker
May 26

THE NIGHT OF MAY 2 WAS a joyous one in Poundmaker's camp. The fires burned brightly and everyone had a story to tell. There was Jacob with Long Tangled Hair, surrounded by yet another awestruck crowd, explaining how he hadn't been able to sleep the previous night, recounting how he had turned this way and that way until he realized that Old Man Stone was prodding him, telling him to get up. Jacob was the keeper of this object, which was regarded as a sacred stone. He made offerings to its spirit, and Old Man Stone had spoken to him many times, telling him when visitors were coming, for instance, or a storm was imminent.

So Jacob got up and ascended to a lookout above the camp. He sat with his back to the west. He felt the wind rise to greet the dawn. He stared as far as he could see, to the grey line where land met sky, then directed his gaze to the marshy, meandering creek below him. That's when he saw the wagons, filled with soldiers, coming straight toward the camp, and he raced off to sound the alarm.

The story of the battle was told again and again. It had been a thrilling victory. But few slept well that night. People kept hearing wagons rumbling in the distance, and occasionally someone would yell, "The soldiers are coming." Everyone knew the whites would want revenge for their defeat at Cut Knife Hill. They knew the camp would have to move. The question was: where should they go?

Two days after the battle, Metis emissaries arrived with a letter from Louis Riel and a council was held to discuss it. Riel was looking for two hundred men. His representatives, seven in all, assured the Indians that the Metis would defeat the Canadians and capture Middleton. They provided rousing accounts of the fight at Fish Creek. Many of the Cree leaders, including Poundmaker, were unimpressed. They wanted to move west, away from the conflict. Poundmaker, his family and a few loyal followers even packed their possessions and started to ride away from the camp. But they were forced to return by a group of armed Metis and Stoneys. Warriors and militants were in control. They had decided to go east and join Riel.

And given the rules that governed Indian camps, that meant everyone would go east.

The Indians began travelling toward the Eagle Hills, moving every other day or so and cutting a wide arc across the prairie until they were sixty miles south of Battleford and the Canadian soldiers. But collisions occurred anyway. The Crees and their allies encountered three white scouts, two of whom escaped on horseback. The third was left behind and, rather than surrendering, died in a shootout with the Indians. Later the same day, they met a train of horse-drawn wagons, driven by teamsters hauling supplies north to Battleford from the railway. Native and Metis fighters seized the wagons and made prisoners of the drivers.

The column of more than a thousand people was still in the vicinity of the Eagle Hills when Metis messengers arrived with news of the fight at Batoche. A day later, there was more news. The Metis had been defeated and Riel had surrendered. This led to a final council for there were many in the camp who remained defiant, who knew they could be starved out but did not believe that they could be beaten in a fight. Finally, Poundmaker rose. He stood amid the multitude seated within the circle of tepees, a tall, slender, dignified man, a blanket draped over his shoulder and thick, braided locks cascading down to his waist.

"You all, as many as you are, behold me. You all call me your chief. Listen carefully to my words. Today, it is no more a question of fighting. You who have committed murders, who have plundered the innocents, it is no more time to think of saving your own lives. Look at all these women and children. Look at all these youths around you. They are all clamouring for their lives. It is a case of saving them. I know we are all brave. If we keep on fighting the whites, we can embarrass them. But we will be overcome by their numbers, and nothing tells us that our children will survive. I would sooner give myself up and run the risk of being hanged than see my tribe and my children shot through my fault, and by an unreasonable resistance see streams of blood shed. Now, let everyone who has a heart do as I do and follow me."

The time had come to surrender and the people stood behind him. Poundmaker dictated a letter to Jefferson asking Middleton for terms. Jefferson left with the document the next day, accompanied by a party of Metis and Indians. They went north to Duck Lake, on to Prince Albert, and southwest to Fort Carlton before catching the general, who was travelling by steamer up the North Saskatchewan to Battleford. Middleton's response was brief and menacing. The Indians could surrender unconditionally or face the consequences. "I have men enough to destroy you, and your people, or at least to drive you away to starve," he wrote, "and will do so unless you bring in the teams you took, yourself and Councillors, to meet me at Battleford on Tuesday, the 26th."

And so they marched north to Battleford, making their final stop eight or ten miles out. "It was a sad camp," Jefferson later wrote. "Gloom of the deepest clouded every face. All conversation was direful speculation as to the form the General's vengeance would take." The next morning, the men filled two wagons with their weapons, over three hundred in all. They walked with empty hands and heavy hearts. Poundmaker led them into the soldiers' camp at Battleford, past dozens of tents pitched on the flats between the Battle River and the police barracks, to Middleton's quarters.

When all were seated, the Cree leader went forward to greet the silent and glowering general who remained in his chair, with

Steamer North West

May 25th 85

Poundmaker

I have utterly defeated the Half-breeds
And Indians at Batoche, and
have made prisoners of Riel,
And most of his Council, I
have made no terms with them,
neither will I make terms with
you, I have men enough to
destroy you, And your people
Or at least to drive you away
to starve, and will do so unless
you bring in the teams, you took
And yourself, And Councilors,
to meet me at Battleford on
Tuesday, the 26th with your arms, I am glad
to hear that you treated the
prisoners, well and have
released them.

Fred. Middleton
Major General
Comdg N.W. Field Force

officers behind him and soldiers back of them. Poundmaker surrendered his gun, a sleek Winchester rifle with a polished brass breech and a stock studded with brass tacks representing hail, a potent natural force revered by the Plains Cree. Then he extended his hand but Middleton refused to shake it.

"Is it usual," the general asked through an interpreter, "for Indians to go about pilfering like rats?"

"I felt that I had a rope about my neck and something drawing me all the time."

"Has a chief no power?"

"I am not sure that I am a chief."

"Who murdered Payne and Tremont?"

"I cannot name them, and I would not tell the great chief a lie."

Middleton interrogated Poundmaker about every incident of the past two months attributed to his followers, and concluded with a warning against future transgressions. "Let all Indians understand that if one white man is killed, ten Indians will suffer for it."

Then the arrests began. Middleton had Poundmaker and his brother, Yellow Mud Blanket, taken into custody. Itka and Waywahnitch, or Man Without Blood, were next. Itka, an old man with a bandage around his head and a tattered blanket drawn over his shoulders, came forward to confess to the murder of Payne. The younger Waywahnitch, resplendent in beads and plumage, admitted slaying Tremont. As the prisoners were led away, whites and natives began to disperse. An old Stoney woman had the final word that day. "The Almighty sees," she wailed in a wrenching voice. "Our children and country have been taken."

Frenchman's Butte
May 28

THE THIRST DANCE BEGAN as evening settled over Big Bear's camp on Red Deer Creek at the foot of Frenchman's Butte, fifteen miles northeast of Fort Pitt. A young man scaled the centre pole of the large, circular lodge—built that day of poplar branches and brush—and seated himself amid the sheared-off crown. He chanted in a slow, melancholy voice, and soon the circle of drummers at the foot of the pole began pounding the big skin instrument from all sides. Warriors danced around the drummers, singing of old raids and fights, while others lay amid the brush that formed the walls, only their heads visible, blowing on shrill goose-bone whistles.

"It was a glorious night," one of the white prisoners, William Bleasdell Cameron, would later write in his book, *Blood Red the Sun*, "the air soft and balmy, not a cloud flecking the high dome of the sky in which the pale, May moon rode majestically, flooding the scene with mellow light. Behind the dancing lodge towered the lofty butte of the... Frenchman, its poplared sides glancing through all their leaves in the shimmering effulgence."

Later, the stars blazed with startling brilliance. Meteors lit the sky. And within the lodge, the Plains Cree warriors and their more northern brethren, the Woods Cree, tried to dance away the animosity that had arisen between them. They had been living together in one large camp, run by Wandering Spirit and his fellow warriors, since the massacre at Frog Lake. They had taken Fort Pitt, and then everyone, about a thousand people, including seventy white hostages, had left for Poundmaker's camp, although they were not kept abreast of developments there, or the fact that he and his followers had surrendered. When they reached Red Deer Creek, messengers arrived with the news that there were soldiers to the east in Battleford and to the west at Fort Edmonton.

These morale-shattering reports nearly led to open conflict. The Woods Cree were ready to go home. Big Bear's warriors insisted that they should all continue. The thirst dance was hastily organized to prevent a rupture. But as dawn broke after the first night of the dance, scouts arrived with more bad news: there were soldiers at Fort Pitt. "Instantly, all was excitement," according to Cameron. "The Indians tumbled out of their lodges, caught up their horses and began to prepare for flight and battle.

"The thirst dance ended abruptly. Wandering Spirit appeared riding [a] tall, gray mare, her sides streaked with paint, eagle feathers floating from her tail and foretop. Naked except for his breechclout and moccasins, his curling, black hair tossing in the wind, his strange eyes flashing, at a mad gallop he circled the camp, shouting the long war-cry of the Crees. He was belted with cartridges: across his chest like the sash of some military order hung a second band. He carried the Winchester without which he never left his lodge."

The Indians moved their camp about three miles from Frenchman's Butte, but that night the first skirmish with the Canadians occurred. A warrior named Maymenook set out for Fort Pitt with about twenty young men, hoping to steal horses from the soldiers. They had not travelled far when they encountered a Canadian scouting patrol. Maymenook charged on his black stallion, fired twice, then slumped over dead, having taken a bullet in the neck.

The following morning, Wandering Spirit put the camp to work, prisoners included, digging a line of rifle pits across the brush-covered summit of Frenchman's Butte. They cleverly disguised the pits with branches so they were not visible from the flat, open field seventy-five to a hundred feet below. By day's end, the defences were complete, and Wandering Spirit's warriors ready to make their last stand.

They did not wait long. Just before sunset, Canadian troops arrived under the command of Major-General Strange. He had led the third, and most westerly column to march north from the CPR line. He left Calgary April 17, with two battalions, the 91st Winnipeg Light Infantry, the Mount Royal 65th Rifles, a troop of mounted police scouts under Inspector Sam Steele, and a single nine-pound gun. They reached Edmonton May 1, after an arduous journey, and departed for Pitt two weeks later, travelling overland and by flat-bottomed river barge. Strange arrived May 25, and on the morning of May 28 fought the Cree at Frenchman's Butte with a small, under-equipped force of 165 soldiers and 27 police officers.

The battle lasted three and a half hours, and ended indecisively. Wandering Spirit and his men fired at Canadian soldiers exposed on the field below, wounding three enemy troops. But with the shorter range of their weapons, they could not cause serious damage. The Canadians could only guess at the position of the Indians and fire at the smoke from their guns. However, shells from the nine-pounder ripped into two pits, exploding and mortally wounding one of the warriors. Their old guns were no match for a cannon, and they quickly abandoned the hill. Strange assumed that the Indians were trying to outflank him and ordered a retreat. The Canadians headed west to Pitt to await the arrival of Middleton and reinforcements. Most of the natives fled north into the bush, seeking refuge and respite. But they found neither.

The Flight of Big Bear's Cree
May 28–July 4

WANDERING SPIRIT LED the flight of Big Bear's Cree from Frenchman's Butte to Loon Lake, a distance of forty miles. The journey took four days, and it was an ordeal. The war chief stayed off trails and waterways to avoid detection, leading women and children, youthful warriors and elderly men through bush and forest. Most were on foot and most had left their possessions behind. Some had nothing but the clothes they were wearing. A few had blankets. Others had a little food. Cold rains drenched them as they trudged through a dense, gnarled wilderness. Fear, hunger and fatigue gnawed at them. And the Canadians pursued them.

Inspector Steele, at the head of a squad of sixty-five officers and soldiers, led the chase. He and his men caught the Cree at the narrows between the two basins of Loon Lake on the morning of June 3. Some of the refugees had already crossed the swampy channel when the Canadians arrived with their guns blazing. Bullets whizzed by women and children, including some of the white hostages. Cree warriors, poorly armed and short of ammunition, fought vigorously, driving off Steele and his men after a short, brisk skirmish. They wounded two Canadians, but five of their own, including a chief named Cut Arm, died. When the shooting stopped, the Cree and their prisoners completed the crossing and buried the dead. By then, despair had overtaken an elderly woman named Standing in the Doorway. She looped a piece of rope over the branch of a tree and hung herself.

The Cree kept moving. They knew that there would be

more soldiers on their trail. Middleton was already en route from Fort Pitt with over 200 mounted men, 150 foot soldiers and a Gatling gun, although he would give up the chase at Loon Lake rather than cross the narrows. The general had sent Strange from Pitt to Beaver River to cut off any escape to the west. He had dispatched Otter from Battleford to Turtle Lake and the mounted police commissioner Acheson G. Irvine from Prince Albert to Green Lake to close off the eastern flank. In all, four columns of men were relentlessly pursuing the tattered, dispirited refugees.

Hunger and desperation finally shattered the large, disparate assembly on June 9. As Big Bear's Cree pushed on north of Loon Lake, the Wood Cree went west, their departure unnoticed until the end of the day. Wandering Spirit and another leader named Dressy Man pursued them and then stayed with them rather than returning to their own bands.

With the war chief gone, Imasees took control of his father's band. Two weeks later, after a futile march east toward Batoche, the final rupture occurred. On June 25, the head men held a council. Imasees and several others, including Little Poplar, Four Sky Thunder, Lucky Man and Miserable Man, declared that

National Archives of Canada PA27861

they would never surrender to the Canadians. Instead, they would flee to the United States. Big Bear and many others refused to join them.

Imasees headed south with about 140 followers, eluding the Canadian forces as they travelled through forest and parkland before reaching the prairie. They travelled some 250 miles—mortally wounding a settler whom they encountered on the South Saskatchewan and slaying a few stray oxen for food—before crossing the border in mid-July. Along the way, however, Four Sky Thunder and Miserable Man turned back and surrendered at Fort Battleford, the former to face a charge of arson and the latter a murder charge for acts committed at Frog Lake.

Those who remained with Big Bear began surrendering after the council of June 25. Forty people turned themselves in to Otter at Turtle Lake. Another seventeen gave up when they encountered Irvine. Fifty more, starving and beaten, walked in to the Indian agency at Duck Lake. Big Bear's wife was among them. But the old chief remained adrift in the bush with only two companions, his twelve-year-old son, Horse Child, and a former councillor named Two and Two. Big Bear had once been a prominent leader whose physical presence, commanding personality and powerful oratory had earned him the respect and recognition of his people. Now, he had lost almost everything a man can lose: his wife, his family, his followers and his country.

In the dark hours before he finally surrendered near Fort Carlton on July 4, Big Bear must surely have wondered how the Creator could allow such things to happen. He had been a good man. He had followed the teachings and traditions of his people. He had revered the Creator who had placed his people on these plains and provided them with the buffalo. He had loved this land in all its beauty, bounty and diversity.

Big Bear's faith had been sorely tested. And it would be tested again, when he was shackled and jailed. When he and his brethren were put on trial. When they were made to sit in prisoners' boxes while strange men speaking a foreign language argued their cases. When they were convicted. When they were imprisoned. And when those who had taken the lives of white men during the troubles of '85 were led to the gallows and hung from the neck until dead.

PART

THREE

A *New World Rises*

Glenbow Archives, Calgary NA-448-6

P*oundmaker*
Died July 4, 1886

"HERE SHE COMES," shouted one of the men on the platform, and at that, people leaned forward, craned their necks, and squinted toward the western horizon. The crowd of Winnipeggers had come to the station to meet the 6:30 P.M. train from Regina, the one carrying the Indian and Metis prisoners destined for Stony Mountain Penitentiary where they would serve prison terms for their roles in the Troubles of '85. Everyone rushed forward when the train rolled in, clanging and hissing and belching out billowy clouds of dirty, black smoke. All were eager for a glimpse of the men who, to quote the *Manitoba Daily Free Press*, "had caused so much commotion in the land."

The prisoners had ridden in their own heavily guarded coach near the front of the train, and remained seated as the regular passengers disembarked. Afterward, the engineer shunted the train backward until the prisoners' car was opposite the door of the station. Mounted police officers had to push the crowd back before they could begin escorting the convicted men across the platform. The Metis went first, a total of fourteen of them. They were, for the most part, short, stout, heavily bearded men. They had dark eyes and gloomy expressions on their faces, having been sentenced four days earlier, on August 17, to terms of three to seven years. When the last of them had cleared the platform, the police brought out the next prisoner, and a spectator exclaimed, "There's Poundmaker."

The Cree chief made a big impression on the crowd. "He is a fine-looking Indian, over six feet in height, with exceedingly fine features for a man of his race . . . and his high, well-developed forehead indicates sagacity and intelligence," the *Free Press* reporter wrote. "He was coatless, but sported a waistcoat, artistically bedecked with small brass nails. A blanket was pulled loosely above his waist which, along with his long braids of jet black hair gave him every appearance of the Indian. He was the centre of attention and saluted to the multitude with a wave of his hand and a smile as he stepped manly from the car to the platform."

The authorities loaded the prisoners into wagons outside the station for the final leg of the journey, the fifteen-mile trip north to the penitentiary. "Poundmaker gazed in rapt astonishment at the buildings as the procession moved along Main Street," the *Free Press* reporter continued. "When . . . he returns to his far off wigwam, he will be able to entertain his allies with tales of the white man's home."

Poundmaker had been in custody since his arrest at Battleford in late May. Then, there had only been a few prisoners confined to the guardhouse at the mounted police post. There was Poundmaker, his brother, Yellow Mud Blanket, and the accused murderers, Itka and Waywahnitch. But the makeshift jail had quickly become crowded as men wanted for looting, stealing and destroying property surrendered or were arrested.

The Canadian authorities wasted little time bringing the men to trial. A man named Tahkokan was convicted of larceny in Battleford on June 27 and received a two-year sentence. On June 29, four more Indians, Natoose, Chesenus, Mistatimawas and Charles Pooyak, appeared on a variety of charges, including horse stealing, larceny and assault. Each was sentenced to six years.

Less than a week later, on July 4, Poundmaker and twenty-three other native and Metis prisoners began the next stage of their strange and unnerving odyssey through the Canadian justice system. Superintendent William Herchmer and a contingent of mounted police shackled the men, loaded them into wagons and left Battleford for Regina. The five-day journey took them across some of the flattest land in the Saskatchewan country, across Eagle Creek, past the Bad Hills and the Coteau Hills to the landing where they crossed the South Saskatchewan River and on to the railway village of Swift Current. The next morning they boarded a train for Regina, the rickety capital of the North-West Territories, and by nightfall, Poundmaker and the others were back behind bars.

The Regina jail was large and crowded. There were prisoners from across the territories, including Louis Riel, whom Poundmaker had never met. He had been at the jail only a few days when he was informed that a letter had arrived for him. It was from one of his children, Jean-Marie Lestanc Poundmaker.

The boy, according to some accounts, had been adopted by an Oblate priest named Father Joseph Lestanc, and was living at the order's St. Albert mission, ten miles northwest of Edmonton. "Learning that there has been fighting in your lands," the boy wrote, "I have been much troubled, but I am glad to know that you were not killed.

"Be grateful father to the Great Spirit who has protected you. I also thank him for having spared my father, whom I love. I have heard the priests; that is why I am glad now. Believe me, father, do as I do, hear the priests and their teachings. God grant that you may be baptised. If you do that, I shall be glad; the Great Spirit will love you and bless you on earth and still more in heaven. I desire also that all my relations may be praying people, as well all the Indians who are upon your lands.

"I wish to be a carpenter. I am learning the trade. When I know it well I shall be able to earn a little money to provide for my subsistence and to be useful to my father. If everything turns out thus, I shall be happy but I shall be more so if you will give yourselves to prayer. I embrace all my relatives and especially you, my beloved father."

The letter, written in French, was signed "Your loving son" and dated July 2. It undoubtedly provided a little relief from the tedium and anxiety of jail, for Poundmaker had learned that his trial would not be held for several weeks.

Riel was the first of the Regina prisoners to go before judge and jury. His trial began July 28 and ended August 1. The justice system next turned to Riel's Metis associates. A total of forty-six Metis faced charges; twenty-eight were convicted; and eighteen went to jail or prison. By comparison, eighty-one natives were charged; fifty-five were convicted; eight of those received the death penalty and the remainder wound up behind bars. On the fourth of August, twenty-six Metis appeared before Judge Hugh Richardson and pleaded guilty, one by one, to charges of treason felony. According to the *Free Press*, this was the result of "a consultation between counsel for the Crown and counsel for the prisoners that has taken place within the last few days." In exchange for their guilty pleas, the men were to receive short prison terms.

The following day, Philip Garnot and Moise Ouellette pleaded guilty to the same charge, but they had been pushed into it. "The pressure of the Crown was brought to bear upon the case, as they threatened to indict them for high treason," the *Free Press* noted. And there was only one penalty for that offence: death by hanging.

Two weeks later, the convicted Metis returned for sentencing. Eleven of them, Riel's councillors and close associates, received seven-year terms. Three others were given three years each. Four got a year in the Regina jail and eight were discharged. This hearing effectively concluded the prosecution of the Metis. At the end of a brief, bite-sized item about the proceedings, the *Free Press* noted: "The Indian One Arrow, convicted of treason-felony, was sentenced to three years in the pentitentiary, despite an eloquent appeal to the court before sentence was passed."

One Arrow, chief of the Willow Cree, whose reserve was located on the eastern margins of the settlement of Batoche, was the first Indian to go to trial in Regina. The indictment, read to the court, charged that the elderly leader "feloniously and wickedly did conspire, consult, confederate, assemble, and meet together with diverse other evil-disposed persons . . . to raise, make and levy insurrection and rebellion against our said Lady the Queen within this realm."

Providing an accurate translation proved to be beyond the

capabilities of the court-appointed interpreter because there were no Cree equivalents for many of the words and concepts in the indictment. The man got around the problem by telling One Arrow he was accused of "knocking off the Queen's bonnet and stabbing her in the behind with the sword." Hearing this, the chief apparently turned to the interpreter with a startled look on his face and asked, "Are you drunk?"

One Arrow's offence was to be seen in Batoche, armed and talking to Riel during the siege of the settlement. The Crown's three witnesses had no idea what One Arrow said to the Metis leader since they did not understand Cree, nor could they say that he had actually participated in the fighting. But one witness did testify that the accused man was "a worthless hound," which brought an outburst of laughter from those in the court.

Despite the lack of evidence, the six-member jury deliberated for only a few minutes before returning with a guilty verdict. And Judge Richardson was unmoved by the impassioned plea of the aging chief. "I know that I have done nothing wrong," One Arrow said before he was sentenced. "I can't see where I have done anything wrong against anybody. So, I beg of you to let me go, to let me go free."

Poundmaker was charged with the same offence as One Arrow and the Metis: treason felony. A few days before his trial began on August 17, he met Beverly Robertson, a Winnipegger who called himself a lawyer and said he was here to defend Poundmaker, which was a strange notion for someone raised in a world where men were expected to provide for and defend themselves. But the Cree leader knew that the ways of his people had been swept aside and that the white man's peculiar rules and rituals now prevailed. He was taken to court and placed in the prisoner's box. He was asked to enter a plea— Poundmaker declared that he was not guilty—and then listened as witness after witness—nine for the prosecution and six for the defence—testified about his actions.

The indictment outlining the Crown's case against Poundmaker, read to the court by prosecutor David Scott, charged that the Cree chief had conspired to make war against the Queen and had actually taken up arms three times—during the looting of Battleford in late March, during the battle at Cut Knife Hill on May 2, and when the teamsters were robbed in the Eagle Hills on May 14. Scott told the six-man jury that to convict Poundmaker they only had to be certain that the defendant had conspired with others and intended to make war. "We are going to go further than that," he assured them. "We are going to show that on these three occasions he actually levied war."

Scott opened the Crown's case by focusing on a letter to Louis Riel, dated April 29 at Cut Knife Hill, and signed by Poundmaker along with four others. The contents, he said, clearly proved that the signatories intended to go to war and conspired to make it happen. "I want to hear news of the progress of God's work," the letter began. "If any event has occurred since your messengers came away, let me know it.

"Tell me the date when the Americans will reach the Canada Pacific Railway. Tell me all the news that you have heard from all the places where your work is in progress. Big Bear has finished his work. He has taken Fort Pitt. If you want me to come to you, let me know at once. I will be four days on the road."

The letter contained many such incriminating statements. The authors admitted to taking all the horses and cattle in the vicinity of Battleford. They said they had guns and rifles of many sorts, but were short of amunition and added: "If it be possible, we want you to send us ammunition of various kinds. We are weak only for want of that." The next segment appeared to confirm the dark designs of those who signed it. "You have sent word that you would come to Battleford when you had finished the work at Duck Lake. We wait still for you as we are unable to take the fort without help. We are impatient to reach you. It would give us encouragement as much to see you and make us work more heartily."

The Crown's first witness was Robert Jefferson, Poundmaker's brother-in-law and the farm instructor on his reserve. He was a prisoner in Poundmaker's camp during April and May 1885 and, according to his testimony, had written the letter as it was dictated to him by a number of Indians. Jefferson told the court that in mid-April a mixed-blood named Norbert Delorme and a Cree called Chicicum had arrived in the camp with a written message from Riel. Delorme read the missive to an assembly of about fifty chiefs and councillors crowded into a large lodge within the centre of the circle of tepees. Afterward, a member of Red Pheasant's band summoned Jefferson to the lodge to write down their response. Poundmaker was present but his role was never clearly established.

"Who wrote the name 'Poundmaker' signed at the bottom of that letter?" Scott asked.

"I did," Jefferson responded.

"By what authority?"

"By the authority of the men that told me to write the letter."

"Had you any authority from the prisoner?"

"Well, I consider I had. I would not have written it if I had not had authority, that is very certain."

"You say the letter was dictated by those who were present in the tent; did the prisoner dictate any portion of it?"

"Well, I believe he did."

"You believe he did. Do you remember that he did?"

"Well, I would not be very positive about it. I think he did."

Robertson's cross-examination of Jefferson raised additional questions about Poundmaker's role in the composition of the letter. The farm instructor testified that a head man of the defendant's band, Oopinowaywin, or Sheds the Hair, told him to sign Poundmaker's name. Furthermore, when Jefferson last saw the letter, a group of Metis were looking it over and seemed to be making revisions. He stated that they had added a highly incriminating postscript, which read "When this reaches you, send us news immediately, as we are anxious to hear the news. If you send us news, send as many men as possible."

The questions about the authorship of the document, along with the fact that it had been altered, should have reduced its value as evidence. Another part of Jefferson's testimony should also have aroused doubts in the minds of the jurors. He told the court that Delorme had used intimidation and outlandish claims about Riel to convince the Indians to join the uprising. The emissary warned them that they would lose all their lands if they did not support the Metis. Delorme went on to say that Riel was a "sort of God," who could foresee the future and was expecting help from south of the border. According to this scenario, American soldiers would take control of the CPR and prevent any more Canadian troops from reaching the North-West by train. The letter, then, may have been little more than an attempt to appease the Metis in the camp.

Jefferson was the only witness to testify about the letter. He, along with three mounted police officers, gave evidence pertaining to Poundmaker's role in the Battle of Cut Knife Hill. The strongest testimony came from Superintendent Herchmer. He told the court he had seen the Cree leader twice during the seven-hour fight. He first observed him riding about in a wagon, which was fifteen hundred to two thousand yards away. Herchmer said he could recognize Poundmaker from that distance because he had known him for several years, ever since they had travelled a long distance together one summer, which was undoubtedly a reference to 1881 when the Marquis of Lorne, the governor-general of the day, had made a vice-regal tour of the North-West, and Poundmaker had guided the distinguished visitor and his party from Battle River to the Blackfoot Reserve on the Bow River, downstream from Fort Calgary.

On the basis of a naked-eye sighting, from a distance of one to one and a half miles, the police superintendent concluded that Poundmaker was directing the native forces, who routed the Canadians that day and forced them to flee. "He looked to me as if he was general in the whole party because after the different positions he would take, the fire would come from fresh ravines, new ravines."

Herchmer next spotted Poundmaker, with the aid of binoculars, at the summit of the actual Cut Knife Hill, which overlooked the entire area and was about one and a half to two miles south of the battlefield. This time, the chief was in the company of an Oblate priest, Father Louis Cochin, the women and the children. "What was he doing there?" Scott asked, to which Herchmer replied, "I should judge it was too far off to tell what he was doing. I should judge he was generalling the whole party."

Having presented their evidence on the Cut Knife fight, the Crown lawyers turned their attention to Poundmaker's first alleged act of war—the looting of Battleford. The basic facts were not in dispute. Poundmaker and several young men from his band had left their reserve on March 29, a Sunday, to go to Battleford. Their objective was to seek information from

Indian agent John Rae about the battle three days earlier at Duck Lake, the first skirmish of the Metis uprising, and to ask for tea and tobacco. Along the way, Poundmaker acquired additional followers from the Sweet Grass and Strike-him-on-the-back reserves. When he reached Battleford on the morning of March 30, he had about 120 men with him, most of them armed. Meanwhile, the residents of the settlement, having heard that the Indians were coming in from the country, had fled to the NWMP post located on a promontory overlooking the confluence of the Battle and North Saskatchewan Rivers.

The Crown called three witnesses to testify about Poundmaker's actions at Battleford. The first, Peter Ballendine, was the former Hudson's Bay employee who had served as Dewdney's informer among the Indians the previous winter. He had gone out from the mounted police post to speak to the Indians and spent several hours among them. Ballendine testified that Poundmaker said he was sorry to see the town empty, but otherwise said very little. The next witness was William McKay, the Hudson's Bay agent in Battleford, and his testimony was just as weak. "He told me he had come down to see the agent and ask for some tea and tobacco and moccasins and some other things they were in want of," McKay said. "He told me he didn't mean any harm when he came down."

The Crown's best witness was William Lightfoot, a fellow Cree and a member of Red Pheasant's band, who had taken part in the uprising by guiding some of Riel's emissaries to the Stoney reserves in the Eagle Hills where they hoped to recruit native warriors. In any event, Lightfoot placed Poundmaker inside a store while the looting was going on. "What was he doing in the store?" Scott asked.

"He was looking over the store, the things in the store, one thing and another."

"Is that all Poundmaker did there? Look over the things?"

"That is all I seen him do there," said Lightfoot, who made one more damaging allegation. He said he later saw Poundmaker seated on a hill overlooking the settlement with a bundle of goods nearby. However, the witness could not say how the goods got there, or whether Poundmaker had taken them from one of the stores.

The final accusation in the indictment stated that Poundmaker had levied war by participating in the seizure of the supply train that was travelling from Swift Current to Battleford in mid-May. Both Scott and Robertson questioned Jefferson about the incident but the farm instructor could not say if Poundmaker was directly involved. The Crown also questioned one of the teamsters, John Shera, who did nothing to strengthen the prosecution's case.

"I don't know whether he was with the Indians or not when we were caught," Shera testified. "I did not see him."

Robertson opened the defence by calling Joseph McKay, farm instructor at the Strike-him-on-the-back reserve who had encountered Poundmaker when he was on his way to Battleford. McKay was born in the North-West and had known Indians since childhood. Robertson questioned him about the role of a political leader like Poundmaker when an Indian band felt it was in danger of being attacked and the warriors had erected a soldiers' tent.

"What is the effect now when a soldiers' tent is pitched in a camp? What effect has that upon the authority of the chief?"

"Well, if any Indians would want to go away, if the soldiers would not let him go, they would go and kill his dogs or cut up his tent. He could not go off unless the soldiers let him go."

Robertson pursued the cultural defence further with his third witness, a member of Poundmaker's band named Grey

Eyes, who testified that the Stoney warriors from the Eagle
Hills had erected a soldiers' tent after arriving at Poundmaker's
camp in early April. He also told the court that Poundmaker
had tried to leave on three occasions, but each time was turned
back by the Stoneys.

"What power has the chief among the Crees and Stoneys
when a soldiers' lodge has been put up in the camp?" Robertson asked.

"The chief has no control over anyone when that soldiers'
tent is up."

"Who has control?"

"The soldiers. The dancers of the lodge."

"Was Poundmaker one of the soldiers?"

"No."

Grey Eyes also testified about events in Battleford and flatly
contradicted Lightfoot's evidence. He said that, with the exception of two brief intervals, he and Poundmaker had spent the
entire night together seated on a hill overlooking the settlement, and that Poundmaker had tried to stop the looting.

"Did Poundmaker have any goods at any time that night?"
Robertson asked.

"I saw nothing."

"What did Poundmaker do, or did he do anything beside
calling out to them to stop?"

"I heard him calling out to the people, stopping them, and
with that there were three or four men along with him that
went down the hill then to go and stop them and speak to them
down the hill."

Robertson next called teamster Wesley Fish, who was driving one of the twenty-nine wagons seized along the trail to
Battleford. He portrayed Poundmaker as a generous and com-
passionate man who seemed more intent on saving lives than

making war. Moreover, he laid the blame for the incident squarely with the Metis.

"Who was in command of the camp?" Robertson asked.

"The breeds," Fish replied.

"The half-breeds?"

"Yes."

"Was Poundmaker there when you were taken prisoner?"

"No."

"Where were you taken on that occasion?"

"We were taken to the half-breed camp."

"Now, tell me, what was the first you saw of Poundmaker when you were taken in?"

"Well, we were taken down hill into a kind of ravine, and Poundmaker came up and shook hands with us all around and said that he knew there was a God and he thanked Him for saving our lives. He did not thank [the] braves. He had no control over them."

Robertson concluded his examination of Fish by asking him to recount an incident involving a pocketknife. "Well," he began, "when we were taken to the camp, the young braves started to search us. They wanted to see what we had, I suppose, and just as Poundmaker came up one of them was taking a pocketknife from one of the boys and Poundmaker saw him do it, and he did not say anything at the time. But as soon as the Indian got away with the pocketknife he took his own knife out of his pocket and gave it to the boy in exchange for the one the Indian had taken."

The final two defence witnesses, Solomon Desjardins and Father Cochin, reinforced the image of Poundmaker as a man of peaceful intentions. Desjardins, an Indian Department employee who worked on Little Pine's reserve, testified that prior to the battle at Cut Knife Hill, several Metis were pestering

Poundmaker to go down to Batoche. But he repeatedly put them off by saying that he would wait until Big Bear arrived from the Fort Pitt area. Desjardin said that the Cree leader finally made it clear he did not want to go to the Metis capital.

Father Cochin told the court that in mid-April Delorme and a large party of Stoneys had forced him and several neutral Metis families from the community of Bresaylor to join the Cut Knife camp. The priest also testified that Poundmaker had protected these families from harm and had saved his life. "Did the Indians, on any particular occasion that you remember, threaten to murder any of the half-breeds who had been taken from the settlement?" Robertson asked.

"I heard the Indians saying to the half-breeds that if you go on giving suspicion there will be damage done. It appears some of the half-breeds... wanted to desert, so the Indians told them if you want to keep deserting that way, at last something bad will happen between us, meaning they would fight them or kill them, and in those circumstances I have seen Poundmaker many times sending them away, Indians, and protecting the prisoners."

"Was your own life in danger at any time?"

"From the beginning until the second [of] May I thought my own life was in danger, and during that time I was threatened now and then, and once there was twenty Stoney Indians that were surrounding and trying to strike me, but Poundmaker came to them and they scattered away."

"What did Poundmaker say to them?"

"I can't say, but I heard some words, I understood a few words and heard Poundmaker saying to them that—his meaning was that they had nothing to do there, and he threatened them."

"Did you ever have a guard standing over you to protect you?"

"Yes. Poundmaker went there to my tent several times to see that nothing had happened to me and others in the camp."

After being cross-examined briefly, Father Cochin stepped down. All the evidence had been tendered, but Poundmaker had no idea what some of the witnesses had said about him since the interpreter translated only key portions of the testimony. Furthermore, he had been forced to remain silent throughout the trial because, in those days, Canadian law prohibited an accused person from testifying in his own defence. Now he had to sit and listen again. It was time for the lawyers to make their arguments to the jury.

Robertson went first. His address was concise and workmanlike, and almost devoid of eloquence or emotion. He began with Jefferson and the letter. The farm instructor, he pointed out, was confused about some things, uncertain about others. Jefferson was unable to say who had dictated the letter or whether Poundmaker had contributed anything. Then the Metis had revised it. They had tailored the message to suit their own ends. They were determined to create the impression that an important Cree leader and his followers were backing their uprising.

Robertson moved from the letter to the looting at Battleford. All the evidence, he said, showed that Poundmaker had gone to the settlement with peaceful intentions. He only wanted to find out what had occurred at Duck Lake. He had no intention of intimidating or harming anyone, nor was he trying to take control of the settlement. The looting was simple robbery, not treason felony. It was the work of young men who could not be controlled by their leader.

"You must remember," Robertson told the jurors, "that an Indian chief, no matter how influential, is not like the commander of an organized or disciplined force. He is nothing of that sort. The influence he has is just such an influence as his personal character and perhaps a knack of speaking may give him. He cannot, with all his influence, so control the young men, the braves of his tribe, as to prevent them, if they are bent upon mischief, from committing it. He has no court of justice; he has no means of punishment; he has nothing whatever to enforce his authority except such persuasive powers as he may have."

Poundmaker possessed great persuasive powers. He had risen to the pinnacle of the Plains Cree world, not because he was a great warrior or a famous shaman or the prosperous head of a large household, but because he was an orator who could move men with his words. But in the spring of 1885, during the days of defiance and resistance, this peaceful man was up against armed and unscrupulous Metis rabble-rousers like Norbert Delorme, who knew that their uprising would succeed only with Indian support. When Riel's men failed to convince Poundmaker, or any other prominent Cree leaders from the Battleford area, to join them, they used guns and force to hijack their bands.

Robertson made all of this clear in his address to the jury. He argued that the Metis had recruited the Stoneys and together they had joined Poundmaker's camp, erected a soldiers' tent and taken control. "Poundmaker's influence, such as it was, was always exercised in the interests of peace and humanity—always," he told the jury. "But there was a stronger influence that he could not countervail, the influence of those half-breeds with the Stoneys at their back. That, I take it, was the true position of the matter."

B.B. Osler spoke for the Crown. He portrayed Poundmaker as clever, devious and disloyal. He described him as "chief of probably the best known of all the Indian tribes of Canada."

He ranked his case as second in importance to Riel's. And he said that Poundmaker could have been charged with treason. "If it were not for circumstances favourable to the prisoner, such as his not allowing those in his power or in the power of the camp to be killed, but for those circumstances which surrounded his actions personally, it would have been the duty of the Crown, in all probability, to put him on trial for his life."

The cornerstone of the Crown's case, said Osler, was the letter to Riel. It revealed the treasonous intentions of those who dictated it to Jefferson. Equally serious, it showed that Riel, Poundmaker and Big Bear had communicated with each other for the purposes of co-ordinating their actions. The language of the letter proved that they had been part of an organized attempt to overthrow the Canadian government. The only issue was Poundmaker's role in preparing this document, and the only evidence before the jury came from Jefferson.

Osler wisely steered clear of the substance of Jefferson's testimony, which was full of doubts and equivocations. Instead, he focused on the farm instructor's character and credibility. "Have you reason to doubt the honesty of Jefferson's evidence?" he asked the jurors. "Consider how he comported himself in the box. Did he give his evidence with animus, without care, or did he give it with care, stating fairly that which was for as well as that which was against the prisoner? How did he strike you as a witness? Have you reason to disbelieve his story?"

For six white jurors sitting in judgement of a supposedly treasonous Indian leader, an alleged confederate of the traitor Louis Riel, the answer to Osler's loaded questions was obvious: of course they believed Jefferson. And if they accepted Jefferson's testimony, they had no choice but to convict. "Upon that letter," the prosecutor thundered, "the case is, in my view, almost unanswerable."

Having upheld Jefferson's integrity, he went on to impugn Poundmaker's. Osler warned the jurors not to be fooled by his seemingly peaceful and humanitarian gestures. They were, he said, the acts of a man who was clever to the point of being devious. "As events changed, as he thought the rebellion was strong, so he was strong; as he thought the rebellion was weak, so he was weak," Osler reasoned. This explained why Poundmaker had tried to leave on three occasions. This explained his kindness toward the prisoners. "It was very easy to set works and do acts which would save him in case the Government ultimately succeeded and asked him to give an account of his chiefship."

Finally, Osler attacked the heart of Robertson's argument that Poundmaker had no control over the camp. He had wielded enough influence to save Father Cochin, the prosecutor noted, and to protect the Bresaylor mixed-bloods from the Stoneys. "Now do you believe," Osler asked rhetorically, "that he was helpless in the hands of the young braves, or if he had chosen to break that tent up, he had not all the influence necessary to do it? If he hadn't that influence, if he was no longer chief, there still was a duty upon him as a loyal Indian. No man can excuse his treason to the Crown unless his treasonable act is produced by fear of death; fear only of death absolves a man from a treasonable offence."

The jury next heard from Judge Richardson. He explained the law under which Poundmaker was charged, and he summarized the evidence for and against him. Then the jury retired to deliberate. They were back in a few minutes.

"Gentlemen, are you agreed upon your verdict?" the clerk of the court asked, once the jurors were seated. "How say you, is the prisoner guilty or not guilty?"

"Guilty," they replied in unison.

Justice Richardson turned to Poundmaker and asked him if he had anything to say before being sentenced. Poundmaker rose slowly. He glanced at the spectators and journalists behind him. He saw the looks of anticipation. Then he faced the judge. He spoke slowly at first, allowing the interpreter to translate his words. He had his left hand on his breast and his right extended toward Justice Richardson. As he warmed up, the words came quickly. His white listeners could not understand him, but they could feel the power and passion in his voice.

"I am not guilty," he declared. "Much that has been said against me is not true. I am glad of my works in the Queen's country this spring. What I did was for the Great Mother. When my brothers and the pale faces met in the fight at Cut Knife Hill I saved the Queen's men. I took their arms from my brothers and gave them up at Battleford. Everything I could do was done to prevent bloodshed. Had I wanted war, I would not be here now. I would be on the prairie. You did not catch me. I gave myself up. You have got me because I wanted peace."

Poundmaker finished his oration with a flourish, throwing his arms open, glancing at those behind him, and shouting, "I cannot help myself. But I am a man still. You may do as you like with me."

He had spoken. Now Justice Richardson would pass sentence. "Poundmaker, you have been convicted of a very serious offence," he said. "The evidence was so strong against you that I cannot see how the jury could have brought in any other verdict than they did. Had the higher charge of treason been laid, a verdict pronouncing guilt upon you would have been sustained, and in that event you would have to leave this courtroom today as Louis Riel left it... under sentence of death."

The judge acknowledged that Poundmaker had saved lives and prevented bloodshed. He had protected Jefferson. He had stood up for the Metis families of Bresaylor. He had prevented the slaughter of Otter's men at Cut Knife Hill. He had been cordial with the teamsters. But his generosity, compassion and heroism were not evidence of loyalty to the Crown. They were treated as mitigating circumstances that would affect his term of incarceration.

"The sentence which the court pronounces upon you, Poundmaker, for the offence of which you have been convicted, is that you be imprisoned in the penitentiary at Manitoba for three years."

Those should have been the final words of the trial. But Poundmaker could not suppress his revulsion. "I would prefer to be hung at once than to be in that place," he shouted as he was led away.

BACK AT THE REGINA JAIL, he learned that a fresh indignity awaited him. His jailers at Stony Mountain would be cutting his hair. It was a regulation: everyone who entered that place had his hair cut. But Poundmaker objected, and when word of his discontent reached Dewdney, the lieutenant-governor of the territories, he intervened on his behalf. It would be best, he reasoned, to appease Poundmaker so he could use his influence to keep the other native inmates in line. Dewdney went right to the top, telegraphing a request to the prime minister on August 19: "If possible would strongly recommend that instructions be sent to Manitoba Penitentiary to dispense with the regulation of cutting hair in Poundmaker's case. Think this important."

Sir John A. Macdonald apparently agreed. It was a small concession to a proud man who was coping with a bewildering ordeal. But it improved his spirits, as he explained to a reporter from the *Toronto Daily Mail*, who met Poundmaker and the

Metis prisoners at the Regina train station near midnight on August 20, as they were embarking for the journey to Stony Mountain.

"Did you really mean," the journalist asked him, "that you would rather die than be locked up for three years as you said in the courthouse?"

"I meant it then," Poundmaker replied through an interpreter. "But now I hear that my hair won't be cut and if I can live to see my children again I would rather not die."

Then the journalist questioned him about his actions at Battleford, one of the four events that had led him to be charged with treason felony. "Why did you go down to Battleford that first time?"

"I came down to see the agent."

"But why did so many of you come?"

"Because the government agent will never listen to one Indian. A chief is no more to them than one of his band. They tell him to get out when he says his children are hungry. But when a lot go, they listen to us. Then they don't tell us we lie or are lazy dogs. They give us a little food and that is all we really want."

As the interview ended, the reporter said goodbye to Poundmaker. And the Cree chief indicated through the interpreter that he wanted to give him a gift. What could that be, the reporter asked.

"Some of his hair," the interpreter responded.

The reporter handed his pocketknife to Poundmaker, who cut "a long lock from his really beautiful hair and handed it to me." A few minutes later, the train thundered in and the Cree chief, along with his fellow prisoners, left for the penitentiary.

The Canadian government had made a small humanitarian gesture toward Poundmaker. But it was too much for P.G. Laurie of the *Saskatchewan Herald*. He denounced the exemption, as well as the sentence, in the September 24, 1885, edition of the paper. "Nominally, Poundmaker was sentenced to three years imprisonment in the penitentiary; in reality he is provided with what is the Indian's highest ambition to attain—plenty to eat and nothing to do. He goes to prison exempt from the treatment accorded to other prisoners; his hair is uncut."

Laurie concluded on the following note: "The country would have been better served had the court complied with his wish, when sentence of imprisonment was pronounced, and taken him out and hanged him at once. He said he preferred death to imprisonment, and it is a pity he was not accommodated."

The forty-three native inmates incarcerated at Stony Mountain following the uprising looked to Poundmaker for leadership. Samuel Bedson, the warden of the institution, visited Toronto in late 1885, and told the *Daily Globe* that the Indians employed in the prison shops were productive workers who handled tools well, and mostly accepted the rigidities of institutional life, although they longed for their homes and families. As for Poundmaker, the warden reported that he "moved from shop to shop, watching and issuing orders to the Crees, over whom he exercises a general superintendency. He has great influence over these people and fulfills his trust faithfully."

In late February, the *Toronto Daily Mail* reporter George Hamm visited the prison while touring the North-West to check on reports that a new Indian uprising was imminent. Hamm interviewed Poundmaker, among others, and noted that the Cree leader seemed to be in good spirits, although his health had deteriorated. "He has not been well lately, and is now suffering from a severe cold," Hamm reported. "He told me that he was treated well by everybody, and especially Warden Bedson, but that he felt lonesome and wanted to get back to the prairie."

By the time Hamm's story appeared, Dewdney was already working to secure Poundmaker's release due to his deteriorating health. He had nearly died of a bleeding lung three years earlier and the psychic shock of incarceration may have left the Cree chief vulnerable to any number of insidious and debilitating ailments. Dewdney and other Canadian officials did not want Poundmaker to die in jail. This, they feared, would make a martyr of him and lead to unrest on the reserves around Battleford.

And so, on March 4, 1886, after six months in Stony Mountain and a total of nine months in custody, Poundmaker was set free along with seven other native inmates and four Metis. If prison had broken his health, it had changed him spiritually as well. Poundmaker received religious instruction from the chaplain and was baptised with twenty-eight of his brethren on February 18. When he left, he left a Christian.

Poundmaker and the others spent their first night of freedom at the residence of Archbishop Alexandre Tache in St. Boniface, near Winnipeg. According to a report that appeared in the March 18 edition of *Le Manitoba*, a francophone weekly, the men talked of the troubles of 1885, their losses and their suffering. At one point, Poundmaker stood and addressed the others. "God has rewarded us in the midst of our suffering," he said. "He has made us see clearly. He has given us light. He has taught us a good religion. We are good Christians now. Let us pray to God to enlighten those who do not yet see clearly."

The men and their escorts, Fathers Lestanc and A.H. Bigonesse, took the train to Regina. Poundmaker met briefly with Dewdney, then the party set out for the Saskatchewan country where they would rejoin their people. They reached Battleford on March 25, just as spring was blossoming on the northern prairie. The gophers were up and there were geese in the skies and yellow plovers in the marshes, the *Saskatchewan Herald* reported. Farmers were ploughing their fields and breaking new lands. Battleford had rebounded from the destruction of the previous spring and newcomers were arriving in the North-West. "The immigration into the territories has opened very briskly, hundreds of settlers leaving Winnipeg by every west-bound train," Laurie told his readers.

A new west was rising from the ashes of the old, but Poundmaker and his people were not welcome in it. "He has no regrets for the evils that he wrought, no compassion for those who suffered through his revolt," Laurie wrote in an editorial, two full columns long, announcing Poundmaker's return. "The mood of this petted savage shows that he is more dangerous now than ever, because he is beyond local control." The editor concluded by referring to some of Poundmaker's alleged atrocities, "the memory of which," he said, "is not smoothed over by the lapse of a year."

The *Herald* carried several brief items that spring which reflected the new reality facing the Indians of the North-West. In early March, the mounted police arrested a native man in Battleford under the provisions of the Vagrancy Act. His offence was that he did not have a pass signed by the district Indian agent authorizing him to be off his reserve. Several times that month, the town was "cleared of stragglers" who were without passes, the *Herald* reported. On one occasion, the police hauled a woman to the barracks under the same pretext and shaved hair from both sides of her head before releasing her. "An hour later," Laurie wrote, "there was not a straggler in town."

The police were enforcing new regulations adopted by the federal government in the fall of 1885. They flowed out of a memorandum that Hayter Reed, assistant commissioner of Indian Affairs, prepared for Dewdney. Reed made fifteen recommendations, directed primarily at rebellious natives, although some came to be applied generally. He suggested disarming all rebels, though shotguns used for hunting were to be marked as Indian Department property and loaned back to their owners. He proposed that "the tribal system should be abolished," along with the offices of chief and councillor, and favoured "careful repression of those that become prominent... by counselling, medicine dances and so on." Finally, he wanted to confiscate the horses of rebellious Indians. "They would be retained on reserves too, with greater ease, if the means of travelling expeditiously are taken from them," he reasoned.

The world had changed irrevocably in the nine months Poundmaker spent locked up. He could see the effect the white man's new rules had had on his people. He could see it in their eyes. He could hear it in their voices. Through all the adversity they had endured since the treaties were signed, through hunger, homelessness and poverty, people had dreamed of recovering their country and returning to their old lives. But the dreams and the defiance were gone.

He, too, had lost much during his imprisonment. His second wife, Grass Woman, had gone to live with another man. And his health had not improved since he returned. Still, he was better off than some native inmates who were freed around the same time. One Arrow, the old chief who had pleaded for his freedom in Judge Richardon's court, died at Archbishop Tache's residence a few days after getting out of prison. And the following short item appeared in the *Saskatchewan Herald* that spring:

"Three Indians sent to the penitentiary for criminal offences, rather than rebellion offences, were released and reached home all sick and weak. One had to be lifted from the wagon in which they travelled. There were four in their party when released but one succumbed to disease and set out from St. Boniface for the happy hunting ground."

Within a few weeks of his return, Poundmaker had seen and heard enough. He could see that, even if he were healthy, he would not be allowed to play a leadership role in the affairs of his people. The Dominion of Canada was in charge now. Government agents would decide how they would live. But Poundmaker would not stand for this and decided to visit his old friend and adoptive father, Crowfoot.

He left on May 18, pass in hand. He was accompanied by Stony Woman, described by Laurie as "his newly acquired and youngest wife," and a nephew. They had one horse between them so they mostly walked the more than two hundred miles to Crowfoot's reserve. They travelled through country he had known since childhood, past old river crossings and former camps, battlefields and buffalo wallows.

Poundmaker's reunion with Crowfoot was surely a joyful event for both men because they hadn't seen each other for many years. But life had been hard on the aging leader of the Blackfoot. He was ill and his children were dying. He no longer had the will or the strength to lead his people.

The two old friends spent five or six weeks together. Then, on July 4, while participating in a Blackfoot sun dance, the famous Cree burst a blood vessel and hemorrhaged to death within minutes.

Poundmaker was buried atop a bluff overlooking the Bow River, at a place the Blackfoot knew as *soyohpoiwko*—ridge under water. The ridge was a crossing, and the Blackfoot had used it for generations. When they signed the treaty in September 1877, they had insisted on meeting Canadian authorities on the flats at the southern terminus of the crossing. And now Poundmaker had departed from here on his journey to the Sand Hills.

In the weeks after his demise, newspapers across the North-West reflected on the character and career of this compelling young man. Laurie and many other editors remained churlish and uncharitable, reflecting, no doubt, the sentiments of many readers. But one editor, Nicholas Flood Davin of the *Regina Leader*, broke with his colleagues. "He will always be remembered in Canadian history as one of the heroes of the insurgent side of the North-West rebellion. A man with a large, generous heart, the nobleness of his nature was written on his lofty and handsome face. He looked a chief, every inch of him. He was a born leader of his people. A great man has fallen and we pay him, with genuine regret and respect, this last tribute—Poor Poundmaker."

He was lamented by Davin, mocked by Laurie, and mourned by his people, who knew they had lost their most impressive leader. But among the aging and out-of-touch Conservative politicians in far-off Ottawa, and the eastern railway tycoons who dreamed of filling the North-West with farmers, there was relief. To them, he was a threat. He was young, handsome and articulate. He could move men with his words. He had the presence and stature to impress both natives and whites. Poundmaker was the man to succeed Big Bear as the most powerful voice for his people. He could have kept the fires of discontent and drums of defiance burning.

Unrest among native people was the last thing the Canadian government needed in the late 1880s. The buffalo were gone, the railway was finished and the Dominion government was anxious to fill the territory with settlers. But how many would come if the government could not control the Indians? Who would believe the government brochures and marketing if the newspapers of eastern Canada and even Europe were telling a different story about the Canadian North-West, a story of cantankerous and unhappy Indians? How long could the CPR survive without hordes of homesteaders on its trains? How many corporate fortunes and political reputations were riding on the government's grand gamble in the North-West?

Far too many to contemplate failure. The unrest had to be suppressed and the leaders, those who were established and those who were emerging, had to be crushed. So it made no difference how Poundmaker had acted in the spring of 1885. It made no difference whether the evidence against him was shaky or the witnesses confused. It made no difference that he had saved many lives. He was declared disloyal. He was branded a rebel. He was charged, put on trial, convicted and imprisoned. And prison did the government's dirty work: it destroyed his health and broke his spirit. It robbed the Cree people of their finest leader, in the hour of their greatest need.

Saskatchewan Archives Board R-A8812

B*ig Bear*
Died
January 17, 1888

BIG BEAR SAT WITH A
frayed Hudson's Bay Co. blanket draped over his stooped and
slender shoulders. His hands were concealed under the
woollen folds, but his feet were showing. He was barefoot and
shackled. He looked withered, withdrawn. His eyes and mouth
were thin lines in a face heavy with melancholy. Four white
men—a smartly attired mounted police sergeant in a pillbox
cap and three civilian associates—stood behind him. The
sergeant's left hand rested on the revolver at his hip and two of
his men clasped the barrels of the rifles that stood at their
sides. All four stared straight ahead with pride and certainty.
The notorious Big Bear, the man who had dominated the front

pages of the largest newspapers in the Dominion for the entire month of June 1885, was finally in custody. This was a moment worthy of a photograph.

Big Bear's Crees had led three columns of Canadian soldiers under the command of General Middleton and a contingent of mounted police under Commissioner Acheson G. Irvine on a wild chase that began at the end of May, following the skirmish at Frenchman's Butte, and ended July 4 when the old man, his youngest son and one of his councillors surrendered near Fort Carlton. Each new twist, each fresh turn in the pursuit of Big Bear was worth a blistering headline. "General Middleton Still in Chase of Big Bear," said the *Toronto Globe* of June 11, adding on the next line: "THROUGH AN UNKNOWN COUNTRY." The Cree Chief was said to be leading his followers and the pursuing Canadian troops through "unsurveyed and densely wooded" lands. A few days later, the headline read: "General Middleton Comes to an Impassable Muskeg. BIG BEAR GETS ACROSS." The commander of Canada's citizen soldiers was stalled seventy miles northeast of Fort Pitt by an expanse of muskeg four miles wide that would not support the weight of his wagons and equipment.

Below the headlines were the stories of the havoc and mayhem wrought by Big Bear's warriors. An early dispatch told of the arrival of the Winnipeg Light Infantry at the Frog Lake settlement, on the Queen's birthday, no less. It was written by a correspondent for the *Globe* who told of peering into the cellar of the parsonage, "guided there by the terrible stench," and being greeted by "one of the most awful sights I ever witnessed." He saw the bodies of Fathers Fafard and Marchand, and two others he couldn't recognize, piled in a corner. The feet and hands of some of the men were missing. Their bellies had been slit open, their hearts ripped out, and their faces charred beyond recognition.

Two days later, the *Globe* carried an account of the skirmish at Loon Lake between Big Bear's men and Inspector Sam Steele of the North-West Mounted Police. Steele was said to have raised a white flag and sent an Anglican clergyman forward to demand Big Bear's surrender. "Never," he reportedly responded. "I will fight to the last." With that, firing "recommenced and was kept up hotly for two hours."

On June 13, the *Globe* told its readers that "Col Irvine and 150 men left Prince Albert yesterday, via Carlton, for Green Lake to intercept some of Big Bear's band." And a few days later, the headline read: "Col. Otter Gets a Glimpse of Some Indians. SUPPOSED TO BE BIG BEAR'S." The accompanying story reported that the colonel's scouts had found a two-day-old camp where the renegade Cree may have rested briefly. By this time, Middleton had given up the chase and returned to Fort Pitt. But Otter, Irvine and General Strange were still pursuing their quarry, and this led to one overly optimistic report headlined: "BIG BEAR APPARENTLY CORRALLED." The trail quickly went cold, however, and the *Globe* headed its next report, on June 20: "NO SIGNS OF BIG BEAR."

Forty-eight hours later, the unfolding story took a dramatic turn. Defence Minister Adolphe Caron announced the latest development from the floor of the House of Commons. "I desire to communicate to the House news I have received from General Middleton," Caron told his Conservative colleagues and Liberal opponents. "The McLean family and two others, who were prisoners, are now free and were expected at Fort Pitt at nine o'clock this morning." At that, cheering erupted on both sides of the house.

The white prisoners eagerly provided waiting journalists with first-hand accounts of the atrocities at Frog Lake, the looting of Fort Pitt and their excruciating trek through the bush. "BIG BEAR'S CAPTIVES," the *Globe* trumpeted on June 23, "Terrible experiences of Mrs. Delaney and Mrs. Gowanlock."

The *Globe* devoted nearly three full columns to the story of the two young widows who had lost their husbands at Frog Lake. Mrs. Delaney declared that John Pritchard, who had served as the interpreter there, and several others mixed-blood prisoners had saved their lives. "I wish to state that I believe both Mrs. Gowanlock and I owe our escape from terrible treatment to John Pritchard and the other friendly breeds, prisoners like ourselves," she said. "Big Bear's treatment of us would have been cruel in the extreme but Pritchard spared us from the agony and torture of forced marches through sloughs, bush and rough land."

But Mrs. Gowanlock suggested that Big Bear was not as monstrous as Mrs. Delaney and others had portrayed him. "For two months, we travelled on, going long and short distances by daylight according to the instructions of Big Bear," Mrs. Gowanlock said. "I frequently saw him. He would come into our tent and talk to us, with Pritchard translating. Big Bear professed sorrow, telling us it was all the fault of his young braves, whom he could not control. I did not believe him altogether, although he had very little control over his band. Wandering Spirit seemed to have more influence with the tribe than anyone."

The big Toronto daily followed up two days later, on June 25, with a long story from another of the former prisoners, the wife of Reverend Charles Quinney, an Anglican minister stationed in the Fort Pitt area. Mrs. Quinney told how local Indians had forced her and her husband from their home on the reserve at Onion Lake the day after the Frog Lake massacre and taken them to Pitt for protection from Big Bear's followers. The Quinneys spent eleven days there, until the mounted police evacuated the fort. At that point, they and four other couples, along with seventeen children, became prisoners of the Crees.

"The first night in Big Bear's camp was a terrible one," Mrs. Quinney said. "The night was intensely cold and it was pitiable to see the suffering of us all. We had no covering at all and while the Indians were revelling in the stores and supplies in the fort, we were suffering intensely from the rough weather. The children suffered fearfully and it was heartrending to see them and feel we could do nothing."

Three days later, they went through the settlement at Onion Lake while travelling to a new camp. Homes had been burned to the ground and marble grave stones knocked over and destroyed by Big Bear's band, she said. Throughout the ordeal, Mrs. Quinney added, Cree braves continually threatened to kill them, and the men slept with guns at hand to protect their families. The ordeal finally ended when they walked into General Strange's camp and were greeted by "three hearty British cheers."

The *Toronto Daily Mail* had followed the Big Bear saga with the same vigour as the *Globe* but had been beaten to the story of the prisoners by its crosstown rival. The *Mail* finally prevailed with a long, emotional account of the rescue of twenty-eight hostages, including the McLean family, written by a correspondent who was travelling with a contingent of troops led by Major Samuel Bedson, later to become warden of Stony Mountain. The Canadians were patrolling the south shore of Loon Lake one day in late June when a hatless and coatless man emerged from the bush, with his arms extended, and shouted, "God bless you, Sam. God bless you."

He then led the soldiers to a nearby clearing where he and his fellow prisoners, including William McLean, the Hudson's Bay factor at Fort Pitt, his wife, Elizabeth, and their nine children, were camped. The troops soon found themselves among "ladies, little toddling youngsters and young and middle aged men, all of whom welcomed our coming with genuine delight." The *Mail* correspondent named each of the prisoners, including the McLean children—Miss Amelia, Miss Eliza, Miss Kitty and their brothers, Sapoomin, Willie, Angus, Duncan, John Rose and baby Ewan, a "fat, chubby little fellow not two years of age." Their mother, Elizabeth McLean, undoubtedly spoke for all the prisoners when she said, "It's all like a horrible dream to me and I can scarcely realize that our troubles are ended. It has been terrible. Thank God, thank God it's all over at last."

The final twist in the story occurred in early July when the newspapers reported that Big Bear had surrendered near Fort Carlton along with his boy Horse Child, and a councillor, Two and Two. The mounted police shipped Big Bear to Prince Albert and then to Regina, where he was detained with several dozen other Metis and natives awaiting trial. At that point, the newspapers and their readers immediately lost interest in Big Bear. A man perceived as a menace had been removed and that was all that mattered.

BIG BEAR'S TRIAL TOOK PLACE on September 11. He faced the same charge—treason felony—as Poundmaker and many others accused of rebellion crimes, and the Crown alleged that he had committed the offence on four occasions: at Frog Lake on April 2, the day of the massacre; at Fort Pitt in mid-April when that Hudson's Bay post was sacked and seized; at Frog Lake on April 21 when he allegedly helped dictate a seditious letter; and at Frenchman's Butte on May 28 when Cree warriors fought the Canadian troops under General Strange. Big Bear chose trial by six-man jury and pleaded not guilty.

Prosecutor D.L. Scott laid out the government's case against him, explaining to the jury that the Crown had only to prove that the defendant intended to make war. "You will see by the evidence given in this case that we go further than is actually necessary," he said. "We show that he not only designed to levy war, but that he actually did it, and that is the best evidence of intention—the fact that he actually did levy war."

Scott called three witnesses, who had been prisoners in Big Bear's camp during the troubles: John Pritchard, the Indian Department interpreter at Frog Lake; James Simpson, the Hudson's Bay clerk at the settlement; and Stanley Simpson, the company clerk at Fort Pitt. The first two could well have passed as defence witnesses since they spoke highly of Big Bear's character and provided no evidence to support the Crown's charges. The third man made one highly inflammatory accusation but his credibility went up in smoke when he was shown to be a liar and a bigot.

The prosecutor opened his case by questioning Pritchard about a meeting on the evening of April 1 at the office of Thomas Quinn, the Frog Lake Indian agent. Quinn had summoned Big Bear and the leading men of his band to discuss the Metis uprising at Batoche and to seek assurances that they would not take up arms. Big Bear spoke first, Pritchard said, avowing that "he was not going to rise, he was going to remain loyal."

The interpreter went on to testify, while being cross-examined by defence lawyer Beverly Robertson, that Big Bear was in the settlement the following morning when the massacre occurred, but took no part in the attacks. He said the aging leader was in the home of James Simpson, having a conversation with the clerk's wife, Catharine, when the first shots were fired. This led Robertson to question Pritchard about Big Bear's ability to rule his followers.

"Who were the leading spirits in the band that took you prisoner?" he asked.

"Big Bear's son."

"What is his name?"

"Imasees."

"Is Big Bear's son a good son to his father?"

"No, I don't think so, because when the father said any-thing the son bucks against it."

"Did he do that through the whole of this trouble?"

"Yes."

"And it was he who took you prisoner?"

"Yes."

"Can you tell me who else were the leaders . . . throughout the whole of this business?"

"Wandering Spirit."

"Any other?"

"Little Poplar."

"Was Big Bear one of the leaders of the band of Indians, did he incite them to wrong?"

"No, I never saw Big Bear incite any Indian."

"You never heard him inciting any wrong?"

"No."

Pritchard was the only witness who testified about a letter purportedly composed by Big Bear, Wandering Spirit and two Metis at Frog Lake on April 21. Here again, the interpreter hardly strengthened the Crown's case. He was present in Big Bear's tepee during the composition of the document in which the authors allegedly invited other Indians and Metis from the district to join them. But since the document had gone miss-ing, Judge Hugh Richardson would not allow questions about its contents.

James Simpson followed Pritchard to the witness box. He

could not say what role, if any, Big Bear had played in the massacre because he was in Fort Pitt on the morning of April 2. He returned that afternoon to the silent and deserted settlement. He went to his home, and finding it ransacked like most of the others, he drove a buckboard out to the Indian camp where he kept a tepee. The Cree men, incuding Big Bear, were seated in a circle amid the lodges when he arrived. About an hour later, he and Big Bear discussed the tragic events at the settlement. "I said to him I am sorry to see what you have done. Well, he says, it is not my doings. I said, now this affair will be in your name, not your young men. It will be all on you, carried on your back. He says it is not my doings, and the young men won't listen, and I am very sorry for what has happened."

Simpson gave no evidence about Big Bear's actions during the seizure of Fort Pitt because his Cree captors allowed him to stay behind at Frog Lake. Nor could he shed much light on the defendant's actions at Frenchman's Butte. He told Scott that Big Bear had been around the camp, several miles from the battlefield, during the fight. When questioned by Robertson, he said he hadn't seen Big Bear until about two o'clock in the afternoon, by which time the old man and several families had fled fifteen to sixteen miles away.

The one thing Simpson spoke of with certainty was Big Bear's character. He had known the chief for forty years. He had camped with him and his people many times while trading with them. "What has been his character during all that time?" Robertson asked.

"Always been a good Indian to the white man," Simpson replied.

"A good friend of the white man?"

"Yes."

"And always respected by the white people as being a good friend?"

"Yes."

"Did you ever hear of his getting into any trouble of any kind with the white man?"

"Never any troubles of his own until this."

Scott's final witness, Stanley Simpson, the Hudson's Bay clerk at Fort Pitt, was in the trading post late in the afternoon on April 15 when some 250 armed and mounted warriors appeared on the crest of a hill two thousand yards away. He testified about many of the events that took place over the next forty-eight hours, when the warriors seized and plundered the post. They killed one mounted police officer, Corporal David Cowan, and seriously wounded his colleague, Constable Clarence Loasby, both of whom had inadvertently ridden into the Indian camp while returning from a scouting expedition. The warriors allowed a contingent of mounted police, under the command of Inspector Francis Dickens, to evacuate the post and leave the district by paddling down the ice-clogged North Saskatchewan in a leaky scow. And they took two dozen prisoners, including the Hudson's Bay factor William McLean, his wife, Elizabeth, and their nine children. Simpson witnessed the whole sequence of events, but had next to nothing to say about Big Bear's role. He testified that he had seen him on the hill above the fort after being taken prisoner. And that was it.

Simpson's most damaging allegation pertained to a statement Big Bear allegedly made to a group of warriors during the thirst dance that was in progress when General Strange and his men arrived at Frenchman's Butte.

"He cut up a piece of tobacco, and he said he wanted his

men to cut the head of the white people off the same as he cut this piece of tobacco. He wanted the head. I suppose it is the officer who was commanding the police at that time."

Robertson immediately rose to his feet and interjected.

"Do you understand Cree?"

"I don't understand it clearly. I understand a good deal more than I can speak."

Scott put the question to him again.

"Then you understand Cree?"

"I understand a good deal of it."

"Then you heard him say this that you have been telling us?'

"Yes."

Scott knew he had hit pay dirt here. So he kept going. And Simpson, having caught everyone's attention, felt emboldened.

"What did he say about the master who was over the soldiers?"

"He said that he wanted them to cut off his head, after they were to capture him, cut his head off."

"And he also said he wanted to cut off the head of all the others?"

"He did not say they were to cut off the heads of the white people, but they were to kill them."

Simpson had unwittingly dug a hole for himself. Big Bear spoke only Cree. Whatever the clerk heard was in that tongue. And he professed to understand it. Robertson picked away at Simpson's story and quickly exposed the weaknesses. He asked Simpson for the words Big Bear had used. The witness was unable to supply them. He looked for context—to whom had the Cree leader been speaking and what had they said in response. Simpson could not say.

Scott then intervened. He suggested testing the clerk's

knowledge of Cree and Robertson readily assented. The lawyers prepared a simple statement—If the captain of the soldiers does not give us tobacco, we will cut off the tops of the trees—and interpreter Peter Hourie put it to the witness in Cree. Simpson understood two words: captain and tobacco. At that, Robertson asked Judge Richardson to strike down Simpson's evidence about Big Bear's statement.

Scott had demonstrated that his own witness was a liar. Robertson subsequently showed, through the evidence of defence witness Henry Halpin, that Simpson was a bigot. Halpin testified that he told Simpson he would be appearing for the defence. "He thought it was strange, very strange, any white man should get on the defence of an Indian," Halpin told the court. "His idea was that the Indians should have been hung."

At the conclusion of the Crown case, Robertson asked Judge Richardson a question: Does your honour think there is a case? The defence lawyer had concluded that the evidence against Big Bear was so feeble that the charges should be dismissed. But Richardson maintained that he did not have the authority to halt the trial and ordered Robertson to proceed with the defence. He began by calling Catharine Simpson, whose husband James had appeared for the Crown. She testified that on the morning of April 2, when the first shots were fired at Frog Lake, Big Bear was having something to eat in her home.

"How did you first know that anything had been done outside?" Robertson asked. "Did you hear shots and that, and what took place then?"

"While Big Bear was eating, I was packing up my little things," she replied. "I heard a shot outside, and I ran out to the door and I saw the man fall, so then I went into my house again."

"And what did Big Bear do?"

"Big Bear got up and went out. And I heard him say, don't do so, stopping it."

Robertson's second witness was William McLean, the Hudson's Bay factor at Fort Pitt. His evidence was noteworthy for its precision. He had spent twenty-three years trading among the Indians, though he had known Big Bear only since "the 29th of last October." He and his family had spent sixty-two days as prisoners in what was nominally Big Bear's camp. During that time, he had seen the old man "almost daily, if not daily."

Robertson's examination was brief. He asked McLean if Big Bear had participated in the looting of Fort Pitt—the answer was no—and whether he had received any of the stolen goods.

"Yes," he replied. "I believe he had—not taken by himself, however. I think he had some tea. I am sure he had some tea given him."

"Do you know where he got it?"

"Given him by Little Poplar," said McLean, who later added that he himself had given Big Bear a couple of blankets from the post because "there was no one in the Indian camp so wretchedly poor looking as him."

Robertson asked how Imasees, Wandering Spirit and Little Poplar had treated Big Bear during the troubles. "With utter contempt," he said.

He asked where Big Bear was during the fight at Frenchman's Butte. In the camp, three and a half to four miles from the battleground, said McLean, adding he didn't believe that the chief had taken any part in the fight.

Henry Halpin, the Hudson's Bay clerk at Cold Lake, thirty-five to forty miles north of Frog Lake, was up next. He took the jury back to March 19 and a brief conversation he had had with Big Bear that day at his camp on the trail between the two lakes. The old Cree was out on his own, hunting in the bush, and Halpin informed him that there was trouble at Batoche, that Riel had stopped the mails.

"I think it is very curious," Big Bear replied, and that was all. He expressed no interest in Riel, or what he was doing. Before departing, Halpin invited Big Bear out to his home. The chief arrived late on March 21 and spent the night. But he never once discussed the Metis leader, Halpin told Robertson. The following evening, Big Bear left for home intending to hunt for moose on the way.

Halpin testified that he was taken prisoner early in April, and saw Big Bear soon afterward at the Cree camp near Frog Lake. He met him again on the way to Fort Pitt "away at the back of the caravan." He also attended most of the councils held while he was a prisoner. Robertson wanted to know what part Big Bear had played at these gatherings, which were forums for discussion, debate and decision-making.

"I don't suppose anybody could think he took any part at all as he never said anything."

"He took no part at all in the councils?"

"No."

"Who were the men that took any leading part in the councils?"

"Wandering Spirit, Big Bear's son, Imasees, and Louison Mongrain and another old chief, and Big Bear sometimes said a word or two. He seldom spoke."

Big Bear spoke out at least once during that spring of turmoil and bloodshed, and it made a powerful impression on one of the white prisoners, William Cameron, a twenty-four-year-old native of Trenton, Ontario. Cameron had ventured west in July 1881, lured by the promise of freedom and adventure. He worked at various jobs, landing at Frog Lake as a clerk in the

Hudson's Bay store there a short time before the trouble started. He was an astute observer of men, a talented writer, and later wrote a captivating book about his experiences entitled *Blood Red the Sun*.

Cameron often heard the speeches of his captors as they sat in the council circle, but he usually paid no attention to what they were saying. "It is customary," he testified, "for different warriors and headmen to proclaim what they have done, and their big deeds, and I never cared to hear what any of these fellows said because I knew they were red-handed murderers, a great many of them."

One afternoon, while lounging in a tepee, Cameron heard a different voice at the council. This time, the young white prisoner listened. "I went up and laid down in the grass at a short distance from where Wandering Spirit and two more of Big Bear's councillors and some of the other men were sitting in a half circle. I was lying opposite on the grass, and Big Bear was standing in the centre and a lot of young men were there too, and he was making a speech."

Cameron admitted that his understanding of Cree was not perfect. "The words, as near as I can tell that he used, were these. He said: Long ago I used to be recognized by all of you Indians as a chief, and he says there was not a bigger chief among you than I was, and all these southern Indians knew it, the Piegans and Sarcees, and the Sioux and the Blackfeet, and all the rest of those southern Indians knew it, and he says when I said a thing at that time there was some attention paid to it, and it was acted upon. But, he said, now I say one thing and you do another."

Cameron's testimony concluded the defence. Robertson then began his address to the jury. He appealed to the six white, male jurors "to mete out to this poor old man, tottering now almost on the brink of the grave, fair British justice, and the same clemency, and the same merciful consideration of his conduct that you would mete out to any white man."

He cited the evidence of Big Bear's character. Without Simpson's dubious evidence, Robertson said, "you have one unbroken stream of testimony that that old man has been a good Indian."

He next asked the jurors to judge the case solely on the basis of the evidence, urging them to set aside any preconceived notions they may have had about Big Bear based on the inflammatory newspaper coverage. "You must know, as I know, the outrageous reports we heard about this old man, Big Bear, all the sins of his tribe, and a great many sins they never committed, were laid upon his shoulders, in the public print. We now know that many of those things are now publicly known to be falsehoods."

Then he walked the jurors through the charges cited in the indictment and argued that the evidence showed Big Bear neither intended to make war, nor did he levy war. At Frog Lake, he had warned Catharine Simpson to pack some belongings and leave for a place of safety. And when he heard shots fired, he ran down the road screaming, Stop, stop. But he had no power to prevent the shootings. Wandering Spirit, Little Poplar, his son Imasees and the Metis Louison Mongrain were in charge. As for Big Bear, he was "nothing more than a feather in the blast before their influence."

During the march to Fort Pitt, he had walked at the back of the caravan. During the negotiated surrender of the fort, he had used his scant influence to ensure that the police and civilians got out alive and unharmed. During the pillaging of the Hudson's Bay store, he had remained at the camp. His only sin was to accept some tea from Little Poplar. "Well, gentlemen, it may be that a poor unsophisticated Indian, an old man hungry and cold, probably ought to have refused to take a cup of tea because it had been stolen from the Hudson's Bay Co., but I don't think my learned friend will contend or ask you to say that he was guilty of a desire to levy war against the Queen because he accepted a cup of tea that another man had stolen."

The final charge in the indictment accused him of making war during the fight at Frenchman's Butte. Yet, he had remained four to five miles back of the battleground and had taken no part in the skirmish. All the evidence showed, Robertson said in conclusion, that "the old man was helpless in his own band, that what little influence he had, he used to save the lives of the whites and keep these people quiet, that he avoided every act of wrongdoing, that he tried to prevent others from committing those acts, and I think you will say in your verdict, that throughout they show that he was a loyal and innocent man."

Scott's argument for the Crown was a slick piece of legerdemain. As he stood before the jury, he faced a daunting problem. He had called three witnesses. The first two had provided no evidence that Big Bear ever took up arms against the Queen. Nor was there anything in their testimony to suggest that he had intended to make war. On the contrary, they portrayed him as a man of good character. Finally, there was Stanley Simpson, who accused Big Bear of inciting his followers to violence but was proven to be a liar and a bigot. Despite the holes in his case, Scott soldiered on.

He started with the Frog Lake massacre, the first charge in the indictment. Scott told the jurors they should judge Big Bear not on what he did, but what he ought to have done. He reminded them of the meeting between Thomas Quinn, Big Bear and the leading men of his band, Imasees, Wandering

Spirit and several others, the evening prior to the killings. "Now, gentlemen," the prosecutor began, "you have heard... that on the 1st of April the prisoner came in with his son and spoke to the Indian agent at that part of the country, and said he heard that there was trouble but that he was going to remain loyal.

"Imasees apparently assented to the statement made by Big Bear, yet we find that on the 2nd April, although, perhaps, Big Bear did not assist in killing, and perhaps wanted to prevent it, his son Imasees was one of the worst in the crowd. If Imasees on the 1st April had any intentions of committing those depradations, Big Bear, the prisoner, would have known it, and it would have been his duty at that time, if he had remained a loyal citizen, as my learned friend tries to make him out to be, he would have given warning the night before to these men, in order that they might be prepared for some defence."

The further Scott went, the more preposterous his arguments became. His learned friend had shown that Big Bear had used his limited influence to save the lives of the prisoners. But the prosecutor pointed out that all those prisoners were associated with the Hudson's Bay Co. and concluded that Big Bear's friendliness "was not extended to the government." Clearly, he had not taken part in the pillaging of Fort Pitt. No matter. "As long as we can show that he was associated with those who did that, and after the act was done he continued to associate with them, and during that time they committed fresh acts which come within the nature of the charges contained in the indictment against the prisoner—then he must be held responsible for those acts to that extent."

Scott admitted that perhaps his witness, Stanley Simpson, was biased against Indians. "But is that any reason why he should not come in that box and tell truthfully all he knew about the circumstances during the time he was imprisoned with them?"

Finally, there was Frenchman's Butte. Of course Big Bear had been nowhere near the battlefield, Scott said. His role in such a situation was to advise his young men, and "having been with them at that time in the camp shows conclusively that he was counselling." Scott repeated that point, saying, "He was there always giving his opinion as far as we have heard, he was always giving his advice." Robertson rose to object, insisting, "That was not what the witnesses said," and Scott retreated a little, admitting, "It is possible that I may have overstretched the thing a little." But he did not withdraw the point.

Scott had begun the trial with a roar, promising, in his opening address to the jury, to show that Big Bear was guilty and then some. But the prosecutor ended limply, endeavouring to prove only that Big Bear was connected with a band that had committed atrocities and levied war, and that he was acting with his band throughout the troubles.

The weak Crown case made no difference to the jurors. They deliberated for fifteen minutes before returning with a verdict of guilty, their decision softened a little by a recommendation of mercy. Judge Richardson dismissed the jury. He would not pass sentence that night.

Two weeks later, on September 25, Big Bear returned to court to learn his fate. Judge Richardson asked him if he had anything to say before being sentenced. There was quite a crowd in the public gallery, including a few reporters who would file brief accounts of the day's proceedings. The youthful trader William Cameron, who had testified for Big Bear, was there too.

"The old man drew himself up with that imperious air that proclaimed him a leader and fitted him so well," Cameron recalled in *Blood Red the Sun*, "the nostrils extended, the broad, deep chest thrown out, the strong jaw looked aggressively prominent, the mouth was a straight line. He gave his head the little characteristic toss that always preceded his speeches."

Only then did he begin to speak. "I think I should have something to say about the occurrences which brought me here in chains. I knew little of the killings at Frog Lake beyond hearing the shots fired. When any wrong was brewing, I did my best to stop it in the beginning. The turbulent ones of the band got beyond my control and shed the blood of those I would have protected. I was away from Frog Lake a part of the winter, hunting and fishing, and the rebellion had commenced before I got back.

"When the white men were few in the country I gave them the hand of brotherhood. I am sorry so few are here who can witness to my friendly acts. Can anyone stand out and say that I ordered the death of a priest or an agent? You think I encouraged my people to take part in the trouble. I did not. I advised them against it. I felt sorry when they killed those men at Frog Lake, but the truth is when news of the fight at Duck Lake reached us my band ignored my authority and despised me because I did not side with the half-breeds. I did not so much as take a white man's horse. I always believed that by being the friend of the white man, I and my people would be helped by those of them who had wealth. I always thought it paid to do all the good I could. Now my heart is on the ground.

"I look around me in this room and see it crowded with handsome faces—faces far handsomer than my own," a remark that brought a round of laughter from those present. "I have ruled my country for a long time. Now I am in chains and will be sent to prison, but I have no doubt the handsome faces I admire about me will be competent to govern the land.

"At present, I am dead to my people. Many of my band are hiding in the woods, paralyzed with terror. Cannot this court send them a pardon? My own children, perhaps they are starving and outcast too, afraid to appear in the light of day. If the government does not come to them with help before winter sets in, my band will surely perish. But I have too much confidence in the Great Grandmother to fear that starvation will be allowed to overtake my people. The time will come when the Indians of the North-West will be of much service to the Great-Grandmother. I plead again to you, the chiefs of the white man's laws, for pity and help to the outcasts of my band.

"I have only a few more words to say. Sometimes in the past I have spoken stiffly to the Indian agents, but when I did it was only in order to obtain my rights. The North-West belonged to me, but I will perhaps not live to see it again. I ask the court to publish my speech and to scatter it among the white people. It is my defence. I am old and ugly, but I have tried to do good. Pity the children of my tribe. Pity the old and helpless of my people. I speak with a single tongue; and because Big Bear has always been the friend of the white man, send out and pardon and give them help.

"*How. Aquisanee*—I have spoken."

A heavy silence hovered over the courtroom for a few moments. Then Judge Richardson spoke. "Big Bear," he said, "you have been found guilty by an impartial jury. You cannot be excused from all responsibility for the misdoings of your band. The sentence of the court is that you be imprisoned in the penitentiary at Stony Mountain for three years."

Big Bear's sentencing lasted only a few minutes. Afterward, mounted police officers whisked him back to jail, then filled the docket with seventeen other native prisoners awaiting sentencing. Most were members of Big Bear's band and their trials had been a travesty. On September 16, nine men charged with treason felony were put on trial at the same time. The defendants were assigned numbers since the Canadian lawyers could not keep their names straight. Nevertheless, the lawyers asked witnesses questions about the wrong defendants and witnesses testified about the wrong men. Robertson, assigned the job of defending them, called no witnesses and passed on a final address. All nine were convicted, and a day later another five men went through the same charade. Again, all were convicted.

At one point, an exasperated Robertson told the court, "Since the conviction of Big Bear, I have felt that it is almost a hopeless task to obtain from a jury in Regina a fair consideration of the case of an Indian. It has seemed to me only necessary to say in this town to a jury, there is an Indian, and we will put him in the dock to convict him."

The sentencing of Big Bear and the seventeen other men brought to an end the Regina Indian trials. But legal proceedings against twenty-five natives being held in Battleford were just beginning. Judge Charles Rouleau, who had fled Battleford in late March at the outset of the troubles and returned to find that his large, comfortable home had been torched, presided over the trials. Most of them lasted only a few minutes. The Indians appeared without defence lawyers and pleaded guilty.

Wandering Spirit, the instigator of the Frog Lake massacre, appeared first on September 22. Big Bear's war chief had attempted suicide by stabbing himself in the chest shortly before his arrest at Fort Pitt in July. He mistakenly hoped that if he took his own life the Canadian authorities might spare his accomplices. Wandering Spirit spent three months in custody at Fort Battleford and had recovered by the time he appeared before Judge Rouleau. He pleaded guilty to the murder of Thomas Quinn. Two days later, he was back to be sentenced.

Judge Rouleau lectured him on the gravity of his crime, then imposed the penalty. "The sentence of the court is that you, Wandering Spirit, be taken back to jail till Friday the 27th day of November, and then be taken to the scaffold and there be hanged by the neck until you are dead; and may God have mercy on your soul."

Before the day was over, Judge Rouleau had sentenced seven others. Four Sky Thunder got fourteen years for burning the Catholic Church at Frog Lake. Two men, Toussaint Calling Bull and Little Wolf, each got ten years' hard labour for arson. Another two, The Idol and Old Man, were convicted of horse theft and sentenced to six-year terms. God's Otter got four years for the same offence because his accuser, the Reverend Charles Quinney, spoke well of him. And a man named Little Runner also received four years for stealing a horse.

The Battleford trials ended October 21. All told, eleven men received death sentences and one got twenty years for manslaughter. A few days before the executions were to take place on November 27, the government granted reprieves to three prisoners and commuted their sentences to life imprisonment. But there would be no mercy for the others: Wandering Spirit; five of his warriors convicted in the Frog Lake killings; and the two Stoneys, Itka, who had killed farm instructor James Payne, and Man Without Blood, who had murdered rancher Barney Tremont.

As the appointed date drew near, the condemned men became fearful and despondent. They spent their last days seated on the floor of the guardhouse at Fort Battleford, blankets draped over their shoulders, balls and chains shackled to their ankles. They could hear the hammers and saws of the workmen building the giant gallows—twenty feet long, eight feet wide and ten feet high—in the northwest corner of the barracks yard. Some of the prisoners succumbed to the entreaties of the Oblate priests, Fathers Bigonesse and Cochin, and converted to Christianity.

On the afternoon of November 26, Superintendent Leif Crozier, the mounted police commander at Battleford, allowed P.G. Laurie and William Cameron to interview the prisoners. They were naturally interested in Wandering Spirit, the once flamboyant and fearsome war chief who now lay wasted and emaciated. He remained silent a long time, but finally spoke.

"Four years ago we were camped on the Missouri River in the Long Knives' land," he said. "Big Bear was there, Imasees, Four Sky Thunder and other chiefs of the band. Riel was there, trading whisky to the Indians. He gave us liquor and said he would make war on this country. He asked us to join him in wiping out the Canadians. The government had treated him badly. He would demand much money from them. If they would not give, he would spill blood, plenty of Canadian blood.

"Last fall, Riel sent word to us that when the leaves came out the half-breeds would rise and kill all the whites. The Long Knives would come. They would buy the land, pay the Indians plenty of money for it, and afterwards trade too, and help rid the country of Canadians. At the time of the massacre, André Nault, a half-breed, told me he had in his pocket a letter from his cousin, Riel, telling him to stay with Big Bear's band and he would be safe. We would never be tried for what we did. 'Anyway,' he said, 'the Canadians can't beat us.'

"Imasees told me at a dance one night before the outbreak that he depended on me to do this thing. I fought against it. I wished last winter to leave the band and go to Duck Lake. My relatives lived there. Imasees nor the others would let me go. Kapwatamut, the Indian agent [Thomas Quinn] would give me no provisions. It seemed it was to be. I was singled out to do it."

Wandering Spirit asked Cameron to tell his Cree brethren not to rise again. He wanted the young white trader to tell his daughter that he had become Christian. He thanked the mounted police for their kindnesses toward him. And he told Cameron there was only one thing bothering him: the thought of dying and having to make the long journey to the Sand Hills with a ball and chain attached to one ankle. When he learned that the shackle would be removed, he was immensely relieved.

"Then I will die satisfied," Wandering Spirit said. "I may not be able in the morning, so now I say again to you all—Goodbye. *How. Aquisanee.*"

The executions were set to take place at 8 A.M., and the condemned men were up early. Outside, it was cold and a sharp wind blew. The prisoners ate their last meal. They said their goodbyes. And they bowed their heads. Mounted police officers cut their hair, removed the shackles and fitted each man with a black veil. Then the men began to sing. Death chants filled the air as they prepared to march across the square from the guardhouse to the gallows.

Miserable Man, who had wounded Charles Gouin, the carpenter at Frog Lake, stood at the head of the line. Bad Arrow, who had finished off Gouin, was next, followed by Round the Sky, who had fatally wounded Father Fafard. Wandering Spirit was fourth. Iron Body, who had murdered the trader George Dill, went fifth, and his co-accused, Little Bear, who maintained his innocence till the end, stood behind him. Itka and Man Without Blood completed the column.

One hundred and fifty mounted police stood at attention around three sides of the square. Dozens of Cree and Stoney people squatted on the grass below the gallows where eight nooses swayed in the wind. Natives were no longer welcome around Battleford. But this was a special occasion. They had been summoned from the reserves around the town to witness the deaths of their brethren.

The square was utterly silent as the prisoners marched out of the guardhouse, each with a mounted police officer to the right and left. One by one, they mounted the steps and took their places. The two priests, Fathers Cochin and Bigonesse, an interpreter and deputy sheriff A.P. Forget stood behind them as the executioner Robert Hodson bound their hands and feet. The short, chubby Hodson, a former cook at Fort Pitt, had been a prisoner of Wandering Spirit's that spring and an object of ridicule. Now, he would be sending his tormentors to their deaths.

Forget read the death warrants then asked the condemned men if they had any last words. Most of them expressed remorse. But Itka was filled with fire and anger. Resist the white man, he told the Cree and Stoney witnesses seated below him. Reject his ways. Make no peace with him. Remember this day, and remain defiant for the rest of your days. Itka began his death chant, and the others joined him.

Hodson worked quickly as the condemned men sang. He pulled the veils over each man's head. He tightened each noose. He drew the bolt. "There was a sharp sound of grating iron, the trap dropped and eight bodies shot through it," Cameron later wrote. "A sickening click of dislocated necks, and they hung dangling and gyrating slowly. A few convulsive shudders and all was over.

"The bodies were dropped into rough wooden boxes and buried in a common grave on the hillside below the police barracks overlooking the broad, wild valley of the Saskatchewan. We certified to the death of the murderers in fulfillment of the sentences passed upon them, and thus closed the last tragic event in the occurrences of the year 1885."

The hangings brought to a close a much larger conflict: the Canadian government's long fight to assert its control over the North-West, the vast territory it had acquired from the Hudson's Bay Co. in the winter of 1869–70. As Sir John A. Macdonald put it in a letter to the Indian Commissioner Edgar Dewdney: "The executions... ought to convince the Red Man that the White Man now governs."

Many years earlier, Big Bear had foreseen the day when the white man would rule. He was an adolescent then, and he had a *niwitcewahakan*, a mentor who was teaching him to hunt buffalo and make war, two skills a boy had to acquire to succeed as a man among the plains Indians. His people were free and sovereign. Yet he had had a vague but disturbing vision of hordes of white men arriving in his country and pushing the Indians out. This and much more had happened in the intervening years. The Blackfoot and the Plains Cree had been subdued and confined. His band had been obliterated. His war chief and some who had listened to him had been hanged. Imasees and his small band of followers had fled to Montana where they would wander as outcasts, homeless and friendless, begging and stealing to survive until desperation drove them home a few years later. And Big Bear had become Convict Number 103 at Stony Mountain Penitentiary.

He served his time quietly, working briefly in the prison carpentry shop before transferring outside to tend the farm animals kept at the institution. He liked the fresh air but was not fond of pigs and chickens. They were noisy and smelled unpleasant. Whenever he could, Big Bear watched the animals in the warden's little menagerie. Bedson kept four buffalo and two bears. The sight of listless buffalo brought him no joy, but the bears made his adrenalin flow. He could see the fire and tenacity in these creatures as they paced in their enclosures.

The bear had been his spirit helper in the old Indian world. It gave him power and protected him from his enemies. Now, he saw in these captive bears something he admired. He saw that they could be caged but never tamed.

By the summer of 1886, Big Bear wanted out. The authorities had pardoned other inmates convicted of rebellion offences, men younger than himself and most serving longer sentences. If they were being released, why not him? He was no threat to white society, and never had been, according to most of the witnesses at his trial. Besides, he was an old man. He pleaded with his jailers to let him go, but the federal cabinet refused to grant him parole.

By year end, Big Bear's health was declining. Dr. W.R. Sutherland examined him and concluded that he was seriously ill. "Although not asked to report on the condition of Convict No. 103, I desire to say that he is very sick and rapidly getting worse," the physician wrote in a memo to the warden. "He is weak and shows signs of great dibility by fainting spells which are growing more frequent. Undoubtedly his further confinement here will aggravate this condition and possibly lead to a fatal termination. I would therefore urge most strongly that he be released as soon as possible."

Prison authorities and the federal cabinet did not want native inmates, especially prominent figures like Big Bear, dying in custody. Indian Department officials prepared a petition and had two loyal chiefs from the Prince Albert area—Big Child and Star Blanket—adopt it as their own in order to protect the government from criticism. "Although we have no sympathy with the heinous crimes laid to his charge," the petition stated, "we humbly submit that it would be very gratifying to the Cree nation if her Majesty's Government would extend to this criminal the clemency shewn from time to time to other prisoners, and grant his pardon for the unexpired term of his sentence."

With this in front of them, Sir John A. Macdonald and his cabinet approved the release of Big Bear, effective January 27, 1887. The old chief left Stony Mountain a week later, when he was well enough to walk, and spent nearly a month travelling to Battleford by train and freight wagon. He had no reserve and no home, but decided to go to the Little Pine reserve, in the valley of the Battle River, about forty miles west of Battleford. His daughter, Earth Woman, was living there and so was his wife, although she had taken up with another man.

Big Bear hardly spoke when a friend of many years, chief Thunderchild, came to visit one day. "You must wonder why I don't speak," he said at last. "My heart is broken. All I can think of are my past deeds and the misfortunes which have happened to me. I have had a hard time. My sons have gone to the States. I am alone.

"The jail was so different from the old times. I did the dirtiest work. One night I was put in a bad place, a dungeon; it was dark and I felt something, a snake perhaps. I did not sleep at all that night. I hated it there, but I would not kill myself for I am not a coward. Now I will not last long. I am broken down."

Big Bear lived to see another cycle of the seasons. He saw the grass grow and heard the rivers run. He saw the prairie summer arrive with the suddenness of a hawk swooping down on its prey. He saw autumn settle with the softness of a sigh, and he felt winter land with a frosty thud. There were, after all, some things the white man couldn't change.

Big Bear had always lived at the centre of his community. He had been the son of a chief and a leader of war parties. A skilled hunter and a good provider. A sponsor of sun dances and finally a chief himself. Now he wanted nothing to do with the world. He took no part in the affairs of his people. And who could blame him? He had been the greatest Indian activist of his time, a leader who wanted a homeland rather than a bunch of scrawny reserves.

But his final years were filled with heartbreak and tragedy. He had been spurned by his son Imasees, rejected by his followers, shafted by a Canadian court and abandoned by his wife. He went to his grave a lonely man and a convicted felon. Big Bear died peacefully January 17, 1888, amid the wind, the whiteness and the savagery of a western winter storm. Sometime that day, he lay down in Earth Woman's flimsy shanty and curled up beneath a blanket. He fell into a deep sleep, and slipped away without a twitch or a sound.

National Archives of Canada c1873

National Archives of Canada PA45666

I sapo-Muxika

Crowfoot
Died April 25, 1890

ONE EVENING IN EARLY
September 1881, a few weeks after the Blackfoot had settled on
their reserve, Crowfoot stood on the south bank of the Bow
River and watched as a cavalcade arrived from the north. It was
an impressive spectacle and hundreds of his fellow Blackfoot
stood with him. Fifty mounted police officers in scarlet tunics
followed the bumpy and rutted trail that descended sharply
some 250 feet from the prairie to the flat valley bottom.
Behind them came the wagons—twenty-seven in all—and then
the scouts, a Metis who called himself Johnny Saskatchewan
and the Cree chief Poundmaker. It was nearly midnight before
the visitors had pitched their tents and made camp opposite the

huge Indian village of hundreds of lodges and twenty-five hundred people. And it was some time after that before quiet settled over the valley and both sides rested for the big day ahead—the day the Blackfoot would meet the governor-general of Canada.

Crowfoot and his fellow chiefs had been informed well in advance that they would be receiving this distinguished visitor. Officials with the Indian Department had advised them that the son-in-law of the Great Mother, Queen Victoria, was on a tour of the North-West and would visit them as he made his way from Battleford to Calgary. He was an important man, they were told, with a title, the Marquis of Lorne, but Crowfoot's people called him their brother-in-law since they saw themselves as children of the Great Mother.

The Blackfoot were up early the next morning for their council with the governor-general and they forded the river at *soyohpoiwko*, the ridge under water. W.H. Williams, the *Toronto Globe* correspondent who was covering the vice-regal tour, watched in amazement for almost an hour as hundreds of Indians navigated the chilly waters on horseback, sometimes two or three per animal. At the deepest part of the river, only the heads of their mounts remained above the surface. The Blackfoot wore glistening brass ornaments and brightly dyed feathers. Most had striped blankets draped over their shoulders, and they greeted Williams warmly as they emerged from the waters.

The council was held beneath bright, blue skies, on a broad, flat stretch of land south of the camp and began with a mock battle, performed by young Blackfoot men, who were mounted and armed with Winchester rifles. They formed opposing lines about two hundred yards apart and charged each other at full gallop, whooping loudly and firing their guns in the air.

Afterward, everyone took their places. Lord Lorne and the Canadians accompanying him, including Indian commissioner Dewdney, sat under a blue and white tent that had been erected as an awning. On either side of this, a dozen or more mounted police stood at attention, their uniforms clean and crisp, their polished buttons, belt buckles and weapons sparkling in the late summer sun. The Blackfoot head men sat in a semi-circle opposite the Canadians. Crowfoot was in the centre, with Old Sun, chief of the northern Blackfoot, on one side and Bull Head, the leading chief of the 450 Sarcees camped in the valley, on the other. The men who had participated in the mock battle sat behind them, and the women and children formed the third row.

Some of the young men performed a dance to complete the ceremonial part of the council, then Crowfoot rose to shake the governor-general's hand and to introduce his wife. He was a striking figure in the eyes of some of the white participants. His clothes were ragged, far worse than those of his followers, yet he was a handsome man with an engaging smile and pride in his bearing. He leaned on a staff, he had his treaty medal pinned to his chest, and in one hand he held a teacup. "He made a telling point concerning the shortness of his rations," according to the *Globe*'s correspondent, "by flourishing a large granite ware teacup and declaring that it could not possibly hold one pound, enough flour to support an Indian for 24 hours. He also complained that a pound of meat, when containing a large piece of bone, was an insufficient supply for a like period of time."

Others who rose to speak were also preoccupied with inadequate rations, but Lord Lorne was unmoved. He had heard such speeches before, and they had all begun to sound the same to him. "Usually, amid much flowery rhetoric, the speech resolves itself into a demand for more favours and is, in short, nothing but an exclamatory beggar's oration," he later wrote.

Lord Lorne had only one response, a line the Blackfoot had heard many times. They must take up agriculture. And Crowfoot assured him that he would heed the advice of the white man. "Hitherto I have been first in fighting," he told the governor-general. "Now I will be first in working."

At the conclusion of the council, Crowfoot offered Lord Lorne one of his last horses as a gift, but the British aristocrat would not accept it. However, he had a gift for the Blackfoot leader—a shotgun he could use for hunting ducks and geese. Before the two parties dispersed, the Blackfoot men held a series of horse races, and Crowfoot had the pleasure of a brief reunion with his old friend and adopted son, Poundmaker, who had helped guide the governor-general and his entourage across the two hundred miles of prairie wilderness that lay between Battleford and Calgary.

All in all, the governor-general's visit had been a colourful and enjoyable occasion. But Crowfoot and the other leaders had hoped the meeting would produce some tangible benefits that would ease the transition to life on the reserve. The twenty-five hundred Blackfoot and Sarcee camped at the Crossing in the fall of 1881 were poorly clothed, poorly housed, frequently hungry and constantly worried about food.

Not surprisingly, relations between them and their new white overseers began poorly and deteriorated quickly. The Indian agent for Treaty Seven, Norman Macleod, was based ninety miles to the south in Fort Macleod, a town named for his brother James, commissioner of the NWMP from 1876 till 1880. Several government employees, including a farm instructor, were stationed at the reserve, along with a few police officers. In addition, there were employees of I.G. Baker &

Co., of Fort Benton, Montana, who had been hired by the government to supply the Blackfoot with food.

Several times during the autumn of 1881, rations were reduced when food supplies became low. On two occasions, the contractors ran out of flour and beef, raising the spectre of starvation. Even when the stocks of food were adequate, the rations barely quelled a person's hunger, which led to discontent and complaints.

As the days became shorter and colder, and winter fell on the prairie, the anger and resentment of the Blackfoot grew. Crowfoot twice led delegations to the farm instructor to plead for more generous rations. He got nowhere, so the warriors resorted to intimidation. They threatened the government employees, and someone fired a gun at the rations house while the instructor was inside distributing food. He fled and reported the incident to his superior at Fort Macleod, who turned to the mounted police for help. The commanding officer, Superintendent Leif Crozier, sent ten men north, under the command of Inspector Francis Dickens, but they were unable to maintain order for long.

On January 2, 1882, a dispute occurred between a secondary chief named Bull Elk and two I.G. Baker employees over the sale of a steer's head. The government employees were allowing the contractors to sell the heads and offal of slaughtered animals, a practice the Blackfoot firmly opposed. They believed they were being forced to buy parts of animals the government had already purchased and felt the contractors were charging exorbitant prices.

On the day in question, Bull Elk paid one of the contractors a dollar for a steer's head but had to wait for his wife to arrive to help him carry it home. In the meantime, a second Baker employee, Charles Daly, sold the same part to another customer. When Bull Elk tried to leave with his purchase, he was accused of stealing and thrown out of the rations house. The enraged chief raced back to his lodge and grabbed his gun. He fired two shots at Daly, who was by then outside the building. One hit a log lying nearby while the other sailed harmlessly overhead.

Within minutes, Dickens arrived with a fellow officer, Sergeant Joseph Howe. They arrested Bull Elk, who was still armed, and began escorting him to the police building. They did not get far. A mob of angry warriors, seven hundred strong according to one estimate and all armed with Winchesters, surrounded the officers. Dickens and Howe tried to push through the crowd. But a scuffle broke out. Dickens was knocked to the ground and Bull Elk slipped away.

At that point, Crowfoot arrived. He denounced the whites for mistreating his people and declared that Bull Elk had done no wrong. He said he would take charge of Bull Elk and turn him over to the authorities when they were prepared to put him on trial. Dickens, seeing he had no choice, agreed. At that, Crowfoot told everyone to go home.

Dickens, meanwhile, sent Sergeant Howe to Fort Macleod for reinforcements. Superintendent Crozier left Macleod as soon as possible with twenty men and rode almost non-stop to the Crossing. They arrived to find that Dickens and his officers had fortified the police building, piling sacks of flour along the walls and cutting small holes in the wallboards so they could fire from inside. When Crozier immediately arrested Bull Elk for a second time, the Blackfoot warriors were enraged. They wanted to attack the police with every weapon and all the firepower they could muster.

Crowfoot was also furious. He had promised to turn over Bull Elk upon request. But Crozier hadn't bothered asking.

The officer had marched into the Blackfoot camp and seized the wanted man. Crowfoot set off, with several hundred warriors behind him, to confront Crozier and demand the release of Bull Elk. Crozier turned him down. "Do you intend to fight?" the Blackfoot chief asked after seeing police guns protruding from the loopholes. "Certainly not," Crozier replied, "unless you commence."

Crowfoot was undoubtedly tempted to unleash the warriors. But he would not let rage get the better of his judgement. He knew the warriors could wipe out the police, although many of them would die or be wounded before the battle was won. Yet their triumph would be short-lived. A victory today could only mean defeat tomorrow. The whites were more numerous than his people. They would want revenge, and they would have it. And even if his people fled, they could not survive on the prairie because the buffalo were gone. Crowfoot again sent the warriors home, and the mounted police took their man to Fort Macleod. Bull Elk was tried before James Macleod, who found that the accused had done nothing wrong in the rations house but was guilty of dangerous use of a firearm. The judge sentenced him to fourteen days in the guardhouse, concluding afterward that "it has been a nasty business."

Crowfoot had once respected and admired the redcoats. They had come into the country and driven away the whisky traders. They had saved his people from ruin, protected them "as the feathers of the bird protect it from the frosts of the winter." Those were the words he had used in the fall of 1877, when the treaty was signed. But those days were long gone. And so was Crowfoot's respect and admiration for the police. Never again would he see them as protectors of his people.

The near disaster on the Blackfoot reserve sent a clear

message to Indian commissioner Dewdney. Changes had to be made, or there was bound to be bloodshed. Dewdney dismissed the farm instructor and replaced him with William Pocklington, a man the Indians knew and trusted. He accepted the resignation of Norman Macleod, the agent in charge of the tribes of Treaty Seven—the Blackfoot, Bloods, Piegans, Sarcees and Stoneys. He replaced Macleod with Cecil Denny, a mounted police officer then stationed at Fort Walsh, and a veteran of the Long March of 1874, the force's epic trek from Fort Dufferin, Manitoba to the foot of the Rocky Mountains.

Crowfoot had met Denny in those days and over the years had come to know him. He was a good man, and Crowfoot welcomed the news of his appointment. By early February, Denny had visited the Crossing. He had met Crowfoot and the other chiefs. Denny listened carefully and acted decisively. He made certain that the food supplies were adequate. He changed the government's arrangement with the contractors, prohibiting the sale of heads and offal. He heeded the wishes of Old Sun, leader of the Northern Blackfoot, and allowed his following of about nine hundred people to establish their own settlement in a valley fourteen miles to the west.

Finally, Denny brought in tools and farm implements, and in the spring had fields ploughed for the Blackfoot, as well as the other Treaty Seven tribes. "It was astonishing to see with what a will they went to work," he later wrote in his annual report to the minister in charge of Indian affairs, Sir John A. Macdonald. "Houses went up thick and fast at the Crossing, Blood and Sarcee Reserves, and really the houses built are most creditable, in many cases the logs are hewn and in nearly all the houses fireplaces are built."

The Indians diligently worked their fields that summer and harvested bountiful crops in the fall of 1882. The Bloods grew

200,000 pounds of potatoes and turnips, along with small amounts of wheat and barley. The Piegans produced more potatoes than they could consume and earned upwards of $1,000 by selling the surplus to settlers. The Blackfoot harvested about 100,000 pounds of potatoes, of which 30,000 pounds were saved for seed and the remainder consumed, allowing Denny to trim their rations.

Denny had much to be pleased with as he wrote his first annual report to the minister. The Blackfoot had spent their treaty money wisely on blankets and clothing. He had no serious crimes to report, nor had there been any problems with liquor. But the new agent saw the world with clear eyes. He knew that the tribes of Treaty Seven had only begun a long journey from the old ways to the new. He had seen poverty and sickness among them. He had seen women clothed in rags fighting for discarded flour sacks that could be turned into dresses. He had seen grieving parents, funereal processions and compact coffins bearing the bodies of children carried off by disease.

Sickness and death were prevalent again the following year. In his annual report for 1883, Denny spoke of a "dangerous fever" that claimed many lives. Sub-agent Pocklington, who spent most of his time on the Blackfoot reserve, noted that in the spring a disease "taking the form of cholera" appeared among the children, and several victims died. The summer brought an outbreak of erysipelas, a contagious disease that left the skin red and swollen in spots, and it claimed the lives of several middle-aged and elderly people. An Anglican cleric named John Tims, who was visiting the reserve at the time, later recalled that "day and night the most hideous cries of lamentation were to be heard as the mourners followed the dead to burial upon the hills or went out at night to visit their resting places."

Crowfoot himself was struck by erysipelas and had a pretty good idea what had made him and many of his people sick. It was the railway. Denny had begun extolling its virtues in the summer of 1882 when surveyors and engineers arrived to chart a route through the northern portion of the Blackfoot reserve. Pocklington repeated the message again in the early months of 1883 to counter the inflammatory reports of several itinerant Metis who passed through the reserve and stirred up the Indians.

In the spring of 1883, a thousand labourers arrived to lay track, and among them were many unsavoury characters. "Gamblers, thieves, bootleggers and bad men generally were to be found in close proximity to the construction camps," Denny later wrote in *The Law Marches West*, his book about the opening of the Canadian frontier. Construction began near the place on the South Saskatchewan the Blackfoot called *saamis*, which took its name from an apparition that had once appeared there to a chief who was on a vision quest. As he gazed at the river from a solitary perch high above it, the chief saw the figure of a male, adorned in the stately, plumed headdress of a medicine man, rising toward the heavens. The railway builders established a community at this place and named it Medicine Hat. By the end of the summer, trains were running from there to the Rocky Mountains, and many Blackfoot were sick.

"Crowfoot told his people that the smoke of the fire wagon was getting down their throats and causing sickness," the Anglican clergyman Tims later recalled. "The Indians became very unsettled and declared that if their chief decided they would tear up the railway and drive all the white people out of the country. So serious did matters become that the interpreter slipped away by night on horseback to notify the mounted police at Calgary more than 50 miles away."

The commanding officer at Calgary immediately sent an inspector and two men to the Crossing. They visited Crowfoot's lodge and explained that the Great Mother had received news of his illness. She had sent them to watch over him and to report back once he had recovered. Fortunately, Crowfoot's condition improved and the crisis passed.

The railway had come into the lives of the Blackfoot with astonishing speed. One summer, the Indian agent was talking about it. The following summer, it was there. And the railway was just one element of the new world rising all around the Blackfoot and their brethren on the other reserves. Ranches, some owned by individuals, others by corporations, now occupied almost two million acres between the Bow River and the U.S. border, and forty thousand cattle grazed on these lands. Towns had sprung to life on the prairie and, with them, newspapers—the *Edmonton Bulletin* in 1881, the *Macleod Gazette* in 1882, and the *Calgary Herald* a year later.

But the newcomers saw no place in their world for the original inhabitants. "The white settler coming into the country to farm or raise cattle cared little what became of the poor Indian," Denny wrote. "If a cow was killed or a horse stolen, the Indians were to blame. Their land was looked upon with covetous eyes and they were regarded as a nuisance and expense. The right of the native red man was not for a moment considered or acknowledged."

Government officials could be just as cold and hard edged, a lesson the Blackfoot soon learned. In late 1883, the Deputy Superintendent-General of Indian Affairs, Lawrence Vankoughnet, visited Fort Macleod while on a tour of the North-West Territories. He met several Treaty Seven chiefs, who had come to Macleod for the occasion, but he was awkward and uncomfortable in their presence. He resisted Denny's entreaties to inspect some of the reserves. Instead, he hastened back to Ottawa and, early in the new year, ordered Indian agents across the country to trim their staffs and reduce expenditures. These measures were deemed necessary because the Canadian economy had gone into recession and government revenues were falling.

For his part, Denny was in charge of five reserves that were home to nearly seven thousand people. His personal staff consisted of a clerk and a driver. Each reserve had a farm instructor, an assistant instructor and a storekeeper who issued rations. In addition, there were usually a few lesser officials employed at the reserves. Vankoughnet ordered Denny to dismiss his clerk, who had only recently completed a long journey to take up his position. The assistant instructors and some of the storekeepers were to be let go as well. To ensure that the government's budgetary objectives were met, Vankoughnet also ordered a reduction in the rations.

Denny would have nothing to do with these austerity measures. He wrote the deputy superintendent a letter of resignation, asking to be relieved of his duties effective March 1, 1884. He addressed Vankoughnet in polite, professional language. But privately, he viewed the directives as disastrous. "The short-sightedness and absurdity of the order is . . . evidence of a lamentable ignorance of western Indian reservations and conditions," he later wrote.

The government's austerity measures led to two violent confrontations between Indians and police, the first in February 1884 on a Cree-Saulteaux reserve at Crooked Lake, about a hundred miles east of Regina, and the second in June while two thousand Cree were camped at Poundmaker's reserve for a sun dance. Another potentially explosive showdown occurred in the spring of that year on the Blackfoot reserve—this one

connected to Louis Riel and the discontent among the Metis—
and Crowfoot was at the centre of it.

The Blackfoot leader and his people did not go looking for
a fight. In fact, the Indian agent reports for 1884 indicate that
they built fences, repaired existing ones, seeded their crops and
generally worked with as much energy and enthusiasm as they
had in previous years. The trouble began when a lone Metis
named Bear's Head rode north from the Judith River basin in
Montana. He had been sent by Riel, and he had a message for
chief Crowfoot. Riel was returning to Canada to lead his
people after nearly a decade and a half in exile south of the line.
They were going to rise up against their new Canadian masters. Riel wanted the Indians to join them. Together, they
would drive out the whites and take back the country that was
rightfully theirs.

Bear's Head made a poor emissary. He revealed the purpose
of his mission, and much more, to the first Blackfoot he met, a
group of hunters searching for game at least a day's ride west
of their reserve. Bear's Head told these men that they were
entitled to kill settlers' cattle and that the country belonged to
them. A mounted police scout was among the hunters, and he
promptly reported Bear's Head, who was arrested on a charge
of vagrancy and taken to Calgary for trial. He was jailed for a
month and told to keep the peace or he would be dealt with
severely the next time.

Upon being released, the Metis agitator headed straight for
Blackfoot Crossing, where Crowfoot welcomed him and made
him a guest in his lodge. Bear's Head quickly stirred things up.
The new Indian agent, Magnus Begg, saw the mood of the
Blackfoot change from friendly to surly overnight. He felt
hostility in the air, and he became nervous. Begg rode to Calgary and reported his observations to Inspector Sam Steele,

the mounted police officer in charge of the detachment there. Steele sent a sergeant and a constable by train to arrest Bear's Head.

The Blackfoot camp was nearly deserted when they arrived because the annual sun dance was being held. The two officers ordered the interpreter Jean L'Heureux to lure the trouble-maker away from the dance lodge. They arrested him, held him overnight at the CPR's Gleichen station and caught the morning train back to Calgary. But they arrived empty-handed. Along the way, Bear's Head slipped off the handcuffs, grabbed the sergeant's gun and jumped from the moving train. The officers gave chase, but one sprained his knee while leaping to the ground, and Bear's Head easily outran the other.

The escape of the Metis rabble-rouser threatened the credibility of the force. Hence, Steele decided to make the arrest himself. He drove out to the Blackfoot camp in a carriage, along with two constables. The officers arrived amid a downpour that had halted the sun dance and driven everyone back to their lodges. They located L'Heureux, who took them to Crowfoot's tepee. Steele announced his arrival, then strode in. He found himself standing in the centre of a circle of men who were seated around the perimeter of the lodge and looking up at him. Crowfoot sat opposite the entrance. Bear's Head was immediately to his right, in the place of honour. The Blackfoot chief glared at Steele without addressing him.

Steele spoke in a firm, steady voice. L'Heureux stood next to him, his legs trembling, and interpreted. Bear's Head would be taken to Calgary, Steele said, and would receive a fair trial. When Crowfoot spoke, his voice was filled with defiance. He was outraged. The Metis was his guest. He had done no wrong. He would remain where he was. The men in the tepee nodded in approval.

Crowfoot sprang to his feet. He made a move toward Steele, who held his ground and warned his adversary there would be grave consequences if he attacked an officer. There was a lull. Steele told L'Heureux to throw open the entrance flap. He put his right hand on the butt of his revolver and, with the other, grabbed Bear's Head by the collar and dragged him outside.

By the time the prisoner was cuffed and shackled, several hundred angry warriors had surrounded the three officers in their carriage. Steele stood to address them. He told the warriors that anyone who interfered with an arrest would suffer for it. Then he summoned Crowfoot. He accused the chief of behaving badly when the police had always treated him fairly. And he wrote a note instructing the CPR agent at Gleichen to issue Crowfoot a return ticket to Calgary so he could witness the trial.

"You may go up to Calgary and hear the half-breed tried by Ho-mux-a-stamix [Lieutenant-Colonel Irvine]," Steele said. "If you think the prisoner will not be fairly dealt with, then, perhaps, you may explain your conduct in the tent. In future, I should advise you to maintain the law as you promised to do. When you . . . attend the trial, you will find that you have been harbouring a disturber of the peace."

Crowfoot caught the train the following morning and arrived in time to witness the trial. Steele was not there to testify. Nor was his report on the incident available. Irvine, who was doubling as a magistrate, realized that there was no case against Bear's Head. In fact, there had been no grounds for arresting him. Irvine freed the prisoner, but persuaded him to leave the country.

Crowfoot returned to his reserve feeling vindicated. But the incident was deeply disturbing. Once again mounted police officers had barged into his camp and hauled someone away. The officers had not questioned anyone or made any effort to find out what was going on. They had acted arbitrarily, and in this case their actions were wrong. As far as Crowfoot was concerned, the police could no longer be trusted to do what was right.

The Canadian authorities were equally perturbed by this confrontation and the others that had preceded it. The mounted police were convinced that an Indian uprising was imminent. They petitioned the Macdonald administration for more officers, and by the end of 1884 were authorized to hire a hundred new recruits. Dewdney was worried too, and he intervened, wisely, to defuse tensions. In the summer of that year, he organized a tour of Regina and Winnipeg for several leading chiefs of the Blackfoot nation. The objective—to impress upon the Blackfoot the might of their new rulers—was evident from a memo Dewdney wrote on July 19 to his superiors in the Indian Department. In it, he said he hoped to counter "the influences brought to bear upon the Indians of Treaty 7 . . . to join in a general stand against the government."

Crowfoot and his foster brother Three Bulls went on behalf of the Blackfoot tribe. Red Crow represented the Bloods and Eagle Tail the Piegans. Regina, the territorial capital, was hardly the place to impress these aging wanderers, who had never learned to read or write, or lived in any structure more grandiose than a tepee. They knew this site was an old Cree hunting camp. Their former enemies had called it *oskana*, which meant bones. White men had named it pile of bones and turned *oskana* into wascana.

Crowfoot and his mates chuckled at the folly of the white man as they got off the train, for this was no place to live. A man could gaze at the horizons all round him and squint till his eyes hurt and never see a tree. He could ride all day to reach the nearest hill. The winds filled the air with dust, and the rains turned the earth to mud so gooey that many a moccasin was lost in the aftermath of a thundershower. The place had one thing going for it—a tiny meandering creek, which had made it an ideal camp for summer buffalo hunts, and which accounted for the huge pile of bones that had accumulated at this spot. Regina had been founded two years earlier as a tent town and now boasted a few frame houses, a rudimentary mounted police headquarters and the lieutenant-governor's residence.

But Winnipeg was big enough to impress. It was a thriving city of 22,000 people, three times larger than the entire Blackfoot nation. A few of its residents were wealthy enough to live in mansions, and its streets were lined with sturdy brick homes. Winnipeg boasted five bank branches and a horse-drawn street railway, and the cornerstone had recently been laid for a grand new city hall—topped by turrets and an ornate clock tower.

The trip served its purpose. Crowfoot and his fellow chiefs returned home knowing that their people would never prevail in an armed conflict with the whites. Dewdney hoped the chiefs would convey this message to their followers and that it would lead to more settled conditions on the reserves. But his superiors in Ottawa undermined his efforts. They cut the rations, which most of the Blackfoot already regarded as inadequate. Twice a week, the Treaty Seven Indians were to get bacon instead of beef, a move that caused outrage.

Bacon was greasy. It smelled strange. It tasted salty. One Blood chief threw his at the storekeeper who issued it. Red Crow complained that the terms of the treaty were being violated. Eagle Tail showed his displeasure by refusing to accept any, and Crowfoot told the Blackfoot agent that his people would die if they ate bacon in the summer. Dewdney quickly went back to all beef rations rather than risk a prolonged confrontation.

But for Crowfoot and his band, another irritant soon appeared. The locomotives that rolled past the northern limit of their reserve every day exhaled dense clouds of ugly, black smoke that hovered over the tracks long after the train was gone. Sparks and cinders fell from the smoke, like rain that glowed, igniting the prairie and leaving behind swaths of scorched land.

Crowfoot remembered these things as he sat in his lodge one day in the fall of 1884 and listened to the promises and pretty phrases of Hayter Reed and Albert Lacombe. The two white men were visiting the Stoney, Sarcee and Blackfoot reserves to sell the natives on another of civilization's blessings: education.

Father Lacombe had started an industrial school at High River, south of Calgary, and he needed students willing to learn trades such as harness making, carpentry and shoemaking. Crowfoot was not interested, nor were any of his brethren. They did not want their children in the care of strangers. They did not want them raised in the ways of the white man. Nevertheless, Father Lacombe managed to take in twenty-three students from the three reserves. They were either orphans or older children who decided on their own to attend. The priest later complained in his annual report to the minister that "not one Indian is willing to part with young children or allow them to remain here for any length of time." The solution, he said, was to pressure the parents "by threatening to deprive them of their rations."

In the spring of 1885, Crowfoot received visitors of a different sort. Cree and Metis messengers brought him news of the uprising on the Saskatchewan. They hoped that Crowfoot would turn his warriors loose, and he was sorely tempted to do so. As a young man, he had absorbed the values and the spirit of his people. He had been fearless and powerful on the battle-field. He had risen to prominence as a warrior. He was leader of a proud people, and he must surely have longed to see his young men ride again and strike fear into the hearts of their adversaries.

But Crowfoot was an old man. He had been a chief for many years. He had a reputation for being wise and generous. Many of his followers called him *manistokos*, the father of his people, because he had always provided for the weak and the disadvantaged. In former times, he ensured that everyone had meat in their pots after a successful hunt and horses to ride when the band was on the move. With the arrival of white rule, he had acquired new, more complex challenges. His biggest was to ensure that the Blackfoot survived as a people. So he would not send his young men off to a war they could not win, even though many of them, and some of the secondary chiefs, were eager to fight.

Crowfoot did not disclose his position immediately. Instead, he kept everyone guessing. He welcomed Cree runners and refugees into his camp. He sent his own runners to Red Crow and Eagle Tail, bearing offerings of tobacco, which they refused to accept, meaning they would remain loyal to the Queen. As the days passed, Crowfoot's silence unnerved Canadians far and wide. The prime minister and his colleagues weathered blister-ing attacks in Parliament and the Liberal press while waiting to learn how big a war they had on their hands. Settlers in the countryside around the Treaty Seven reserves were terrified that their Indian neighbours would rise. And on the evening of March 27, rumours of an imminent Blackfoot attack produced panic in the tiny settlement of Calgary.

The citizens hastily organized a one-hundred-man armed guard to protect their community. They summoned Father Lacombe from his school at High River and asked him to meet the Blackfoot leadership. The CPR ferried the priest out to the reserve in a locomotive and he held councils with Old Sun and Crowfoot along with their lesser chiefs. Father Lacombe concluded that the whites had nothing to fear. On March 30, before returning to Calgary, he sent a reassuring telegram to the prime minister from the CPR station at Gleichen, just outside the reserve. "I have seen Crowfoot and all the Blackfeet," he wrote. "All quiet. Promised me to be loyal no matter how things turn out."

The government took its own measures to ensure that the Blackfoot kept the peace. Dewdney put the trusted and respected Denny back in charge of the Treaty Seven Indians and gave him a free hand to keep them happy. Denny promptly increased the daily rations to a pound of beef and an equal measure of flour per person from half a pound of each. And on April 11, Dewdney, along with Denny, Father Lacombe and an interpreter, held a large council with Crowfoot and the other Blackfoot leaders. The lieutenant-governor assured them they had nothing to fear from the government and promised that troops entering the country would do them no harm.

Crowfoot replied for the Blackfoot, and later that day dictated a message to the prime minister, which was sent immediately by telegraph. "On behalf of myself and my people," he began, "I wish to send through you to the Great Mother the words I have given to the Governor at a Council held at which all my minor chiefs and young men were present. We are agreed and determined to remain loyal to the Queen. Our young men will go to work on their reserve and will raise all the crops we can and we hope the Government will help us sell what we can raise."

Macdonald was delighted with Crowfoot's message, and on April 14 sent the following reply: "I have received your good and loyal message by telegraph and I have shown it to the Governor General who is our Great Chief under the Queen. He desires me to thank you for your promise to be a faithful friend to our Great Mother and is sure your words are true. I have also read your message to our great Council at Ottawa which pleased them very much. What Governor Dewdney has promised shall be performed. We will help you sell what you cannot use of your crop and shall never forget the good conduct of yourself, your minor chiefs and warriors."

Macdonald was immensely relieved, and understandably so. The youthful Dominion was fighting what was, in effect, a foreign war. General Middleton and most of his men were more than a thousand miles from home in a land they had never seen before. They were having enough trouble suppressing an uprising by a small force of poorly equipped Metis and natives on one front—the North Saskatchewan. The last thing they needed was war on a second front. Macdonald and the Canadian armed forces were spared such an ordeal because Crowfoot and his fellow chiefs kept the peace on the southern prairie. Crowfoot had the interests of his own nation at heart. He denied his young men a few days' glory on the battlefield, but ensured that they would live to help bring forth a new generation of Blackfoot.

But fate would not be so kind to him. Over the next year, sickness, death and heartbreak visited his lodge. In early May 1885, a daughter developed an ominous cough. She began spitting up blood and, by the end of the month, she was dead of tuberculosis. Over the summer, Crowfoot himself became sick again. At the same time, he had to digest the disheartening news that his adopted son, Poundmaker, was in custody and would soon be tried for his role in the troubles. He appealed to Dewdney for a pardon, thinking his own services to the Queen might carry some weight, but he got nowhere. However, in October, when the Blackfoot received their annual treaty money, the government recognized his loyalty by presenting him with $100 in addition to the $25 he normally received.

It was a feeble gesture, and whatever gratitude Crowfoot may have felt was swept away when another of his children became gravely ill and died of tuberculosis in early December. The ailing and disheartened leader was still grieving when he learned that sickness had struck one more of his offspring. Crowfoot was close to despair, as is evident from a letter to Poundmaker, which he dictated to the agent on his reserve on Christmas Day, 1885.

"Dear Poundmaker," he began, "I send you word that the agent and other white men say you are well used, and I should like you to send word if it really is true. I have such a feeling of lonesomeness of seeing my children dying every year and if I hear that you are dead, I will have no more use for life. I shake hands with the Agent and Mr. Dewdney, and I know they will do what they can for you. I would like to hear from you direct, how you are treated. Your father, Crowfoot."

Poundmaker sent assurances that he was being well treated. A few weeks later, Crowfoot received more gratifying news: the Canadian authorities were going to release his adopted son. But by spring he was grieving again for he had lost two more children to disease. Crowfoot had been a father of twelve when the treaty was signed nine years earlier. Since then, eight of his children had died, leaving him with two adult daughters, a son who was nearly blind when he reached manhood and a baby girl. Tragedy deepened Crowfoot's attachment to Poundmaker. He had feared for him while he was in jail. He had rejoiced in seeing him again upon his release. And he was rent with grief when Poundmaker died before his eyes.

Crowfoot was still grieving when he learned that his people would be receiving more distinguished visitors: Sir John A. and Lady Macdonald were travelling across the country and would stop at the Blackfoot reserve. The Canadian prime minister had come west on the transcontinental railway and his train arrived at Gleichen July 22 at eight o'clock in the morning. Hundreds of mounted and colourfully dressed Blackfoot gathered on the prairie near the station to greet Macdonald. When the train stopped, Crowfoot and Old Sun went aboard to meet the Canadian prime minister. Old Sun, according to a journalist with the *Toronto Daily Mail*, wore garments that "rivalled in brightness the rising sun." But Crowfoot was poorly dressed in the tattered clothing of a man in mourning.

When the introductions were complete, the visiting dignitaries emerged from their car and Lieutenant-Governor Dewdney addressed the Blackfoot through an interpreter. Sir John, as Dewdney called him, was a great chief, specifically charged with the well-being of the Indians. He had come to see the Blackfoot and the Canadian Pacific Railway and to travel from saltwater to saltwater. He was anxious to meet Crowfoot and the other chiefs, who were his friends. If they had any complaints, he would gladly hear them.

Crowfoot rose to speak. He took off his hat. He explained why he was dressed so poorly and asked the prime minister not to take it as a sign of disrespect. He told his fellow chiefs to listen closely. And he told the interpreter to translate his message truthfully. He began with the CPR. The trains had caused many fires on the reserve. He and others had complained, but the men who ran the railway ignored them. If a white man down east had his grass burned by the fire wagons, he would make a row about it, and so, too, would the Blackfoot.

Turning straight to the prime minister, Crowfoot said he and his fellow chiefs feared for their children. They feared that food would not be given to them, and they wanted Sir John to banish those fears. Crowfoot was concerned about how the white world perceived his people. He desired to be friends with the white man, and he was grieved by the reports in the newspapers that had given his men and their families a bad name they did not deserve.

Then Sir John spoke. He, for one, never believed the newspaper reports about the Blackfoot. He and the governor-general had received messages from Crowfoot and had believed them. They had found he was a man with a big heart and had been true to the Great Mother and the treaty. The prime minister had seen with his own eyes how the trains had burned the prairie. He regretted it and would do his best to have the problem addressed. Finally, he advised the Indians to till the soil, to raise livestock and to become like white men.

That is all very well, Crowfoot replied. But when his people grew more potatoes than they could eat and tried to sell them, they got only a small amount of money, the size of a fingernail, for a whole sack. If that was all they got, they would starve.

The prime minister agreed that they should have more rations, but would leave the particulars to Dewdney, who would deal with any other complaints they might have. As for he and Lady Macdonald, they had to continue their journey. That ended the speeches. Before departing, they watched a pow-wow and distributed gifts. Sir John gave Crowfoot a new suit of clothes and his wife presented the chief with a large pipe, the bowl of which was supported by a crow's foot. There were pipes for the lesser chiefs, calico for the women, and tea, tobacco and sugar for all. Then the Macdonalds returned to their train and resumed the trip that would take them to Calgary, into the foothills, over the mountains and down to the sea.

Crowfoot assumed he had seen the last of Sir John. But later that summer, he and a number of other leaders of the Blackfoot, the Bloods and the Piegans were invited by the Canadian government to attend the unveiling of a monument in Brantford, Ontario, to honour Mohawk leader Joseph Brant. Crowfoot had made many journeys during his long, eventful life. As a young man, he had visited the lands of neighbouring tribes, some friendly, some hostile. He had been to the country of the Crows, south of the Yellowstone River, and that of the Crees, north of the Battle River. He had been to the land of the Stoney Indians, in the lee of the *mis stak 'kis*, the mountains that shone on the western horizon. And he had made forays to the country of the Assiniboines, which lay to the east of the Cypress Hills.

He had been to every place of beauty and significance in the land once known as Blackfoot country. He had bathed in the cleansing waters of *ah wy kee miskan*, the lake that runs up and down, and grazed his horses near the low-lying hills known as *masto wy okan*, the crows' stones. He had hunted buffalo in *kasaps ispatsee kwag*, the drifting sand hills, and heard the stories about *ak kao kee neeman*, or dead lodge canyon. And he had on many occasions found himself resting at *oh ma kee ya kotop*, the great cairn.

Now he was embarking on a grander expedition. Crowfoot and two companions, his foster brother Three Bulls and the interpreter Jean L'Heureux, left several days ahead of the others. They boarded the CPR's eastbound transcontinental two miles north of his camp at the Blackfoot Crossing on September 25, 1886. Their train, the Atlantic Express, hurtled across flat featureless expanses, covering as much ground in an hour as they had once traversed in a day, and stopping just long enough to take on coal and water or fresh crews and new passengers at Medicine Hat and Maple Creek and Swift Current, and many other pinpoint railway towns with colourful names and grand ambitions.

Some thirty hours and more than seven hundred miles later, the Express pulled into the station at Winnipeg. From the window of their car, Crowfoot and his companions could see swirls of people on the platform. A buzz swept the crowd as the two Blackfoot stepped off the train. Crowfoot was tall and lean with a handsome face. He wore moccasins, multicoloured pants, a glorious blue shirt with two medals pinned above his chest, and a dark felt top hat adorned with a pair of eagle feathers, one white, the other scarlet. The stout and muscular Three Bulls was just as colourfully dressed, and the two "were stared at as though they were the greatest curiosities in the world," according to a *Manitoba Daily Free Press* reporter.

The Winnipeg stop was just a warm-up. The Atlantic Express reached the Canadian capital on the evening of September 30, and wherever they went over the next two weeks, Crowfoot and Three Bulls were surrounded by crowds and followed by journalists. They visited the head offices of the CPR in Montreal and met the men who ran the railway—Sir George Stephen, William Van Horne and R.B. Angus—although this time Crowfoot did not complain about the fires on his reserve. They were introduced to the premier of Quebec, John Jones Ross. They toured the legislative library at the National Assembly. While in the assembly chamber, Crowfoot was allowed to sit in the Speaker's chair. Later, they had their picture taken at a photo studio and attended a social event at a roller skating rink where two thousand people waited to meet them.

Crowfoot and Three Bulls were worn out by the time they returned to Ottawa to meet the other chiefs—Red Crow of the Bloods, his nephew One Spot, and North Axe of the Piegans. Their hosts had another busy schedule of events planned, the highlight being a meeting with Sir John and Lady Macdonald, which took place at Earnscliffe, the prime ministerial residence, on Saturday, October 9. Crowfoot spoke for his fellow chiefs, and his people, as he had done so often in encounters with white officials and leaders.

"We have come a long way to see you at your house," he said. "We remember you both when you came to our land this summer. We had a good feeling there, and the lady gave our people money and presents. We hope the Great Chief will think of our people. Since the white man came, the buffalo have gone away, and now we need to be helped by the white chiefs. We want big farms, but what shall we do with what we cannot eat? I see . . . that you do not forget your own people, as they sell what they do not want. That is what my people want to do."

Sir John gave the Blackfoot leaders $25 each and advised them to be peaceful and patient and all would turn out well in the end. As the chiefs were about to leave, Crowfoot informed the prime minister that he and Three Bulls were too exhausted to continue with the itinerary that had been set out for them. The following Tuesday, they boarded the westbound transcontinental with Father Lacombe while their brethren, along with four newly arrived Cree chiefs, left for Brantford and the unveiling of the Joseph Brant memorial.

Crowfoot and Three Bulls arrived home on October 20.

Blackfoot agent Magnus Begg, acting on instructions from the prime minister, supplied beef, tea, tobacco and other items for a feast, and the two leaders began telling all they had seen. They entertained band members with tales of their trip for weeks. But as winter arrived, Crowfoot's health failed, and he withdrew to the seclusion of his lodge.

His days as a dynamic leader were over. He had been a chief for two tumultuous decades, during which his world was utterly transformed. He was old and worn out. His people still heeded his word. They loved and respected him. But he had no power. Indian agents on the reserves and other officials now controlled the lives of native people.

Begg filed reports from the Blackfoot reserve in the latter half of the 1880s, the final years of Crowfoot's life, that bristled with news and optimism. New buildings were being erected, new services were available and new enterprises were being created. A Catholic mission and a day school were started to serve Crowfoot's camp. A doctor made monthly rounds to visit the sick and vaccinate the people. A mine, worked by a white manager and his Blackfoot assistants, produced enough coal to meet the annual needs of the reserve, the agency buildings and the Oblate industrial school at High River.

Begg also reported that the Blackfoot were changing. They were abandoning traditional ways and living more like white men. They were beginning to build their homes farther apart and were taking "more pride in having good strong fences [around] their own fields." They were giving up the blanket, their traditional outer garment in cold weather, and opting for the settler's overcoat. They were less interested in the annual sun dance. And they were remaining on the reserve partly because the mounted police, "having a good system of patrolling, assist greatly in keeping the Indians at home."

In his final years, Crowfoot endured prolonged periods of illness due to a number of ailments. But when he was healthy, he went visiting. He renewed old friendships among the Bloods, Piegans and Sarcees, and roamed the land that had once been his. He travelled by foot, by horse and sometimes in a horse-drawn wagon, usually accompanied by a few old men who were especially close to him.

In February 1887, he went south to see Red Crow on the Blood Reserve, 150 miles away on the Oldman River, near the place of his birth. He was surprised by the wild and restless young Bloods, who were still roaming the plains to steal horses and make war on an old enemy, the Gros Ventre. A year later, he visited the South Piegans, now living in Montana, but was twice hospitalized by illness, and turned back shortly after crossing the border. Crowfoot barely left his lodge for the next four months. But by July 1888 he was off again, this time to see the North Piegans, a hundred miles south on the Oldman.

Travel improved his health and lifted his spirits, and October found him out on the prairie again. He made a brief stop at the Blood reserve to recoup his strength before going on to visit the South Piegans. From there, Crowfoot and his companions, including several young men, went on a peace-making mission to a reserve occupied by Gros Ventre and Assiniboines, who were still at war with the Bloods. The Gros Ventre welcomed the Blackfoot. But Assiniboine braves jeered them as they walked through the camp, while their women spat and hurled insults. Crowfoot's young men took offence and a confrontation occurred. Both sides aimed rifles at each other. Crowfoot and an old acquaintance, the Assiniboine chief Black Bear, stepped between the hotheads, linked arms and dared them to fire.

The two leaders prevented a shootout. But the old chief was

stunned by the incident and led his men home. They arrived in December. Crowfoot remained on his reserve until the following November. He was in poor health, and his sight was failing. Yet he was eager for a last glimpse of the land he knew so well and loved so deeply. So he went to visit the Sarcees on their reserve near Calgary, then travelled west to the foot of the mountains and spent a few days with the Stoneys who had once been his enemies.

When he returned to Blackfoot Crossing, he began preparing for his final journey, this one to the Sand Hills, that arid and desolate place where dwelt the spirits of all the people who had come before him, and where he was ready to go without fear or hesitation. Crowfoot's time came as the prairie was greening, the Bow was bursting with spring runoff, and his own people were seeding their modest fields and gardens.

He spent his final days in his tepee—shunning the house the Indian Department had built for him several years earlier in recognition of his peacekeeping efforts. His lodge stood on a magnificent bluff on the north side of the river, overlooking Blackfoot Crossing. According to the Anglican cleric Tims, no fewer than twenty-seven medicine men attended to Crowfoot as his condition deteriorated. They used every device available to them—drums, rattles, whistles and chants—and all their powers to try to scare off the malignant spirits who were carrying away the great Blackfoot leader. Their melancholy music filled the lodge and drifted over the valley to no avail. A physician took his turn at Crowfoot's bedside and left, having achieved nothing.

Crowfoot allowed himself to be baptised by an Oblate priest as death drew near, but Tims later insisted that "he died as he had lived, in the faith of his fathers." In his last hours, he slipped in and out of consciousness. A commander to the end, he issued instructions to family and friends in those moments when he was lucid. He advised his people to take up the ways of the white man, and to forget about returning to the days of freedom, now irrevocably lost. He instructed his wives not to chop off fingers or disfigure themselves as they mourned. He had his favourite horse destroyed so it could accompany him to the Sand Hills. He departed forever in the middle of the afternoon on April 25, 1890, and a camp crier quickly spread the news.

"Men, women and children," he shouted, "mourn over your great parent. You will no more hear his kind voice and its eloquent harangues. In your distress and misery, you will no more rush to his lodge for comfort and charities. He is no more. No one like him will fill his place."

Many would come after him, but there was only one Crowfoot. He had been a warrior, a provider, an orator, a peacemaker and a diplomat. As Dewdney later put it, "Crowfoot died beloved by his people, feared by his foes, esteemed by all." He had been feared for his prowess on the battlefield, for his utter disregard for personal safety when defending his people and their country. He had been loved and esteemed for many things: his courage, his generosity, his dignity, his eloquence and his wisdom. He was a man of many qualities, and he used them all for the good of his people.

Piapot, One Who
Knows the Secrets of the Sioux
Died Late April 1908

PIAPOT AND HIS PEOPLE
had been adrift on the prairie for ten days. They had set out
from Fort Qu'Appelle in search of buffalo and travelled southwest toward the Cypress Hills. They had eaten the last of their
provisions. Hunger forced them to slaughter a horse, something they hated to do. They wandered another seven days and
then they prayed. They danced and sang a night away, appeal-
ing to the Great Spirit for deliverance. Still, the herds failed to
appear. And at the end of seven more days, they prayed again.

Early the following morning, they broke camp and soon
arrived at a well-known lookout. The hunters with the sharpest
eyes scoured the horizons in all directions as the sun climbed

higher and heated the land. Finally, one man discerned a faint cloud of dust, away off to the southwest, and everyone knew the Great Spirit had heard their prayers.

They knew this cloud had risen from the prairie, that it had been created by thousands of hooves scouring the earth. They knew there was a huge herd out there. And they knew the country between the lookout and the cloud. There were rivers to ford, valleys to cross and hills to climb. The buffalo would not arrive until at least sunset. So everyone rested. They gave thanks. And they waited for the day to pass.

As evening rose from the land, the wind brought the sound of hooves. All night, the people lay and listened. And when the first streaks of light appeared in the east, the smell of buffalo filled the air. Hunters went to the lookout and could see that the herd was immense even though it was still some distance away. Scouts mounted their fleetest ponies and rode off to take its measure, to examine the countryside and to determine an angle of attack. They rode eight miles in one direction, and two in another, and returned with astounding news. The buffalo were following a snow-white bull.

People gasped at this. The hunters' eyes lit up. The best were determined to earn the distinction of bringing down this animal. The men killed many buffalo that day and the women busied themselves removing hides and butchering carcasses. That night, a great feast was held. The people rejoiced and filled the lodges with drum and song.

Early the next morning, fifty hunters set out again. They would take as much meat as they could get, perhaps enough for a few bags of pemmican. And besides, no one had killed the white bull. They rode till the sun was high in the sky, following a trail of crushed and tangled vegetation before pausing to rest and water the horses. They rode till midday, and from then till dusk, but still had not caught up to the herd. The trail brought them to the edge of a broad, shallow slough, its amber waters teeming with fowl and its marshy shoreline crackling with the sound of bullfrogs, and the hunters stopped there for the night.

They ate quickly the following morning, saddled the horses and rode around the slough. But when they reached the other side, they could not find the trail. How could this be, they wondered? The trail had been two miles wide. They had followed it all the previous day. The leader of the party ordered his men to search in all directions. But they returned at dusk perplexed and despondent. They had found no trace of the herd.

That night, they made fires, and stretched out under their blankets. The camp was quiet, and the sky exceptionally black, with hardly a star visible. Some talked in hushed tones about this mystery. Most said nothing. Suddenly, every man's eyes were pulled upward by a dazzling light. It was the white bull, leading the big herd across the sky. The hunters gazed in wonder until the buffalo slipped below the horizon, and it was later said that they had disappeared into a hole in the earth.

This was the story Piapot's people told around the fires in those days when they were not far removed from the old way of life, when they were camped in the Cypress Hills and determined to take a reserve there. It was a story that arose out of hardship, hunger and deprivation. Piapot was one of the last of the Qu'Appelle Cree to settle down. He had aligned himself with his brethren from the North Saskatchewan—Big Bear, Little Pine and Lucky Man—to form one large camp of three thousand Indians. They wanted to create a homeland for native peoples, but the Canadian government would not consider the idea. And in mid-1883 the mounted police had driven the Indians out of the Cypress Hills and forced them to go to reserves in other parts of the country.

The authorities had chosen a reserve for Piapot near the village of Indian Head, forty-two miles east of Regina. He would settle on lands adjacent to the reserve of an old friend, the Assiniboine chief Carry the Kettle. Piapot had a following of 430 people, and they left the Cypress Hills in June of 1883 with a police escort. Most were on foot, because the band no longer owned many horses, and they walked thirty miles north to Maple Creek on the CPR line. They were to travel by train, in boxcars rather than coaches, and the police saw that they embarked. The train had covered only a short distance when one of the cars went off the track and slid down the embankment. No one was hurt, but Piapot and his people refused to go any farther by rail. They would make the entire journey on foot.

Piapot's weary and threadbare band arrived at Fort Qu'Appelle in the latter half of August. Most of the chiefs from the surrounding reserves, along with six hundred of their followers, were there to greet him. The Qu'Appelle Indian agent, Allan McDonald, gave Piapot permission to camp for six days on the flats around the fort so his people could rest, recover their strength and visit old friends from the other bands.

But on the seventh day, McDonald ordered Piapot to leave. "I told him all supplies were stopped and that no more would be issued until he and his band reported themselves at the office at Indian Head, where they would get sufficient [supplies] to take them to their reserve," the agent later wrote. "On the 25th [of August], I visited the camp at Fort Qu'Appelle, where I met all the Indians there assembled, and read to them the instructions received that morning from the Honorable the Indian Commissioner in reference to the action that would be taken against Pie-a-pot if he attempted to cause dissatisfaction among the Indians and did not get on his reserve."

McDonald did not reveal the nature of Commissioner Dewdney's threat. But the following day, Piapot led his band out of the Qu'Appelle Valley. By September 1 they had reached their reserve. Piapot did not want to settle on the lands assigned to him, and he made this clear to the Indian agents. He had several objections, the principal being that the reserve included a series of low-lying hills, some of them littered with the bones of people who had died during a smallpox epidemic many years earlier. Since then, the hills had been known as the skull mountains, and events during the winter of 1883–84 confirmed for Piapot their malevolent influence. Many of his people died, up to one-third, according to some estimates, but the exact number is not known.

McDonald made reference to widespread illness in his report for the year ended June 30, 1884, stating: "It was chiefly confined to the families who came on the reserve last summer. The mortality was largely due to consumption. The principal sufferers were Piapot's and the Assiniboine bands." And a youth named W.W. Gibson, whose family was homesteading nearby, later recalled seeing the dead, wrapped in blankets and laid to rest in trees as was the custom among the plains Indians. "Many a time," this pioneer wrote, "while herding my father's flocks . . . I passed aspen groves where there were dozens of platforms lashed to poplar trees with rawhide thongs, sepulchres that bore mute evidence of that tragic winter."

When spring arrived, Piapot was determined to leave. In mid-May, he and the surviving members of his band departed for the Qu'Appelle Valley. They would settle there, where they could be assured of finding adequate supplies of wood and water, fish and fowl, and hay for their horses. They had travelled only a few miles when they were intercepted by assistant Indian commissioner Hayter Reed, mounted police commissioner Acheson G. Irvine and a small corps of officers. Reed had heard that Piapot was on the move and came out from Regina to send him back.

The old chief said he and his people were on their way to a sun dance on chief Pasquah's reserve near Fort Qu'Appelle. But he also made it clear he had no intention of living near the skull mountains. His people had been dying, he said, and they would all be gone soon if they stayed there. Furthermore, the water supply was inadequate and they were being denied fresh meat. Reed warned Piapot that the government would not permit groups of armed men to roam the countryside and urged him to think about what he was doing. Then, seeing that he could not impose his will, Reed returned to Regina, along with the police.

On May 18, Reed and Irvine left the capital again and resumed their pursuit of Piapot. This time they brought fifty-six officers and a seven-pound cannon. They learned of his whereabouts from Pasquah's Indians and timed their movements to arrive at an opportune moment. At dawn on May 21, Irvine ordered his men to halt four miles from Piapot's camp. Then he and an interpreter rode in while the Indians were asleep. Someone immediately sounded the alarm and men spilled from the lodges. They grabbed their rifles, mounted their horses and prepared to defend the camp.

Irvine avoided a confrontation by offering to lead Piapot and his band to Fort Qu'Appelle where they could discuss their grievances with Reed. Negotiations were held that night and the following day. Irvine later told his superiors that he had sent Piapot back to Indian Head, and he said nothing further about the chief who had given him more trouble than any other in this district.

Yet, by year end, Piapot had settled on the south side of the

Qu'Appelle Valley, next to the reserve of another Cree chief named Muscowpetung. The Indian Department had agreed to give Piapot fifty-four square miles of land that started on the prairie, dropped down into the valley and ran out to the river. John Nelson, the Dominion land surveyor who mapped the reserve the following summer, described the soil as sandy and poor, and deemed the wood supply inadequate, except in the coulees. Most important, he observed that "it does not contain the quantity of land to which their numbers entitle them."

Nelson did not elaborate on this point in the report he submitted to the superintendent-general of Indian Affairs, Lawrence Vankoughnet, in Ottawa. But the treaty stipulated that each family of five was entitled to one square mile of land, an allotment that could be adjusted for families that were larger or smaller. And Irvine's report on his confrontations with Piapot indicated that the Cree leader's camp comprised about seventy lodges, meaning there were at least that many families in his band and they should all have been included when the government calculated the size of the reserve.

In the years to come, Piapot complained that the white man had cheated his people on many occasions and could not be trusted. But there is nothing in the Indian agent reports to indicate that he was unhappy with the size of his reserve. In fact, Piapot appears to have lived quietly for a while. He took no part in the troubles of 1885. And the following year, he even tried his hand at cultivating the soil and growing food, according to the reserve's farm instructor, one R. McKinnon.

His accounts for 1886 show that Piapot worked a total of thirteen acres, planting wheat and barley, as well as several vegetables, including potatoes, turnips and peas. And twenty-six other band members followed his lead. McKinnon kept track of every acre sown and every bushel of grain and vegetables harvested. But the summer was hot and dry, and the yields dismal. "The grain sown in the valley did not head out on account of the drought," the instructor informed his superiors. "The root crop was almost a total failure. The land on this reserve is of a sandy nature, consequently not getting any rain this season our crops were burnt up. Too dry for oats, they did not grow. Barley a complete failure."

Crop failure greatly troubled officials at all levels of the Indian Department. It meant the department would be forced to distribute rations for another year and expenditures would remain unacceptably high. Worse still, the Indians were no closer to becoming self-sufficient, and that was one of the primary objectives of the government.

The weather was only one obstacle. Departmental employees saw the tribal system of communal living and community ownership of land as impediments to self-sufficiency, and they were adamant about changing the way the Indians lived. In 1889, the Indian Department sent Dominion land surveyors to reserves throughout the North-West with instructions to begin subdividing them into forty-acre lots. They showed up at Piapot's reserve on June 10, accompanied by Reed, who was there to explain the department's new policy. Pastures and woodlots would remain community property, he declared, but each family would be responsible for a forty-acre plot. They were expected to live on their land and endeavour to meet the requirements for obtaining a certificate of ownership.

This was too much for Piapot. He and his people lived close by one another in a village of log homes at the foot of the valley, where they could walk well-trod paths to visit their neighbours and where a person could usually hear the laughter of children and the talk of adults. Besides, when spring arrived, most people moved out of their homes and into tepees, forming a camp in the lush hay meadows of the valley bottom. They had no desire to live alone on the prairie, separated from neighbours by acres of land and miles of barbed wire, like the white settlers who were trickling into the Qu'Appelle Valley. Piapot could not stop the Indian Department from subdividing his reserve, but he and his people refused to be dispersed to isolated plots of land.

Despite the opposition of Piapot and a few other chiefs in the North-West, Reed boasted at year end of the progress the department was making. "The work of sub-dividing the reserves has begun in earnest," he wrote. "The policy of destroying the tribal or communist system is assailed in every possible way." And he assured the Ottawa bureaucrats to whom he reported that "only the idle-good-for-nothing [band] members offer any objection to what is hailed with pleasure by the better class."

Over the next few years, departmental officials pestered the men and women of Piapot's band about moving to individual lots. But they demonstrated that they could live communally, as they always had, and still be productive farmers. Their 1891 harvest yielded enough wheat to meet their needs until the following summer. They even had surplus grain, which they sold at sixty cents a bushel to a Regina merchant. Indians on the neighbouring Muscowpetung and Pasquah reserves also had wheat to sell that year. Indeed, earnings from the sale of grain, hay and wood netted the three reserves a total of $6,351 and the agent in charge, John Lash, reported that "the past year has been the most prosperous since the agency opened and the Indians have practically supported themselves for the past eight months."

During the winter months, the Indians of these reserves displayed an industriousness that impressed Lash. The women knitted, sewed and mended. The men fashioned harnesses out of leather they had tanned themselves. They made ox collars, handles for rakes and axes, and sleds for their children. Piapot undoubtedly participated because he worked the land alongside his people and needed tools and implements when spring arrived.

But in the winter of 1891–92, he also immersed himself in another endeavour: the preparations for a grand sun dance to be held on the reserve the following summer. A fellow band member had pledged to give the dance. He became the sponsor, or pledger, and he asked Piapot to serve as one of the four assistants who would help him conduct this complex religious celebration. There had been dances on the reserve almost every summer since Piapot and his people had settled, and they usually invited their brethren from the neighbouring Muscowpetung and Pasquah reserves. Now they wanted to hold a larger dance like the one that Piapot and many other Qu'Appelle Cree had attended a couple of summers earlier on an Assiniboine and Gros Ventre reserve in northern Montana. It had been a memorable social occasion and, for Piapot, an opportunity to re-affirm his spiritual powers.

They had departed from a gathering place near Regina, and travelled 250 miles southwest in a cavalcade of thirty to forty wagons, along with riders on their own horses. They followed an old trail, which they knew from the buffalo days, and camped where they liked because much of the country was still unsettled and unfenced. People were happy to be out on the prairie again even though the land was parched. As they travelled farther south, they saw dried-up creeks and sloughs, and grasses that were burned and brown.

When the Qu'Appelle Cree reached their destination, they received a warm welcome, greeted old friends and learned that their hosts had nearly completed the preparations for their annual sun dance. The camp sprang to life early the next morning. An emissary arrived at Piapot's lodge carrying a ceremonial pipe wrapped in expensive cloth. He sat opposite Piapot, set the pipe between them, and began to explain his mission.

He said that the sponsor had spent many years preparing for the day when he could give the sun dance. But he now wanted Piapot to take his place because the land was in the clutches of a terrible drought. The crops were dying. The people were suffering and they would have a hard winter unless it rained soon. The sponsor wanted Piapot to use his unusual powers to appeal to the Great Spirit for deliverance from this harsh, dry season. When the emissary finished speaking, he unwrapped the pipe and awaited Piapot's answer.

Piapot deliberated a long time. He and the emissary sat in silence, while outside the lodge people were busy with the final preparations. The pledger of the dance had selected four young men to cut the centre pole, and they led a procession of children and adults to the designated tree. They burned sweetgrass, made pipe offerings and then wielded their axes. When they returned with the pole, the people began constructing the lodge around it. As this was happening, Piapot gave his answer. He passed his hand over the pipe, with the palm up. He would give the dance.

The emissary left to deliver the news, and Piapot began to get dressed. He looked splendid when the pledger arrived a short time later to escort him to the lodge. A crowd had gathered outside, and inside, every place but one was taken. It was reserved for the giver of the dance. Piapot seated himself there, among a circle of eight to ten singers, each with a willow switch in his right hand, and poised to pound the big drum. He lifted a rattle above his head and there was silence.

Then he spoke. "I can pray to the Great Spirit to help us," he said. "I cannot promise to make it rain. No one can make rain but the Great Spirit. But if the whole community will help me, we can have rain. I will sing four songs. I want everyone to sing these songs with me and to help me by having faith that the Great Spirit will have pity on them. Everyone must think about it and everyone must help."

Piapot shook the rattle again, and a moment later the lodge reverberated with the throb of drums, with the soaring chants of dozens of voices and the swirl of dancers with painted faces and beaded garments. The singers beat the taut, hard hide with remarkable speed and precision. They sang in unison and the entire gathering sang with them. Men and women danced around the centre pole, keeping their eyes fixed on it. As heat and exhaustion overcame them, dancers sat down and others took their place.

The singing of the first three songs took most of the day. By the time the third had been completed, people observed clouds on the western horizon and many believed the Great Spirit had heard their prayers. But Piapot urged them to continue. "I want you all to sing with all your heart," he shouted. "I want you all to cry out as one person."

The people threw themselves into the fourth song. They had reached the mid-point when those outside the lodge observed thick, billowy clouds filling the sky. They heard the rumble and crackle of thunder. They saw lightning, sheets of it first, and then streaks that came out of the clouds to touch the earth somewhere beyond the horizon. They felt the wind become cooler and finally raindrops fell. The rain came harder and harder, yet the people danced until their clothes were drenched and they had turned dirt to mud beneath their feet. The drought was over.

A few days later, Piapot and the rest of the Qu'Appelle Cree set out for home. The rain had brought the prairie back to life. The land was green again, and Piapot was thankful for the faith that had made this possible. As a boy growing up among the Sioux, he had come to believe in the Great Spirit, and his faith had sustained him through a long life. It had made his tribulations bearable and his triumphs possible.

He hoped that the young people growing up on the reserves would believe as he and others of his generation believed. He wanted them to give the sun dance when the old people were gone. And so now, when a member of his band vowed to sponsor a dance in the summer of 1892, Piapot supported him wholeheartedly. Together, they sent messengers with tobacco offerings to Cree bands in the Touchwood Hills and the file Hills, and to the Assiniboines at Indian Head and Moose Mountain. The offerings were accepted, meaning many of these Indians would attend.

As the time of the dance approached, the people of Piapot's band were filled with anticipation. Hundreds of Indians began arriving from other reserves. Tepees went up, a large camp took shape, and the sound of drums boomed across the Qu'Appelle Valley day and night. People danced. They exchanged news and gossip. Everyone was in high spirits. And then John Lash arrived. The agent saw painted faces and colourful clothing and rituals he did not understand. He saw Indians at play and worship. He saw empty fields and work that needed to be done.

Lash sent for Piapot and told him he would not allow the dance to proceed. Piapot objected, and the two had a long discussion. But the old chief eventually "listened to reason," as the agent later put it, and a compromise was reached. The agent would permit the Indians of the Piapot, Muscowpetung and

Pasquah reserves to hold a dance but only after all the others were gone. "The dance which took place at the end of June was a miserable failure," Lash wrote. "The enthusiasm which usually attends Sun Dances was wanting and the intense excitement which prevailed in the early part of the month seemed to have departed with the Indians who left for home very much disappointed."

The agent extracted one other concession from Piapot as part of their compromise: this was to be the last sun dance ever held by the Indians of the three reserves. Lash later had a change of heart because in early June 1894 the ceremony was held again. Over a thousand people participated, according to a journalist from the *Regina Leader* who attended the dance. And they were well-behaved throughout the two-day celebration. A mounted police inspector and two officers maintained a steady vigil but there were no disturbances of any kind. Yet the unnamed journalist cast the participants in an unfavourable light, writing: "The savage was there in all his glory, painted in vermilion and bedecked with feathers, gaudy coloured clothing, in pristine splendour."

The following spring, Piapot's band held a much smaller dance. A local newspaper, the *Qu'Appelle Progress*, reported, "The making of braves and a dog feast were the principal features of the dance." "Making braves" was a white expression for the piercing ritual, an act of self-mutilation performed to fulfil a vow to the spirit powers. A young man would pierce his breasts with two skewers and a cord would be attached from the skewers to the centre pole. He would then dance around the pole until the skewers tore away from his flesh and freed him. Piapot's band risked incurring the wrath of the white authorities by including the piercing ritual. In fact, they were lucky to have completed the dance that spring.

Many other Cree and Assiniboine bands tried to hold sun dances, but Indian agents suppressed them. In one case, the mounted police were called in to back an agent, John P. Wright, who became involved in a dispute with the leaders of a Touchwood Hills band. "Mr. Wright did not use the gentle method," according to a report in the weekly *Qu'Appelle Vidette* on June 27, 1895. "[He] stated plainly that the dance would not be allowed and, to show that he was not trifling, had the leaders arrested and bound over to keep the peace."

The spring of 1895 marked a turning point in the conflict over religious practices, which had begun when the native peoples of the North-West began settling on reserves. Indian agents, along with missionaries, had tried to stop the sun dances because they brought together unacceptably large numbers of people and disrupted the work on the reserves, sometimes for a week or more. As well, they often included the piercing ritual, which many whites found shocking. White authorities were equally opposed to giveaway dances, which involved the ritualistic exchange of goods among band members. This ceremony was seen as detrimental to the accumulation of material possessions needed to help the Indians become self-sufficient.

Try as they might, Indian agents never entirely succeeded in eliminating these practices. Finally, in 1895, the Canadian government came to their assistance by amending the Indian Act. It became a criminal offence to participate in "any Indian festival, dance or ceremony of which the giving away or paying or giving back of money, goods or articles of any sort forms a part or is a feature." The changes also made it illegal to take part in celebrations or dances involving "the wounding or mutilation of the dead or living body of any human being or animal."

This action provoked one of Piapot's most celebrated

outbursts against white authorities. In mid-October 1895, the most senior Roman Catholic clergyman in Manitoba and the North-West, Archbishop Langevin of St. Boniface, came to the Qu'Appelle Valley to celebrate the thirtieth anniversary of the Oblate mission there. He visited the town of Fort Qu'Appelle, the Qu'Appelle Mission Industrial School at nearby Lebret and several Indian reserves. During one of these stops, he met Piapot, and the old chief spoke his mind about white men, and how they had treated his people. "In order to become sole masters of our land, they relegated us to small reservations as big as my hand and made us long promises, as long as my arm. But the next year the promises were shorter and got shorter every year until now they are about the length of my finger, and they keep only half of that."

Piapot refused to abandon his faith. He saw no reason why he should. He had made his terms with the white man in the treaty, and the treaty said nothing about spiritual beliefs or religious practices. So he would continue to worship the Creator, although doing so led to more direct clashes with his white overseers.

In the spring of 1899, his band planned to hold a rain dance, which was a short version of the sun dance. The night before the ceremony was to begin, about twenty young men came to Piapot's home and asked to be pierced. "This is not a laughing matter," Piapot told them. "But since you have asked for this experience, and the Great Spirit has heard you and knows what you ask, you must carry it through. Come back tomorrow before dawn and you will be pierced."

The young men arrived, as instructed, wearing only breech cloths. Another old medicine man was there to perform the ritual. He had with him a bear claw and he went from man to man, lifting the skin of their breasts, piercing it in two places with the claw and inserting skewers. Each took his turn being connected to the centre pole and each danced until he broke free from the skewers.

A few days after the dance, mounted police officers arrived at the reserve and arrested Piapot. They took him to Regina where he was given a trial and sentenced to two months in the provincial jail. While he was serving his term, Piapot received a visit from a young student named Harry Ball, who attended the industrial school in the city. The youth noticed a sign outside Piapot's cell bearing his name and offence, and he drew this to the old man's attention.

"What am I in here for?" Piapot asked.

"It says on the paper outside that you were arrested for being drunk," the youth replied.

"But I never drink," he said. "I know why I am here. It is because of the rain dance and the piercing of the boys."

Piapot was arrested again in late October 1901, at the age of eighty-five, this time after a dispute with white authorities over a giveaway dance. The agent in charge of his reserve was a man named William Graham, who zealously enforced the Indian Act, and he complained to the mounted police about the dance. A sergeant and a constable left the Qu'Appelle detachment with warrants for the arrests of two men believed to be the sponsors of the ceremony. Upon arriving at Piapot's village, they encountered "a large number of Indians, painted up and ready to resist at all costs," according to Graham, and the old chief led the resistance.

The officers wisely retreated and rode to Regina for reinforcements. The next day, they returned, arrested six members of the band, including Piapot, and charged them with various offences. The trials were held in Fort Qu'Appelle and all were convicted. Four men received suspended sentences for participating in the dance. The organizer was sentenced to six months' hard labour at the Regina jail, and Piapot got two months for obstructing justice.

After this incident, Indian Department officials were determined to rid themselves of Piapot. He had tried their patience too many times over the years with his sharp tongue. On one occasion, he accused an agent of being so cheap that he blew his nose in a linen cloth because he was afraid he might lose something of value. On meeting Graham, who had lost a leg in a boyhood accident, Piapot said, "Now I know the government is going to break the treaty because when it was signed it was understood that it would last as long as the grass grew, the winds blew, the rivers ran and men walked on two legs, and now they have sent us an agent who has only one leg."

Even the agents who had never felt the sting of Piapot's wit saw him as a troublesome old man who continually resisted the work of church and state to the detriment of his people. He was the leader of what they referred to as "the pagan element" of the band, and these Indians were more resistant to change than those who had become Christian. As late as 1900, over three-quarters of the band's 180 members were listed as pagan in departmental reports, the remainder being either Roman Catholic or Presbyterian. The heathen majority would not allow churches on the reserve. They sent fewer children to the industrial schools than their Christian counterparts on other reserves. And they refused to abandon their village in order to live on individual parcels of land.

Shortly after Piapot was released from jail, the Indian Department declared that it would no longer recognize him as chief of the band. Piapot's people stood behind him, however, refusing to elect a successor as long as he was alive. Nor would any of his four councillors take his position. Nevertheless, departmental officials were certain they had made a good decision. Graham reported in August 1902 that eighty per cent of Piapot's band had converted to either Roman Catholicism or Presbyterianism while the pagan element was reduced to a rump of thirty members. And Graham had one other thing to boast about. "The dancing, which had always been carried to excess on this reserve, has ceased," he wrote. "I know of one small dance taking place during the year. I have lost no time in doing everything in my power to discourage excessive dancing as it certainly does more to demoralize work on the reserve than anything I know."

Piapot lived quietly after he was deposed. He was an old man then, older than anyone in his band, and likely the oldest Indian in the Qu'Appelle Valley. Age had left him gaunt and stiff. He had always been lean, but now his clothes hung loosely on him, and he walked slowly and with great care. He was still a handsome figure, with two long braids of hair that hung down to his chest, and eyes that sparkled when he talked. His mind was sharp, and he was as witty as ever.

He had three wives, who took good care of him, and he had young children. He developed a friendship with Father Joseph Hugonnard, the principal of the industrial school at Lebret, about forty miles east of the reserve. Father Hugonnard, who was fluent in Cree, frequently visited the reserve to recruit students and he eventually convinced Piapot to send his two youngest sons to the school. He also tried to convert him to Christianity.

"You know, my elder brother," the priest said one day, "you are getting old. We are going to teach your children our religion. They will be telling you how good is our religion. You should take our religion also."

"My younger brother," replied Piapot, "you want to teach

me your religion. Do you know the Great Spirit made that country where you came from and planted you there and gave you this religion. The Great Spirit gave you a land over there and people who grew up there got this religion. Then something got into your head to come to this country—my country—for God gave me this country and all these Indians. The paleface gets so greedy, having a foothold in this country he wants to own the whole country."

"Well, I want you to try to understand my religion," the priest said, "because that's the only way that you will see God."

"Ah, my younger brother, you have nice ideas, but you don't know the first thing of what our forefathers taught us."

"Your religion will just lead you down to the devil where you will be burned forever."

"My younger brother, you are foolish," said Piapot. "You are only a child. You are trying to scare me. In your country, I think you are using the same method—fear. You try to work it on me. I am too old for that. You can't scare me. You are using that method of fear among Frenchmen and you have them so fixed in your hands they dare not open their mouths for fear they are going to hell. What is hell? We have no such thing in our religion."

"That is where you are heading," the priest said.

"Well," replied Piapot, "you will have to show me the way."

The old man was firm in his beliefs yet he would not stand in the way of those who chose Christianity. He even allowed a Presbyterian minister to hold services in his lodge and no longer objected to having a church built on the reserve. But he kept his door open to the young people who wanted to learn about the spirituality of his people. Piapot would teach them as much as he could of the Creator and the spirit powers that inhabited every living creature and even inanimate objects like rocks and stones. He would teach them some of the prayers and some of the simpler rites, such as pipe offerings to the powers.

Piapot frequently received visits from a youth whose Cree name was Watetch, which meant Herald of the Sky. Watetch was born in the fall of 1883 while the band was camped at the skull mountains, but had spent his early years on the reserve in the Qu'Appelle Valley. Then, at age six or seven, his parents had sent him to the industrial school at Lebret. The priests who ran the school named the boy Abel and soon everyone knew him as Abel Watetch. Abel spent twelve years among the priests. He grew up speaking English. He attended Mass, received the sacraments and learned to say the Lord's Prayer. At the start of each school day, he stood at attention before the Union Jack and sang "God Save the Queen." He learned to read and write. He came to know about Queen Victoria and Sir John A. Macdonald. He acquired the rudiments of carpentry and shoemaking. He studied the crafts of the wheelwright and the tinsmith.

Abel finished his schooling as a new century was dawning. He was an educated young man and that was a source of pride to the priests who had taught him. He was prepared, in their opinion, to take his place in the world. He could go to Fort Qu'Appelle or Regina or perhaps farther afield and become an apprentice to some tradesman. But Abel had no interest in following such a path. He wanted to return his people, so he went back to the reserve.

Much had changed in the years that he was away. Childhood playmates had grown up and married. Children had been born. Elders had died. And a few who had violated the new laws of the land had wound up in Stony Mountain Penitentiary. Abel Watetch soon caught up on the news. In doing so, he began to hear the stories, songs and prayers of his people, some that he'd heard as a child but forgotten, others that were completely new to him. He heard them whenever he went visiting and he was captivated. He asked many questions, but often, people were stuck for an answer, and they invariably said: ask your uncle. Ask Piapot.

Abel visited Piapot almost daily when he first returned to the reserve, and he learned many things from the old man. But the big, complex ceremonies like the sun dance could not be taught at a kitchen table. They had to be learned through participation. This faith, like the Roman Catholicism Abel had absorbed at the school, had to be lived. But an Indian who practised publicly risked being arrested and jailed. So Piapot could not pass on much of what he knew.

One day, when Abel and a few others were there, Piapot had said, "I won't be with you much longer. When my time comes, don't bury me in the earth. Don't let them put me in the ground." A few days later, Abel's father sent him to check on Piapot and the youth returned almost immediately. "The old man is dead," Abel said. "There is mourning in his house."

Everyone in the intimate little community quickly learned of their leader's death, but fulfilling his final wish was a delicate matter. He did not want to be interred like a white man. But the Canadian authorities would not permit the traditional practice of wrapping the body in blankets or lodge coverings and lashing it to the branches of a tree. They would have to find a middle way, and quickly, before the farm instructor or some other government official learned of Piapot's death and ordered them to dig a grave six feet deep.

While the elders of the band deliberated, Abel Watetch put to work the carpentry skills he had learned at Lebret and hastily built a coffin of boards ripped from floors and wagon boxes. Piapot's body was placed in the coffin with his knees drawn up the Indian way and the lid nailed shut. The coffin was placed on a wagon, and the old chief was driven to his final resting place with most of the community marching behind.

They took a trail that led from the coulee where Piapot had lived to the prairie above his house and they stopped at the edge of a bluff. They dug a grave six inches deep, deposited the coffin and covered it with stones and rocks. They placed stones in a circle around the grave just as their people had once made circles of stones to denote where their lodges stood. Then they went back to their homes and their fields, leaving Piapot's spirit to gaze out eternally over the valley and the people he so dearly loved.

For years afterward, Piapot's people told their children and grandchildren stories about him and his accomplishments. And Abel Watetch wrote down these tales, as well as those he had received directly from the old medicine man. Almost half a century later, a writer from Ontario named Blodwen Davies visited the Qu'Appelle Valley collecting stories about the people who lived there. The Cree people of the valley sent her to see Abel Watetch, who shared his notes and recollections, and together they produced a slender volume on the life of Piapot. So a little of his story and his beliefs survived, despite the efforts of white authorities to discredit him and to erase all that he held sacred.

"And I Will Be Gone"

THOSE WHO LEAD rarely can choose their time in office, their challenges, or their adversaries. Therefore, leadership is always a test of character, and this was certainly true for Piapot, Big Bear, Crowfoot and Poundmaker. These men and their peoples faced an adversary more menacing than any invading army or competing economic system. They confronted a civilization that was alien and incomprehensible, that threatened all that they knew and loved: a way of life that allowed them to draw strength from the elements, knowledge from the land and wisdom from their dreams; a way of life that, according to frontier journal keepers, kept them healthy, happy and robust; a culture based on motion and mobility, homes that were light, portable and comfortable, villages that flowed with the seasons and the herds of buffalo, nations of the spoken rather than the written word, communities where names were fluid rather than fixed.

Piapot, Big Bear, Crowfoot and Poundmaker fought to preserve what they could of their communities and their cultures, their freedom and their independence, their pride and their dignity, their way of living, thinking and being. They led their peoples during a time of crisis and national catastrophe. To understand the challenge they faced, think of Moses being called upon to lead his people from slavery into freedom, and think of these men being forced to lead their people from freedom into subservience.

Leadership brought them challenges they could not surmount and a cultural conflict they could not win. They were up against a civilization that strove for permanence, that erected fences and fixed structures, that built roads and railways, that adhered to clocks and calendars. It was a world where things were nailed down, driven into the ground, built to last.

The times denied these men the rousing victories and personal glory that leaders so often crave. The times tested them in ways that few other leaders in our peaceful, orderly Dominion have ever been tested. They drew upon their unshakeable courage and integrity to deal with the circumstances that fate had dealt them, and they displayed an adamantine resolve to do what was best for their nations. They were heroes to their people, and justly so, for they were remarkable leaders. They were noble to the end, and fearless even as they faced death, qualities that found expression in Crowfoot's dying words, delivered to his grief-stricken family and friends as he lay in his lodge that overlooked the swift, shallow Bow River and the

Blackfoot Crossing. "A little while and I will be gone from among you, whither I cannot tell. From nowhere we came, into nowhere we go. What is life? It is as the flash of a firefly in the night. It is as the breath of the buffalo in the winter time. It is as the little shadow that runs across the grass and loses itself in the sunset."

Ahenakew, Edward. *Voices of the Plains Cree*. Toronto: McClelland & Stewart, 1973.

Ambrose, Stephen. *Of Courage Undaunted: Meriwether Lewis, Thomas Jefferson and the Opening of the American West*. New York: Simon & Schuster, 1996.

Barnett, Donald C. *Poundmaker*. Toronto: Fitzhenry & Whiteside, 1976.

Beal, Bob and Rod MacLeod. *Prairie Fire: The 1885 North-West Rebellion*. Edmonton: Hurtig Publishers, 1984.

Butler, William Francis. *The Great Lone Land: An Account of the Red River Expedition and Other Travels and Adventures in Western Canada*. Rutland, Vermont: Charles E. Tuttle Company, 1968.

Cameron, William Bleasdell. *Blood Red the Sun*. Edmonton: Hurtig Publishers, 1977.

Catlin, George. *Life Among the Indians*. London and Edinburgh: Gall & Inglis: 1875.

Cochin, Louis. *The Reminiscences of Louis Cochin, O.M.I.: A Veteran Missionary of the Cree Indians and a Prisoner in Poundmaker's Camp in 1885*. Saskatoon: Star Publishing, 1927.

Cowie, Isaac. *The Company of Adventurers: A Narrative of Seven Years in the Service of the Hudson's Bay Company During 1867–1874*. Toronto: William Briggs, 1913.

Dempsey, Hugh A. *Crowfoot: Chief of the Blackfoot*. Norman, Okla.: University of Oklahoma Press, 1972.

——. *Big Bear: The End of Freedom*. Vancouver: Douglas & McIntyre, 1984.

Denig, Edwin Thompson. *Five Indian Tribes of the Upper Missouri*. Norman, Okla.: University of Oklahoma Press, 1961.

Denny, Cecil E. *The Law Marches West*. Toronto: J.M. Dent and Sons, 1972.

——. *The Riders of the Plains: A Reminiscence of the Early and Exciting Days in the North West*. Calgary: The Herald Company, 1905.

Dion, Joseph F. *My Tribe the Crees*. Calgary: Glenbow–Alberta Institute, 1979.

Ewers, John C. *The Blackfeet: Raiders on the Northwestern Plains*. Norman, Okla.: University of Oklahoma, 1958.

Fine Day. *My Cree People*. Invermere, B.C.: Good Medicine Books, 1973.

Graham, William M. *Treaty Days: Reflections of an Indian Commissioner*. Calgary: Glenbow Museum, 1991.

Hassrick, Royal B. *The Sioux: Life and Customs of a Warrior Society*. Norman, Okla.: University of Oklahoma Press, 1964.

Henry, Alexander and David Thompson. *New Light on the Early History of the Greater Northwest*, ed. Elliott Coues. Minneapolis: Ross & Haines, 1965.

Hind, Henry Youle. *Narrative of the Canadian Red River Exploring Expedition of 1857 and of the Assiniboine and Saskatchewan Exploring Expedition of 1858*. Edmonton: Hurtig Publishers, 1971.

Hines, John. *Red Indians of the Plains: Thirty Years Missionary Experience in the Saskatchewan*. Toronto: McClelland, Goodchild & Stewart, 1916.

Hughes, Katherine. *Father Lacombe: The Black-robe Voyageur*. Toronto: McClelland & Stewart, 1920.

Jefferson, Robert. *Fifty Years on the Saskatchewan*. Battleford: Canadian North-West Historical Society, 1929.

Johnston, A., ed. *The Battle at Belly River: Stories of the Last Great Indian Battle*. Lethbridge: Lethbridge Branch, Historical Society of Alberta, 1974.

Kane, Paul. *Wanderings of an Artist Among the Indians of North America*. Edmonton: Hurtig Publishers, 1974.

Kelly, L.V. *The Range Men: The Story of the Ranchers and Indians of Alberta*. Toronto: William Briggs, 1913.

Light, Douglas W. *Footprints in the Dust*. North Battleford, Sask.: Turner-Warwick Publications, 1987.

MacLean, John. *Canadian Savage Folk: The Native Tribes of Canada*. Toronto: William Briggs, 1896.

Mandelbaum, David G. *The Plains Cree: An Ethnographic, Historical and Comparative Study*. Regina: Canadian Plains Research Centre, 1979.

McCourt, Edward. *Saskatchewan*. Toronto: Macmillan Company of Canada, 1968.

McDougall, John. *George Millward McDougall: The Pioneer, Patriot and Missionary*. Toronto: William Briggs, 1888.

Milloy, John Sheridan. *The Plains Cree: Trade, Diplomacy and War, 1790 to 1870*. Winnipeg: University of Manitoba Press, 1988.

Miller, J.R. *Big Bear: Mistahimusqua*. Toronto: ECW Press, 1996.

Miller, J.R., ed. *Sweet Promises: A Reader on Indian-White Relations in Canada*. Toronto: University of Toronto Press, 1991.

Morton, Desmond. *The Last War Drum: The North West Campaign of 1885*. Toronto: A.M. Hakkert, 1972.

Morris, Alexander. *The Treaties of Canada with the Indians of Manitoba and the North-West Territories.* Toronto: Belfords, Clarke & Co., 1880.

Mulvaney, Charles Pelham. *The History of the North-West Rebellion of 1885.* Toronto: A.H. Hovey and Co., 1885.

Pettipas, Katherine. *Severing the Ties that Bind: Government Repression of Indigenous Religious Ceremonies on the Prairies.* Winnipeg: University of Manitoba Press, 1994.

Roe, F.G. *The North American Buffalo: A Critical Study of the Species in Its Wild State.* Toronto: University of Toronto Press, 1951.

Russell, Dale R. *Eighteenth-Century Western Cree and Their Neighbours.* Ottawa: Canadian Museum of Civilization, Mercury Series, Paper 143. 1991.

Sharp, Paul. *Whoop-Up Country: The Canadian-American West, 1865–1885.* Norman, Okla.: University of Oklahoma Press, 1973.

Siggins, Maggie. *Riel: A Life of Revolution.* Toronto: HarperCollins, 1994.

Spry, Irene M. *The Palliser Expedition: An Account of John Palliser's British North American Exploring Expedition: 1857–1860.* Toronto: Macmillan Company of Canada, 1963.

Stanley, George F.G. *The Birth of Western Canada: A History of the Riel Rebellions.* Longmans, Green and Co., 1936.

Steele, Samuel B. *Forty Years in Canada: Reminiscences of the Great North-West.* Toronto: McGraw-Hill Ryerson, 1972.

Stewart, W.P. *My Name Is Piapot.* Maple Creek, Sask.: Butterfly Books, 1981.

Stonechild, Blair, and Bill Waiser. *Loyal Till Death: Indians and the North-West Rebellion.* Calgary: Fifth House, 1997.

Thwaites, R.G., ed. *Travels in the Interior of North America by Maximilian, Prince of Wied.* Cleveland: Arthur H. Clark Company, 1905.

Turner, Peter John. *The North-West Mounted Police: 1873–1893.* 2 Vol. Ottawa: King's Printer, 1950.

Watetch, Abel, as told to Blodwen Davies. *Payepot and His People*. Saskatoon: Saskatchewan History and Folklore Society, 1959.

Williams, W.H. *Manitoba and the North-West: Journal of a Trip From Toronto to the Rocky Mountains*. Toronto: Hunter, Rose & Company: 1882.

Woodcock, George. *Faces From History: Canadian Profiles and Portraits*. Edmonton: Hurtig Publishers, 1978.

GOVERNMENT DOCUMENTS

Canada Sessional Papers. *Annual Reports of the Department of Indian Affairs*. Ottawa, 1875–1908.

Canada Sessional Papers. *Annual Reports of the North-West Mounted Police*. Ottawa, 1875–1908.

PHOTOS